THE GORAKHPUR HOSPITAL TRAGEDY

A DOCTOR'S MEMOIR OF A DEADLY MEDICAL CRISIS

KAFEEL KHAN

PAN

First published in 2021 by Pan
an imprint of Pan Macmillan Publishing India Private Limited
707 Kailash Building
26 K. G. Marg, Delhi 110 001
www.panmacmillan.co.in

Pan Macmillan, The Smithson, 6 Briset Street, London EC1M 5NR
Associated companies throughout the world
www.panmacmillan.com

ISBN 978-93-90742-71-4

3 5 7 9 8 6 4 2

Typeset in Sabon LT Std by SÜRYA, New Delhi
Printed and bound in India by Replika Press Pvt. Ltd.

To the innocent children who lost their lives
at the BRD Medical College, Gorakhpur, in August 2017,
and the brave parents who have endured limitless grief
and a grave betrayal

Contents

PART THREE: DISCOVERY

PART FOUR: DETERMINATION

THE GORAKHPUR HOSPITAL TRAGEDY

Dr Kafeel Khan was born in Gorakhpur, Uttar Pradesh. After completing his MBBS and MD in Paediatrics at Kasturba Medical College, Manipal, in Karnataka, he worked as an assistant professor at the Sikkim Manipal Institute of Medical Sciences in Gangtok, before joining the Baba Raghav Das Medical College, Gorakhpur, as a lecturer.

Since his suspension from the BRD Medical College's Nehru Hospital after the medical crisis of August 2017 and subsequent release from Gorakhpur Jail, Khan, along with his team and the help of ordinary citizens, has been working under the banner of Dr Kafeel Khan Mission Smile Foundation. He has also started a Health for All campaign to demand the Right to Healthcare legislation and has launched a new initiative named Doctors on Road to provide healthcare services to patients in the Indian hinterlands.

In January 2020, Khan was arrested again and charged under the National Security Act (NSA) for his allegedly inflammatory speech at the Aligarh Muslim University; he subsequently spent seven months in prison. On 1 September 2020, his detention was set aside and all charges under the NSA were quashed by the Allahabad High Court.

Khan was terminated from service on 9 November 2021 by the BRD Medical College and, as of December 2021, cases against him are being pursued in lower courts even though the enquiries conducted by the state and central governments have not found any evidence of medical negligence or corruption on his part.

He can be reached at www.drkafeelkhan.org or on email at teamdrkafeel@gmail.com.

Cast of Characters

My Family

Adeel and Kashif: my brothers

Ahmar: my sister Farkhanda's husband

Farkhanda or Farro and Zeenat: my sisters

Nuzhat Parveen: my mother

Samar: my sister Zeenat's husband

Shabista: my wife

Zab and Zain: my children

Ab and Jasir: my nephews

Zara and Rid: my nieces

The Hospital

Balwant and Krishna: oxygen pipeline operators

Dr Satish Choubey: the senior resident who informed me about the oxygen crisis on the night of 10 August

Gajanand Jaiswal: the chief pharmacist in charge of the supply of jumbo cylinders

Dr Ram Kumar Jaiswal: the acting principal

Dr Ganesh Kumar: the new principal

Dr Satish Kumar: head of the Department of Anaesthesia, head of maintenance and nodal officer in charge of oxygen supply

Dr K. P. Kushwaha: the retired principal

Dr Rajiv Kumar Mishra: the principal

Dr Mahima Mittal: head of the Department of Paediatrics

Dr O. N. Pandey: finance officer/drawing and disbursing officer (DDO)

Sudhir Pandey: the senior-most clerk in the accounts department

Uday Pratap Sharma: a junior accountant

Dr Purnima Shukla: Dr Rajiv K. Mishra's wife

Dr A. K. Srivastava: superintendent-in-chief (SIC)

Dr Ramashanker Shukla: chief medical superintendent (CMS)

Sanjay Tripathi: a senior accountant

The Government

Anita Bhatnagar Jain: the additional chief secretary of medical education in the Uttar Pradesh government

Ashutosh Tandon: the minister of medical education of UP

Himanshu Kumar: the enquiry officer and principal secretary to the UP government's Food Protection and Administration

Dr K. K. Gupta: the director general of medical education and training (DGME)

Rajiv Kumar: the chief secretary to the chief minister of UP

Rajeev Rautela: the district magistrate, Gorakhpur

Siddharth Nath Singh: the health minister of UP

Yogi Adityanath: the chief minister of UP

The Prison

Bala: the writer of Nehru barrack

Suresh Dhani: jail superintendent

Surya Pandey: the deputy jailor

D. Ram: a retired PWD employee under trial

Ashish Singh: the deputy jailor

Shailesh Singh: the writer of Millennium barrack

Shukla: the jailor

V. Singh: a retired soldier from Barabanki

Mantri-ji: a politician from Maharajganj in Gorakhpur Jail

Other Characters

Manish Bhandari: the owner and managing director of Pushpa Sales

Dr Harjit Singh Bhatti: former president of the AIIMS Resident Doctors' Association, Delhi

Timeline of Events

2017

10 August:	Piped liquid medical oxygen runs out at the BRD Medical College's Nehru Hospital.
11 August:	The Uttar Pradesh government posts on its official social media account that no deaths have occurred due to lack of oxygen at BRD.
13 August:	Sixty-three infants and eighteen adults die over the course of fifty-four hours after the oxygen shortage at the hospital.
22 August:	The BRD Medical College suspends me from my post at the paediatrics department.
23 August:	The Department of Medical Education of UP files an FIR against me and eight others under IPC sections 409, 308, 120B, 420, the Prevention of Corruption Act, Section 8 of the IPC and Section 15 of the Indian Medical Council Act.
28 August:	I file a plea for anticipatory bail in the Allahabad High Court.
2 September:	The UP Special Task Force arrests and sends me to Gorakhpur Jail.

2018

10 April:	The Indian Medical Association comes out in my support, calling me a victim of conspiracy.
18 April:	I write a ten-page letter detailing the events that transpired on the night of 10–11 August 2017 and ask for justice to be served in the Gorakhpur hospital tragedy case.
25 April:	The high court releases me on bail after eight months in prison, after clearing me of the charges of medical negligence and corruption.
19 May:	I visit the BRD Medical College and hand over a letter requesting the authorities to reinstate me.
10 June:	My younger brother Kashif is shot three times in Gorakhpur by unidentified assailants.
14 August:	An RTI response reveals that the hospital was facing a shortage of oxygen cylinders on the night of 10–11 August 2017. The BRD administration's response states that around six cylinders were bought from other hospitals and I had arranged four oxygen cylinders on my own.
22 September:	The UP police arrests me again and I am sent back to Gorakhpur Jail for allegedly creating a ruckus and forcibly treating patients at the Bahraich district hospital and criticizing the policies of the UP government. On the same day, my elder

brother Adeel is arrested on charges of fraud and let go a month later.

3 November: I am released from prison.

2019

7 March: The Allahabad High Court orders the UP government to conclude their departmental enquiry against me within ninety days, acting on my writ petition to have my suspension revoked.

15 April: A probe panel led by Principal Secretary Himanshu Kumar submits their report, which absolves me of any charges of medical negligence, corruption and dereliction of duty, and acknowledges my efforts to control the crisis but finds me 'guilty' of private practice until 8 August 2016.

10 May: A division bench of the Supreme Court, comprising Justice Sanjay Kishan Kaul and Justice Indira Banerjee, orders for the enquiry regarding my suspension to be concluded in a timely manner and further directs the UP government to pay the subsistence allowances due to me.

31 July: A second suspension order is passed against me for forcibly treating patients at the Bahraich district hospital and criticizing the policies of the UP government while being in government service.

27 September: An internal enquiry committee of the hospital absolves me of the charges of medical negligence, corruption and dereliction of duty.

4 October: The UP government orders a fresh departmental enquiry into my role in the deaths of infants on the intervening night of 10–11 August 2017.

12 December: I deliver a speech against the controversial Citizenship Amendment on the campus of Aligarh Muslim University.

2020

29 January: The Uttar Pradesh STF arrests me in Mumbai, stating that my speech disrupted communal harmony and was likely to create a negative law-and-order situation. I am sent to Mathura Jail.

10 February: Aligarh district court orders my release.

13 February: The National Security Act is invoked against me for my anti-CAA speech at AMU.

24 February: The UP government orders a fresh enquiry, rejecting some points in the report submitted by the Himanshu Kumar-led committee.

1 September: The Allahabad High Court sets aside the UP government's order holding me in preventive detention under the NSA.

17 December: The Supreme Court rejects the UP government's plea to review the high court order quashing the charges under the NSA against me.

2021

30 January: I am added to the list of history-sheeters by the UP government.

3 July: I file a writ petition against my first suspension order.

29 July: The high court questions the delay in ordering a fresh enquiry; also asks the UP government to justify why I am still suspended after four years.

6 August: The UP government informs the high court of its decision to withdraw the second enquiry and promises to complete disciplinary proceedings within three months.

27 August: The high court quashes the criminal proceedings against me for my speech at AMU in December 2019.

9 September: My second suspension in the Bahraich district hospital case is stayed by the high court.

15 September: The high court directs the UP government to conclude their enquiry against me within a month.

9 November: The Department of Medical Education of UP terminates me from my post at the BRD Medical College.

PROLOGUE

A Dream and a Nightmare

> 'We are at pain in observing that ... non-supplying of oxygen to the hospitals is a criminal act and not less than a genocide by those who have been entrusted the task to ensure continuous procurement and supply chain of the liquid medical oxygen.'
>
> – From an order passed by Justices Siddhartha Varma and Ajit Kumar of the Allahabad High Court on 4 May 2021

In August 2017, following the deaths of more than sixty infants at the state-run Baba Raghav Das Medical College in Gorakhpur, Uttar Pradesh, after the hospital's medical oxygen ran out, I was suspended and jailed for more than eight months. The authorities denied that the hospital's oxygen supply had been stopped, failed to identify the real culprits and instead blamed me for the fatalities. Between 10 and 12 August, I worked round the clock, trying to figure out a way to restore the supply of life-giving oxygen to the infants and children admitted in the wards and the intensive care unit of the hospital's Department of Paediatrics. What happened over the course of those two to three days would soon lead to a life-and-death struggle of my own: a fight for my liberty, to remain in the profession of healing and a battle to live and work in the place where I was born – Gorakhpur, the home of my ancestors.

Little did I know at the time that some years after qualifying as a doctor and embarking on my medical profession, I would be forced to newly educate myself through bitter lessons learnt by witnessing negligence and dereliction of duty, corruption and vicious prosecution. It was only after navigating a series of crises in the past four years that I could understand why I had to go through this incredible ordeal. I was meant to become more conscious and aware – for my own sake and that of society.

This book documents the arduous journey I was compelled to undertake after the events of August 2017, which upturned my life forever.

My father, the late Shakeel Khan, was a gazetted officer in the state's Irrigation Department. He and my mother, Nuzhat Parveen, both came from families with roots in Gorakhpur. While my maternal grandfather was a landlord with significant land holdings around Gorakhpur, my paternal grandfather had worked as a gazetted officer in the Indian Railways.

Our home, in the Basantpur locality of old Gorakhpur, had been built by my paternal grandfather first as a sprawling mud-and-thatch dwelling. It was my mother who supervised the construction of a brick-and-cement building that still stands today and provides shelter to our large family. Like any locality of old Gorakhpur, the streets around our home in Basantpur are home to cows and buffaloes, goats, donkeys and dogs, and also provide space for kids to play gully cricket.

I grew up surrounded by families from different castes, communities and classes. The locality was neither a rarefied, gated colony of government officials nor a Muslim-dominated neighbourhood. My friends and neighbours were Dalits, Yadavs, Kumbhars, Christians and Brahmins; I played with children from families of milk sellers, rickshaw pullers, potters, street-food vendors and mithai-shop owners. On Holi, we would frolic together with great gusto, looking like crazed, multicoloured monkeys in torn kurtas. We celebrated Eid by inviting our neighbours to our dinner table, and the gujias they gave us on Diwali were so plentiful that we would be sent to school with tiffin boxes full of sweetmeats for a whole week afterwards.

I first registered the terms 'Hindu' and 'Muslim' when I was around five years old. Right after the assassination of Indira Gandhi, on hearing many conversations about her in the days following her death, I had asked my grandfather, 'Was she a Hindu or a Muslim?'

My grandfather looked into my eyes. He must have understood that my childish question was not about labels as much as it was about determining what we had in common with the former prime minister.

Drawing me close, he said, 'Beta, she was Hindu, Muslim, Sikh and Christian.' This seemed to satisfy me, and I nodded, thinking that she was like us just as much as she was like any of my friends.

In 1984, this answer could not be plastered on social media as a piece of fake news about the Gandhi family's bias for Muslims or their secret Muslim origins. The kind of hate-mongering we see in today's India had not yet become routine.

As a child growing up in the eighties, I was haunted by questions of belonging, but at the time, these had nothing to do with national or identity politics. I was one of six siblings – the second-born child among four brothers and two sisters. The competition for sweets and delicacies in my family was fierce. Every year, we were given a set of new clothes for Eid and our school uniform. Moreover, cloth was bought in long metreage to save money, so all the brothers had to wear similarly patterned shirts and pants. On my father's salary as an engineer in government service, we could eat meat no more than once or twice a week – a single piece for each child. Jostling with one another to get a little bit extra was routine. The most important question was who would get to spend the longest time riding the single bicycle we all shared.

Since I was more fair-complexioned than my siblings, some of my young relatives would tease me about it. 'Don't fret if your elder brother gets a longer turn on the bicycle,' they would say. 'It's only natural. You were picked up as a baby by your parents after they found you abandoned and took pity on you. So just accept what you can get and don't make such a fuss!'

I suspected this to be a lie, but a child's mind relies less on logic and more on emotion. In moments of anger, when I was being denied something, I would cry, throw a tantrum, and accuse my mother: 'I know you treat me like this because I am just a picked-up child!' With her extreme patience and love, she would calm me down.

When I was in class nine, I went to a circus with a friend named Tabrez. There, the bear trainer posed a challenge: 'Can anyone from the city of Gorakhpur tame my bear?' I took up the challenge, even though I weighed just fifty kilograms and the bear was at least ten times my weight. I was roughed up badly and my clothes got ripped; after a long struggle, the trainer and some other men rescued me. I could smell the bear's breath for months. I still think that daring stint – though some may call it foolhardy – is one of the reasons I have had the strength to push myself so hard against several odds in my life.

Apart from this incident, my childhood was mostly uneventful. If we complained about anything, it was the undue emphasis placed on academics in our home. My father, being an engineer, ensured we were devoted to our studies. I went to an English-medium school. But when I graduated to class six, I was admitted to a Hindi-medium school, the Mahatma Gandhi Inter College, where I made many friends.

Long study hours, weekly television sessions and occasional treats and outings were usual in my family. My sister Farkhanda, a year younger than me, was my constant and loyal friend. She had my back in fights or disagreements, laughed at my jokes and kept my secrets. We have remained close all through our lives, even after she moved to another country with her husband and their family. Farro, as I call her, was bitten by the study bug harder than any of us and went on to do a PhD.

I fared reasonably well in school too. After completing class twelve, I took the Combined Pre-Medical Test (CPMT), which made me eligible for admission into various Uttar Pradesh medical colleges – in Jhansi, Azamgarh and Gorakhpur. I also qualified for admission into the Manipal Institute of Medical Sciences in Karnataka, with an all-India rank of thirty. After considerable discussion within my family, it was decided that I would go to Manipal.

The years I spent studying and later working at the Kasturba Hospital in Manipal laid the foundation for my understanding of the medical profession. We were trained to think of our patients above all else. Their religion, caste, gender and economic status were irrelevant. What mattered was the nature of their illness and how they could be brought onto the road to recovery. It was an enriching and illuminating period of my life.

During the second year of my MBBS at Manipal, I dreamt that Abbujaan had fallen sick. I wrote a letter to him on 1 March 2003, asking him to do a complete medical check-up. Tragically, just two days later, he passed away, and I reached Gorakhpur only to receive my own letter in the midst of our grieving family.

For a while, I was so devastated that I would go to the kabristan at night and sleep at my father's grave. I slept there for a whole month, compelling my brothers to come every night to drag me home. My father had wanted me to be a doctor, but he had moved on before he could see me become one.

After my graduation, I also worked at the Sikkim Manipal Institute of Medical Sciences in Gangtok for several years. There I wrote my first medical book, the first edition of the *Manipal Manual of Clinical Paediatrics* for undergraduates and paramedics.

One of the foremost reasons I love the medical profession is my fondness for children. While working in Gangtok, I became keen to advance myself in the field of paediatrics.

In 2015, I moved back to Gorakhpur and married Dr Shabista Khan, to the delight of my family.

On 8 August 2016, I joined the BRD Medical College as a lecturer in the Department of Paediatrics. After clearing the necessary Uttar Pradesh Public Service Commission (UPPSC) exams and processes, I was appointed as a permanent employee on probation. Before that, I had worked as an assistant professor for a few months, from 2 May 2016, under the National Rural Health Mission's (NRHM) contractual employees' scheme.

Situated on the BRD campus, the Nehru Hospital has long been the favoured destination for patients from not only adjoining districts of the state, such as Maharajganj, Basti, Gonda, Bahraich, Mau, Deoria and Kushinagar, but from many towns in Bihar and Nepal as well.

I suffered a huge culture shock when I joined the paediatrics department at BRD. After working at the cleaner, more orderly hospital in Manipal for twelve years, I was horrified to see that the paediatrics ICU here resembled a general ward. Parents could stay overnight with their children, and they all ate together in the wards, surrounded by flies. Some of the staff worked without masks or gloves, while others moved around the ICU with their shoes on. Occasionally, dogs could be seen sitting under the patients' beds. The ratio of nurses and doctors to patients was nowhere close to the norms. It would be difficult to trace the details of the last time the ICU had been fogged and sterilized.

At this time, I was serving a mandatory two-year probation period, as per the UPPSC's criteria for securing permanent employment. For this reason, I did not have any administrative or financial power when I joined.

The circumstances compelled me to recommend masks, gloves and shoe covers for the medical staff. I bought a fogging machine with my own money, as well as a fan for the paediatrics ward. In the early days, I even paid for phenyl, brooms, dustbins, mosquito-eliminating rackets, Hit spray to kill flies, registers, pens, notebooks and files. There were times when I would give cash to sweepers and ward boys who had not been paid their salaries for months. It was of paramount importance to me to have motivated and committed people around the infant patients.

During my probation period, I wrote several proposals to higher authorities but each time I received either a reply stating there was a budget crunch, or no response at all.

As a doctor and a long-term resident of Gorakhpur, I was aware of the recurring annual outbreak of encephalitis. Acute encephalitis syndrome or AES was an annual scourge that had, since 1978, claimed the lives of over 25,000 children in Uttar Pradesh and left more than one lakh permanently disabled.

An acute inflammation of the brain, a case of AES is clinically defined as a person of any age, at any time of year, experiencing an acute onset of fever (for less than fifteen days) and a change in their mental status (symptoms include confusion, disorientation, coma or the inability to talk) and/or an onset of specific kinds of seizures.

It is an umbrella disease in which multiple aetiologies have been implicated, some established (such as Japanese encephalitis, herpes simplex and the enterovirus) and others not yet known. AES is a major public health problem due to its high fatality rate (20–30 per cent) and frequent neuropsychiatric damage (50–70 per cent). It is considered a medical and neurological emergency, requiring urgent consideration of key issues, including immediate life support, the protocol for which is known in the medical profession as ABCD (airway – whereby the patient's airway is to be cleared; breathing – most importantly, oxygen, high flow nasal cannula (HFNC) and mechanical ventilation; circulation using inotropic agents; and drugs – anti-epileptic, anti-edema and anti-pyretic medication – and institution of specific therapy).

It is a disease especially common amongst the underprivileged. Most AES-afflicted children come from poor, marginalized communities. The seven 'P's long associated with AES are population, poverty, poor nutrition (malnutrition), poor supply of safe drinking water, poor vaccination, poor hygiene and poor sanitation.

The virulent Japanese encephalitis is transmitted by mosquitoes as a vector from pigs to humans, but we have a vaccine for it. Still, most of the affected children belong to a low socio-economic stratum. I used to wonder how mosquitoes differentiated between rich and poor kids, or if it was because the health workers responsible for vaccination drives never visited these marginalized groups.

After finishing all my work at the ward and the OPD, I would teach nurses and junior doctors about the protocol for encephalitis treatment – how to handle a ventilator, talk to the patients' relatives and administer medicines.

I even took a course to improve my teaching and public speaking skills.

Soon after, I created a core group on WhatsApp with my colleagues in order to exchange information about AES. Our motto was: 'Let's fight together and eradicate encephalitis.' I also worked day and night for a month in the High Dependency Ward – an upgraded version of the Paediatric Intensive Care Unit (PICU) with better ventilators and modern equipment for taking care of critically ill patients.

On 9 July 2017, during a visit by the newly elected UP chief minister, Yogi Adityanath, I made a presentation before the principal secretary of health and education, the district magistrate, the commissioner, the director of the NRHM and the chief minister himself about overcrowding, staff deficiency, unavailability of medicines and shortage of equipment at the hospital. After the presentation I received several assurances. Nevertheless, I remember running after the chief minister and telling him, 'Sir, the NRHM employees have not got their salary for the past three to four months!'

Within a week of that exchange, those employees received their salaries.

Before the chief minister's next visit, on 9 August 2017, the district magistrate and the principal of BRD Medical College warned me against speaking out of turn in front of him. The previous time, I had broken protocol by mentioning the overdue salaries to him directly. It seemed that the administration had been pulled up thereafter. My intervention had not gone down well with my superiors.

A few days prior, on 31 July, while it was raining and the wards were packed with AES-afflicted children, I had been interviewed on ABP News about the shortage of doctors and nurses at the hospital. Calling it an unethical practice, I had pointed out that around four to six consultants and a few nurses were taking care of 400 children, making proper care impossible.

In August 2017, I was still serving my probation as the junior-most lecturer in my department. I had, however, already caught the attention of the higher authorities at the BRD Medical College and the chief minister of Uttar Pradesh, due to my actions and statements of the preceding weeks. I was entirely unaware of how these actions, combined with the medical crisis at the hospital, would soon change my life.

In the year that followed, I could not have imagined the hatred and harassment that would be unleashed upon me. Or that Gorakhpur, the city where I had been born and raised, would soon become the battlefield on which I would have to fight tooth and nail for my life and my liberty.

PART ONE

Duty

1

Driving into the Cataclysm

It was almost midnight when my phone started buzzing. I picked it up instantly from my bedside table out of sheer habit and squinted at the screen. Someone had sent a message on the BRD Medical College's AES WhatsApp group. It delivered such a jolt that I was fully awake in a second. The sender was Dr Satish Choubey, a senior resident at the Nehru hospital. 'There is no oxygen supply in NICU,' his message read. 'Cylinders out of stock.'

No oxygen? Immediately my mind was flooded with images of the children in the paediatrics ward of the large hospital attached to the college. Alarmed at the thought of what would happen to those young patients, I scrambled out of bed and groped for my formal clothes in the dark.

My wife, disturbed by the sound of my movements, asked in a sleepy whisper, 'Where are you going at this hour?'

'I have to go, my love – it's important.' I got dressed as fast as I could.

'Work, work and work. You think only of your hospital and the patients. Do remember that your own daughter is growing up. Try to spend some time with her!'

I did not want to argue with my wife or remind her that I had spent that whole day at home. Neither did I want to tell her about the situation at the hospital as it would only make her panic.

'It's really urgent – a baby is very sick,' I said, offering a well-practised explanation that was not untrue.

'Okay, but come back soon.'

'*Bas, abhi gaya, abhi wapas aaya* (I will be back as soon as possible).'

Stepping into the night, I walked towards my car, preparing to drive the ten kilometres to the hospital. During such an emergency, I did not want to waste any time calling my driver and waiting for him to arrive. It would have taken him another half an hour to reach my place.

So I drove off in my car, my mind whirling with questions.

Why was it that I did not have any inkling about the oxygen shortage mentioned in that message? It was because I had been on leave on 10 August 2017. My sister had come home from Oman after a year. After being on duty during the chief minister's visit to our hospital on the 9th, for which we had been preparing long and hard, I had taken a day's leave to spend time with my family. I was surrounded by my loving wife, my caring mother, my eleven-month-old daughter Zab – the princess in our lives – and my brothers and their families.

I played for hours with my daughter, niece and nephews. After dinner, my sister Farro and I even found time for a long chat with each other. Later, I enjoyed putting Zab to sleep after trying to teach her how to say 'Papa', not that I minded her adorable childish gurgles.

While I had been thus engaged, away from the hospital for a single day, a crisis had got underway, threatening the lives of hundreds of our patients.

A shortage of oxygen could affect the life-saving processes in any hospital even during ordinary times. But what galvanized me into action at that late hour was the inopportune period in which this particular shortage had occurred. This was August, and it was peak AES season.

What could I do in such a situation? What could anyone do? What would I find when I reached the hospital? I frantically searched my mind for answers. All I knew was that I needed to be present to help save as many lives as we could. As my grip tightened on the steering wheel, my whole being gathered itself into a prayer for those helpless children.

Allah rehem kare!

Pressing hard on the accelerator as I zoomed through the dark, deserted streets, I began calling people at the hospital using my phone's hands-free function. Before I left my house, Dr Satish Choubey, the senior resident who had sent the WhatsApp message, had told me that he had received panicked phone calls from the junior residents on duty. The hospital had run out of liquid oxygen, the fifty reserve cylinders were also exhausted and we had started to lose patients.

The conversations I had on the way to the hospital are seared into my memory. They were strange and surreal – most people I spoke to seemed not to have grasped the urgency of the crisis, except the junior doctors on duty in the wards.

Dr Sakshi and Dr Anil were the two junior residents on duty in the PICU that night.

'What happened?' I asked Dr Anil.

'Sir, there is no oxygen left at the hospital.'

'Did you inform anyone?'

'Yes, sir, I have informed everyone,' Dr Anil said. 'The senior resident, the consultant on duty ...'

'How did you realize that the liquid oxygen had run out?'

'Sir, the ventilators were not working and had begun beeping. I called Balwant Gupta, the central pipeline operator, who told me we have run out of liquid oxygen. He said the jumbo cylinders were not picking up enough pressure and those are also over now. Sir—' I could sense a tremor in his voice as he tried to convey the next piece of news.

'What is it?' I asked.

'Three babies have died.'

I pressed the accelerator harder.

After taking Balwant Gupta's number from him, I ended the call.

Next, I called Balwant. My conversation with him was brief but enlightening.

'What happened, Balwant? Tell me in detail,' I asked.

'Sir, at 7:30 p.m. an alarm indicated that the liquid oxygen gas pressure was low. So I put fifty-two reserve cylinders on the alternative pipeline, but by 11:30 p.m. these, too, were exhausted. I informed everyone that the hospital now had no oxygen supply. I told the junior residents on duty, too. I wrote to Dr Mahima Mittal [the head of the Department of Paediatrics] as well as Dr Satish Kumar [the head of the Department of Anaesthesia], telling them about the impending oxygen shortage this morning itself. They had forwarded my letter to the principal.'

'Okay, so when is the next cylinder arriving?'

'Sir, Imperial Gas is sending a truck with jumbo cylinders from Faizabad. I don't know when it will reach.'

'When did the truck leave? Do you know?'

'Sir, it must have left in the evening. I think Dr Rajiv Mishra sir [the principal] would have spoken to the suppliers, but they have not reached yet.'

As I tried to wrap my head around the communication channels and the chain of command, I fired a series of questions at him.

He repeated to me in a resigned but patient voice. 'Yes, sir, I informed everyone. I gave them this information in writing during the day, and when the oxygen ran out at 7:30 in the evening, I told them that we have only fifty-two cylinders left which would also be empty soon. "Please do something," I said to them ...'

'What did they tell you?'

'They said they will see.'

'Have they called you back?'

'No, sir, they have not called me back.'

'Has anyone come to the ward?'

'No, sir, nobody has turned up. Only the junior residents have been speaking to me.'

As a lecturer in the Department of Paediatrics at the BRD Medical College, I was very low in the pecking order, which began with the head of the department, under whom worked two senior professors and two associate professors. My status as a probationary employee gave me no administrative or financial powers. There was a group of doctors working on contract who had also been given the designation of Lecturer or Assistant Professor. These included three senior resident doctors and a large number of junior residents who were in the process of securing an MD in paediatrics or a diploma in child health.

Out of this pool of doctors governed by professional rules as well as everyday hospital etiquette, I was going to have to stick my neck out, no matter what happened. In my mind's eye, I could envision the tiny, naked bodies in the Neonatal Intensive Care Unit (NICU) and the gasping children in the PICU, and thoughts of designation and seniority vanished from my mind.

I dialled the number of the head of the Department of Paediatrics, Dr Mahima Mittal. She picked up on the tenth or eleventh ring.

'Good evening, ma'am, I'm sorry to disturb you at this late hour. Did you read the message from Dr Choubey?'

There was no reply from her and, for a moment, I

wondered if she was even on the line. I continued talking breathlessly.

'Ma'am, we have run out of liquid oxygen and the reserve jumbo cylinders are also empty. The Imperial Gas truck from Faizabad has not reached yet. There is no oxygen at all in the entire hospital, and all the ventilators in the department are beeping ...'

'Yes, I know. You should tell the principal,' she finally said.

'Okay, ma'am,' I replied, and did as I had been told.

I called the principal repeatedly, but his phone was not reachable. Desperate, I called the HOD again.

'Ma'am, Principal sir is not answering his phone.'

'Then talk to the acting principal.'

Now I felt even more confused. The acting principal? I didn't even know we had an acting principal!

'Ma'am, I don't understand. Where is Principal sir?'

'He has gone to AIIMS Rishikesh for an inspection. Dr Ram Kumar Jaiswal is the acting principal. Talk to him,' she said.

'But ma'am, I don't know him at all! Can you talk to him, please?'

'He is the head of the Department of Ophthalmology.'

'But I don't have his number, ma'am!'

'I'll send it to you.'

'Ma'am, are you coming to the hospital?'

'I will see,' she said, and ended the conversation.

I was still driving when I called Dr Ram Kumar Jaiswal, whose number the HOD had sent me. My mind was spinning in a dozen different directions. What on earth was going on? Why was the HOD speaking so strangely, and where was the principal? Why had none of the senior residents, consultants, the superintendent or anybody else reached the wards, even though most of them lived on campus? I would imagine that if the central oxygen supply was out, the whole hospital should be in emergency mode. What was happening in our department must be taking its toll elsewhere in the hospital, too. After all, it was a 950-bed tertiary-care hospital. I was at a loss.

The acting principal allowed me to introduce myself and explain the situation. I told him I had spoken to the HOD who had advised me to inform him.

He replied, 'Okay, try and talk to Dr Rajiv Mishra, and then I will see. I will talk to Dr Satish, the head of Anaesthesia, who is in charge of oxygen supply, and to your HOD as well.'

That seemed to be the sum and substance of his cold, clipped reaction.

I called the HOD once again and told her that the acting principal would talk to her.

'Sure, I'll speak to him. You keep calling Principal sir,' she said.

'Ma'am, were you able to speak to Dr Satish?' I interjected urgently.

'I'll call him.'

'But ma'am, are you coming?'

'I'll see. Meanwhile, tell the residents to remove the children from the ventilators and perform Ambu until alternative arrangements can be made.'

I was stunned. A thought crossed my mind: Was she talking in her sleep?

The Ambu bag is a bag valve mask (BVM) that is used to manually provide positive pressure ventilation to patients who are unable to breathe properly using the oxygen in the air. It is most often used in the ambulance or during an emergency before the patient can be connected to any oxygen-delivering device. It is a challenge even for trained medical professionals to use it for a sustained length of time.

How long would it be before the oxygen supply was restored? I wondered. *How would we find enough doctors and trained nursing staff to manually keep pumping oxygen into the tiny lungs of all the children who needed it?* The casual manner in which this instruction had been thrown at me had left me speechless.

In the moments before I reached the hospital, I collected myself. I knew from Balwant that the impending shortage of oxygen had been communicated by him in writing to the authorities that morning. I knew from the junior residents that they had informed the consultant on duty, who had neither shown up nor sent any word about the oxygen supply. I knew that the truck with jumbo cylinders was coming from Faizabad, but I did not know why it had not reached yet. The entire trip should not have taken more than four or five hours. As I covered the last stretch before reaching the hospital gates, my sense of urgency while making all the calls to the relevant authorities and my confusion at their mechanical responses had given way to a stark realization.

I was reaching the scene, and it was now up to me to take action.

The screams could be heard even from the gates of the medical college. As I parked and locked my car, I could hear the cries and curses of mothers ripping through the quiet of the post-midnight hour.

I walked towards what seemed like absolute chaos, each step drawing me closer to a site of unimaginable suffering and tragedy.

2

Doctor, Save My Child!

My domain at the BRD Medical College included the Department of Paediatrics, which spanned wards 6, 12, 100, and the paediatrics and neonatal ICUs. There are a hundred beds in the eponymous ward 100, set up under the NRHM scheme in 2013. The building that houses ward 100 and the equipment in it had been donated by the central government, while the state government was responsible for the medicines and maintenance. Across these wards, there were a total of 216 beds in our department. However, we were often confronted with an occupancy of over 400 patients, particularly during the monsoon season of AES. As the sole fully equipped hospital offering free treatment in an area of over 200 square kilometres, it was only natural that the patients should outnumber the beds available for them.

On a normal night, if I had been visiting a patient, I would have walked past parents and caregivers sleeping quietly on chairs or in the corridors, security guards at their posts and the night nursing staff engaged in their work.

That night I made a beeline towards ward 100. At the gate, I passed a small group of people carrying the limp body of a girl about eight to ten years of age.

Three women held one another, crying loudly, '*Mera lala, mera lala.*' They were shedding tears for a child who had either died or was lying unconscious. I was not wearing my lab coat, but had my stethoscope clasped in my hand. While they did not immediately recognize me as a doctor, the look they gave me will haunt me forever. Their eyes full of pain, the faces conveying helplessness as I hurried past is etched in my memory. My body responded physically to their agony.

In the corridor outside the PICU, parents were gathered in small groups, attempting to look inside. The guards, who should have been on hand to prevent them from doing so, were nowhere to be seen. Even as I tried to clear the crowd so I could enter the PICU, I could hear parents crying out around me, '*Mera bachcha! Mera lala!*' I was shaken by their desperation. These were people who had travelled long distances with their sick children. Our hospital granted them hope. I fervently wished to keep that hope alive.

On entering the large room, I was struck by the amount of noise in what should have been a quiet and well-regulated ICU. From the raised voices of those agonized by the condition of their children, others bemoaning their child's death, the continuous beeping of the ventilators that were not receiving oxygen, monitors showing a critical dip in oxygen saturation, to the junior doctors vacillating between patients and checking their falling vital parameters – it was a scene of extreme distress and chaos.

The nurses sprinted from one cubicle to another, and the junior doctors were clearly in a frenzy.

Sister Saumya came running towards me. 'Sir, sir! Please help us! We just don't know what to do!' She seemed close to tears.

I asked her where doctors Anil and Sakshi were.

'They are in cubicle 3, sir.'

As I walked towards cubicles 3 and 4, I could see a crowd of people in cubicles 1 and 2. They were howling, and the beeping of the ventilator monitors added to the commotion. Sometimes I still hear that sound in my dreams.

Dr Anil and Dr Sakshi walked over as soon as they saw me.

'What do we do, sir? All the ventilators have stopped working and eight children have already died.'

Their faces reflected sheer terror and distress. The night had tested their training to the extreme; they were completely unprepared for such a situation.

I was thinking quickly as to how we could start coping with the breakdown of ICU operations.

'Which consultant was supposed to be on night duty when the oxygen ran out at 7:30 p.m.?' I asked the junior residents.

'Dr Sharma.'

'Did you tell him?'

'Of course, sir,' said Dr Anil.

'He said he is doing something about it, but now he is not taking our calls,' said Dr Sakshi.

'Did you inform madam?' I asked to confirm if the HOD, Dr Mahima, had received information about the crisis from them as well.

'Yes, sir. Everyone we called said they would do something, but nobody has turned up. And now they're not picking up the phone, and I don't know how we are going to get through the night ...' the junior resident's voice trailed off, his expression was of extreme distress.

'Calm down,' I told him. 'How many of you are on duty now?'

'There are six of us.'

'Then call the juniors and the nursing staff. We need to decide on a course of action. How many patients do we have?'

'Around 313, sir. We have lost some of them already.'

'How many of them are on ventilators?'

'Around fifty. In the neonatal ICU, sixteen out of eighty neonates are on ventilators, but I haven't been able to go there because I was caught up. There are two doctors and four nurses there, too. Plus six in Emergency and, sir ...' he gulped as he was overcome with emotion again. 'I'm not able to carry out any monitoring. Due to the lack of oxygen, the condition of the children is deteriorating, they are having seizures due to hypoxic damage ...'

I gripped his shoulder. 'I know. Tell me, how many nurses are on duty now?'

'Around twenty-four, sir.'

'Call them all. Call all the interns, all the ward boys and every sweeper. We have to work hard to save each and every life. Each and every life,' I repeated. Both the juniors nodded earnestly.

In a few minutes, we had all gathered in cubicle 3. I gave instructions on how to get through the night, despite panicked parents crowding outside and a large number of children in critical condition.

'Don't show signs of panic, and do your best to stay calm,' I said, looking around at the faces of the scared and anxious doctors, nurses and ward staff.

'Be gentle with the parents. This is like a warzone, and we have to fight for each child's life. Their parents will be emotional. Don't raise your voice or be rude to any of them.'

No one responded to this. I knew this was the most difficult task of all – to handle parents whose children were dying in front of their eyes.

'How many Ambu bags do we have? We need to collect as many of them as we can to save the children on ventilators. I will show you how to start the procedure. We may even find some parents who will be able to learn and perform it on their child themselves.'

I watched the assembled group glance at one another with uncertainty, unsure of whether they would be able to substitute the oxygen supply with a manual technique that many did not know how to carry out with enough dexterity.

'Well, let me demonstrate,' I said, as I led them to the side of one of the children. We removed the beeping ventilator connected to the tiny body, and I performed the Ambu bag and tube ventilation technique. The junior doctors and nursing staff all leaned close and watched, until I handed the bag over to a nurse and gave everyone the remaining instructions.

'We will have one nurse in each cabin to administer medicines, and one doctor to monitor the patients' parameters. Everyone else will perform the Ambu tube ventilation until the oxygen supply is restored. Understood?'

There was a chorus of 'Haan, sir' and 'Ji, sir,' as they began to disperse.

I stopped them and said a few final words.

'This is going to be a long night. Get the Ambu bag to the beds that need it now, and don't forget to note everything you do on paper. Note each process. The truth. No manipulation. If anything goes wrong, please inform me immediately.'

With that, the doctors, nurses and ward staff started hurrying towards the patients.

We had to continue reviewing the delicate conditions of the patients around me and monitoring what treatment was being administered to each of them. I took a quick round of all the ICU cubicles, accompanied by a junior resident who could tell me the details of each case and the medicines that had been given. Most cases had turned critical.

'Sir, Vinita, an eight-year-old female, came with a history of fever for five days, three days of vomiting, two days of altered sensorium, multiple seizures on day five, and one day of loss of consciousness. She's on isotonic fluid with calcium and inotropic support of 10 micrograms, phenobarbitone injection, midazolam SOS as well as Acyclovir, Vancomycin, Amikacin, Ceftriaxone. There have been no fresh seizures, and she is afebrile, but her vitals are dipping ...'

I needed to know more. 'What are the vitals? Which fluid is the patient on? What were the last electrolytes?'

'Change fluid according to serum sodium, potassium,' I continued. 'Inotropes? Dopamine or dobutamine, or both? Is calcium to be administered? Have we taken anti-edema measures? Has mannitol been given? Which anti-epileptic drugs have been prescribed – phenytoin? Valparin? Phenobarbitone? Tell me the infusion and fluid drop rates. If a patient has a seizure, give them midazolam, diazepam, lorazepam on an SOS basis, repeat electrolytes – an arterial blood gas (ABG) analysis if needed – and change the ventilator setting accordingly. What is the urine output? Show me the intake chart. What is her temperature now?'

One of the junior doctor showed me the temperature chart.

'Let's check her pupils. Don't change the antibiotic that was being administered, let it continue. If nebulization was administered every second hour, make it every sixth hour. Continue administering suction and 3 per cent nebulization, changing the posture, performing chest physiotherapy and monitoring the vitals – heart rate, respiratory rate, blood pressure, capillary filling time (CFT), padding of the eyes ...'

My training and education as a doctor allowed me to keep up a stream of enquiries and instructions, even as my thoughts were turning more and more gloomy at the sight of so many vulnerable, malnourished, critically ill children. I walked from one bed to another with my junior doctor, feeling the eyes of anxious parents following me. I wanted to finish my round as quickly as possible, but every patient had to be visited. I had to know what medication they were on, whose condition was critical and to what extent, which patients needed a fluid change or a change of treatment in the event of an oxygen shortage.

When I found that a child had died, I instructed the staff to clean the body properly, carefully remove all the monitoring probes, the IV cannula, the catheter, the endotracheal tube, to clean the bloodstains, and be very gentle and empathetic while breaking the news to the parents.

I listened to each case history and examined each patient but had no control over where I would be called next for an emergency.

Suddenly, the condition of a three-year-old deteriorated. A junior resident started the Ambu tube ventilation, and we all rushed to her bed, but she started bleeding from her nose and mouth. We gave her cardiopulmonary resuscitation (CPR), but it was too late – we could not save her. There was a gush of fresh frothing blood due to a possible pulmonary haemorrhage.

We broke down. Everybody cried – the parents, sisters, junior doctors. I, too, was in tears. It was not just the death that had affected us, but also the sheer frustration, helplessness and fear we were all feeling. We were fighting a monstrous, implacable enemy, and had been denied the most important weapon we needed in the battle – life-giving oxygen.

It was tough to find the words to explain to the parents why their child had died.

Wordlessly, I hugged a few parents before carrying on, because there were still children to be saved. My heart felt heavy as I moved mechanically from bed to bed with my junior.

They now started plying me with questions: What had happened to the oxygen that was supposed to have reached us from Faizabad? How long would it take? What was to be done until then?

I tried to pacify the parents before leaving for ward 12 where there were fewer patients on ventilators. Many of them were stable, but there were still a large number of anxious parents. Some of the children on oxygen were turning blue because of the interrupted supply of oxygen.

'Remove these children from the ventilators and start performing Ambu!' I urged the doctor on emergency duty. I sent the sweeper to ward 6 to get the smaller cylinders and start giving oxygen to the children in ward 12. As I did a quick round of the ward, I noted the condition of each child. I explained to the junior doctors in this ward what we planned to do until the oxygen arrived.

'Try not to admit new patients; refer them to nearby hospitals,' I said. Then realizing the impact this could have on the poor parents who would arrive from faraway places with their beloved children, I added, 'But if they are really ill and don't want to go anywhere else, please admit them.'

Every few minutes, I had to re-evaluate and adapt my strategy to keep up with the rapidly changing conditions of the patients in the wards.

By that point, I had been identified as the single available figure of authority by the parents who waited anxiously for news about their children.

After finishing my round of ward 12, I went to the NICU. A significantly positive feature of the NICU was that nobody was allowed to enter – only babies, doctors and nurses were present. That night, however, several parents had gathered outside the ward.

There were sixteen warmers in working condition, but since there were around seventy to eighty babies, each warmer held four or five of them. Upon asking the doctors on duty about the situation, I discovered that five babies had already died; another twelve desperately needed oxygen. One child had turned completely blue and lay dead.

'Please hand over the body to the parents. Let me talk to them,' I told the doctors. Most of the children in the NICU required oxygen.

When I went to address the concerns of the waiting parents, I discovered that they were all aware that the hospital had run out of oxygen.

'Don't worry, we have jumbo cylinders on the way, which should be reaching any minute now,' I told them.

'Please tell me if my baby will be okay,' someone said.

'Doctor, save my child!' said another.

I tried again to placate them all. 'We are trying our best to save every life. Pray to God, pray to God,' I repeated fervently.

'You don't really have to wait here,' I said. If we have any update, an announcement will be made on the mike. Come to the NICU only when you hear your name being called out.'

I wanted them to stop crowding the area. But they continued to bombard me with questions.

'What if we want to take our child to another hospital?'

'Of course, if you want to take your child to another hospital nearby, you are free to go,' I replied.

While I tried to counsel them, three or four mothers clutched my leg and started begging, 'Doctor, please save my baby!'

'Please understand that we are trying our best,' I said, trying to gently extract my leg from their tight and desperate grip.

'Sir, this child was born after thirteen years of our marriage!' said one woman. Her tearful eyes looked at me so pleadingly that I was shaken to my core.

'This is our only daughter among four brothers!' wailed another mother.

'We were granted a son after many prayers and three daughters!' said a third.

Having grown up in a diverse neighbourhood, I knew the extreme deprivation and poverty against which these people struggled daily. The fact that they reposed such faith and hope in me and that I was unable to help them made me feel utterly frustrated.

My eyes filled with tears again as I left the NICU. I only had one mission now – find oxygen for these gasping babies.

When the mothers pleaded with me to save the lives of their children, I remembered my own daughter, Zab. Would I not be in the same state if it was her life that hung in the balance? The thought reinforced my resolve – I would find and provide oxygen to these children, even if it took me all night.

3

Hunt for Oxygen

Medical oxygen, considered a life-saving drug, features on the National List of Essential Medicines and is also on the World Health Organization's model list of essential medicines. As a doctor accustomed to normal operations in the wards and the ICU, I had never concerned myself with the intricacies of the oxygen supply system. It was taken for granted in a hospital – electricity or water supply could get interrupted but never oxygen.

Every minute of the intervening night of 10–11 August 2017 brought home to me how vital a continuous supply of oxygen was for critically ill patients. I spent hours, until the next morning and even beyond, hunting for oxygen cylinders using every possible source known to me, even if it meant I had to request, plead, beg and give assurances that the cylinders would be returned.

I finished my first round of ward 6, which held patients in a stable condition, most of whom were sleeping peacefully with their parents. I then told the nurses and junior doctors assembled before me not to worry about the oxygen and continue their tasks.

'The jumbo cylinders from Faizabad will reach soon,' I said.

After that, I went to check the oxygen supply in the supply monitoring room behind ward 100. Only one person was there – the central pipeline operator, Balwant. I had met him for the first time in my life, and to him, I was just the doctor who had called him an hour ago.

I introduced myself and asked him to show me the supply system. I wanted to understand for myself how the supply was maintained and measured.

He pointed towards four channels of sixteen cylinders each, and a central panel where the oxygen meter was showing the number zero. After the liquid oxygen tank had emptied, even the replacement cylinders that he had shown me had been exhausted. All the oxygen had run out by 11:30 p.m.

'These sixteen cylinders finish very fast, within forty-five minutes to an hour. Once a channel of sixteen cylinders gets over, we open another channel; meanwhile, we have just enough time to replace those sixteen empty cylinders. This is an emergency system that we hardly use when the liquid oxygen supply is running normally. We had three central pipeline operators, each working in eight-hour shifts, in order for us to maintain a continuous, uninterrupted supply of oxygen. The situation we're in now was not supposed to arise.'

'I understand. But we have to do something now to get these cylinders refilled. I will see what I can get,' I told him.

It was past midnight when I drove to a nearby hospital. I asked the security guard where I could meet the manager of the hospital, but he said the office staff had left and I would have to talk to the doctor on duty.

'Please, I need jumbo cylinders,' I said to the doctor on duty after introducing myself and telling him about the situation at BRD Medical College.

'Well, it is not within my power to give you any cylinders. You will have to talk to the owner of this hospital.'

'All right, please give me his number.'

The doctor obliged, and I called the owner to explain the situation to him.

He was polite but sounded half asleep. 'We don't have many cylinders ourselves, and we also have patients on oxygen. I can give you a maximum of three cylinders. But you must bring back the empty cylinders in the morning, no later. I hope that is clear.'

'Of course,' I said. 'I promise we will return these three cylinders by the morning.'

As soon as the cylinders were loaded into my car, I drove back to the hospital, where, with the help of Balwant, the cylinders were loaded onto a panel. Balwant told me that all three together would last about fifteen to twenty minutes.

'But what else could I do? I couldn't have fit more than three or four cylinders in my car,' I told Balwant. We discussed various other options for a couple of minutes.

'If we can get a mini truck or van, more cylinders can be brought in. But where can we get such transport in the middle of the night?' I asked aloud.

'I know somebody who drives a small truck,' said Balwant.

'Then call him!'

After speaking to his friend on the phone, Balwant turned to me and said, 'Sir, he will come, but he has to be paid right away. He can't wait for the medical college to pay him. What shall I tell him?'

'Ask him to come immediately. I will pay him,' I said.

I had stressed the urgency of the matter, and I was pleasantly surprised to find the van and driver arrive within five to ten minutes. He clearly stayed close to the medical college.

I told him that I needed to go with him to several small and big hospitals nearby, in order to pick up however many cylinders each of those places could provide. He said he was ready, so we set off at once.

In the next couple of hours, we visited some six or eight hospitals, going through a similar process at each one.

I requested cylinders at every hospital. While they generously gave them to us, their only worry was about getting them back. I assured the staff that the cylinders would be returned. When we dropped off the filled cylinders at the medical college, we would load the empty cylinders onto the van and try to return as soon as possible.

I spoke to the doctors on duty, hospital owners and the administrative staff. Even though it was late at night, we managed to round up six cylinders for Balwant to put on another panel and resume the oxygen supply.

At around 1 a.m., I briefly checked on the wards to tell all the nurses and junior residents on duty to not worry, since we had been arranging for oxygen.

It suddenly occurred to me that the jumbo cylinders from Faizabad had still not reached. I got the number of the Imperial Gas Limited (IGL) truck driver from Balwant and called him.

'Where are you now? What is taking so long?'

'I'm near Khalilabad,' he said, which meant he was still around forty minutes from the campus.

'Please drive fast,' I told him. 'It should not have taken you this long. We have an acute emergency.'

After that, I left on another quest for cylinders with the driver of the small truck. This time I managed to get four cylinders from one hospital and eight from another, even though I had to pay up front at some places. This meant that we now had twelve cylinders for Balwant to start some more panels.

It was time to visit the wards once again. Inside, a few parents were performing Ambu, but they were not able to do it properly. I told the doctors to put the children back on the ventilators since we had managed to get some cylinders. But the pressure from these cylinders was not enough for the liquid oxygen to run through the ventilators smoothly, and they continued beeping. Still, it was better than nothing.

It had been a while since I had first arrived at the hospital. My thoughts were with the nurses, doctors and ward staff who had been on their toes all through the crisis. The situation had been so serious that most of them had skipped dinner. I asked one of the ward boys to get tea for everyone and gave him some money. His harried expression turned into a grin as he rushed off on the errand.

Meanwhile, I returned to Balwant in the supply monitoring room.

'What is going on, Balwant? Hasn't it been more than an hour since I spoke to the IGL truck driver? Why hasn't it reached yet? Call him and find out.'

'I just called him. The driver mentioned he was on Bank Road and will reach soon.'

'But why did he even go to Bank Road? He had to come directly from the highway to Medical College Road!' I was baffled by this last-minute complication.

Balwant's expression grew even more resigned. 'They didn't know the way.'

Stunned, I asked, 'What do we do until they reach?'

Fortunately, the driver of the small truck told us he knew of a supplier who could give us cylinders against ready cash.

I gave him ₹10,000. Standing there, holding the money, he then asked me, 'Sir, ₹2,000 out of this is for me, right?' I understood his anxiety about getting paid.

'Yes, yes, you keep two thousand, but please hurry and get more cylinders with the remaining money as quickly as possible.' He left in a trice to begin loading his truck with empty cylinders.

I went back to the wards and found that the OB-GYN (obstetrics and gynaecology) and medicine wards had also been affected by the oxygen crisis. After all, how could they have possibly escaped it, with the 100-foot-tall liquid oxygen tank lying empty? There, too, no senior consultant was present; only junior residents were managing the floor. In the medicine ward, I witnessed the same scene as in paediatrics – the monitors and ventilators were beeping.

I asked the junior resident if he had informed his seniors.

'Yes, sir, but nobody came.'

'So, what are your plans?'

'Sir, we don't know. We have already lost ten patients and ten others are very critical ...'

'Okay, let me see what we can do. We have arranged a few cylinders,' I told him.

The people at the the hospital's Emergency Trauma Centre were embroiled in a similar crisis.

An auto rickshaw had collided with a truck at a very late hour of the night and eight or nine people had arrived with serious injuries – some of them were in a critical condition.

I asked the doctors how they were managing. Their ICU was alongside the casualty ward, and ventilators were beeping there too, but unlike the paediatrics wards, there was a deathly silence in this ICU.

The ICU doctors, for some reason, did not respond when I asked if they had informed their seniors and what they intended to do. I understood the wariness behind their reticence, so I collected the empty cylinders in the corridors and sent them to the small truck to be refilled.

'Just bring as many cylinders as you can,' I told the driver.

The most despairing moment was when the IGL truck finally reached the campus at around 2 a.m. and we realized it was carrying only fifty jumbo cylinders, not 250 as we had assumed.

As I shouted at the driver in desperation, he replied, 'Sir, we received an order for just fifty. I will bring more if you ask me to.'

'What do you mean? You will have to go back to Faizabad to bring more! That will take almost a day!'

'Sir, I will come back as fast as possible,' he said, trying to assure us that he would not lose his way again.

'Fine, just ensure you return with at least 250 cylinders.'

I left to share the news with Balwant. Standing helplessly in the oxygen supply room, both of us had a single thought: What to do now?

In the meantime, the driver of the small truck returned to tell us that the local supplier, Modi Gas, was unwilling to provide any cylinders to us.

'But why? Give me his number – I'll call him,' I said.

The Modi Gas supplier picked up after two rings.

'Modi-ji, we are facing an extreme scarcity – you have to help us.' I explained the problem to him.

'This is not possible, sir. First, you must ask Principal sir to cancel the IGL Allahabad tender and give me the contract; only then can I supply to the medical college,' he replied.

'I am trying to call the principal, but his phone is unreachable. Can you please send us some cylinders now?' I pleaded.

'I can't do that unless the IGL Allahabad contract is cancelled. Why has he assigned the tender to someone from outside the city, and that too as far as Allahabad?'

Although I wanted to bang my head against a wall, I chose to keep persisting instead. 'Look, I don't know about the tender; I am just a doctor.'

'I know you are a doctor, sir. But we have helped you before in an emergency. The last time this happened, we supplied around 200 to 250 cylinders in broad daylight, and yet Principal sir gave the contract to the other supplier.'

My frustration was rising, but his determination seemed to be growing simultaneously.

'Look, I know nothing about this. Please help us tonight – the kids are dying ...'

'No. No, sir, I won't give any cylinders this time,' he said before ending the call.

We continued looking for cylinders, attaching the ones we could source to the column, checking on patients and monitoring if anything needed to be done based on their clinical condition.

By dawn, it was clear that the parents were running out of patience. Four or five men had tried to hit a junior doctor, seeing which a nurse came running to fetch me.

'Sir, they are misbehaving with the doctors!' she cried desperately.

When I reached the ward, the parents rushed towards me and grabbed me by the collar.

'My child has died because of a shortage of oxygen!'

'Can you bring back my child? Are you doctors or demons?

'Who is responsible for my child's death?'

They were agitated, furious, upset and devastated. All of them were shouting at the same time. My shirt was being pulled, and I was pushed once or twice. I tried to stay calm, to not show any fear or anger.

'I understand your pain,' I said, standing before them with folded hands. 'We are doctors, and we are trying to do our very best to save your children. We have been making arrangements through the night to procure oxygen cylinders ...'

'No! No!' a chorus of cries drowned out my voice. 'We will kill you! We heard the ventilators beeping all night. Why was there a shortage? Why have so many children died? Why did you ask us to use Ambu bags? Do you think we don't understand what's going on?'

The questions kept coming. Where were the other senior doctors? Where was the superintendent of the hospital? Where was the principal?

'We want to talk to them – NOW!'

I have never used my persuasive powers with as much determination as I was forced to that night, in order to pacify the distressed parents. Then, by some miracle, they slowly left the ward. The nurses and junior doctors had, by now, grown apprehensive, so I had to convince them to keep going.

'You are doing great work. Let's keep it up. Their anger is natural, but they have realized we are doing what we can.' I tried to reassure them as best I could.

The longest night of my life was drawing to an end, but the horrors it had unleashed wouldn't dissipate anytime soon.

4

Dawn, Death and Decisions

The crowd of parents outside, the deliveries made by the small oxygen truck, the discussion among all those gathered about how the lives of their loved ones had been affected by the lack of oxygen – none of this had gone unnoticed during that long night at the BRD Medical College.

Soon after, I began marshalling the paediatrics department's doctors and staff to deal with the emergency.

'You have not informed anyone outside the hospital, right?' I asked them, seeking confirmation that they had understood the need for this crisis to be contained within the hospital.

'No, sir. But some local reporters have already arrived,' a junior doctor told me.

'What? Who informed them?' I asked. However, even as I framed the question, I was aware this was beyond the scope of the doctor's knowledge. Journalists had their own ways of gathering information, just as we had our means when it came to treating patients.

The doctor's shrug confirmed my hypothesis. 'We have no idea, sir. No information has gone out from any of us.' I patted his shoulder reassuringly before carrying on with our work.

But even when the morning of 11 August dawned, we were far from achieving the oxygen capacity that was considered normal.

I began making calls as soon as there was daylight, hoping for a better response from my seniors and the hospital administration than I had received the night before. The first call was to the chief medical superintendent (CMS), Dr Ramashanker Shukla.

'I am coming,' he said.

But he did not show up.

Next, I called Dr Satish Kumar, an anaesthesiologist appointed by the medical college as the administrator of oxygen supply. 'Good morning, sir, this is Dr Kafeel.'

'Good morning!' he replied. 'Tell me, Kafeel, what is it?'

Shaking off my bewilderment, I told him in detail what had transpired during the night. He heard the whole account, making appropriate sounds at regular intervals to indicate that he was listening. This was followed by a long pause as I waited for his reply.

'Actually, Kafeel, I am on my way to Lucknow. From there, I will take a flight to Mumbai to attend my son's convocation ceremony on the 12th.'

'Shit!' I exclaimed before I could stop myself. 'Okay, sir,' I said in resignation.

Just then, one of the junior doctors came and said to me, 'Sir, a stringer from a local newspaper was taking pictures of us. I didn't talk to them. I've asked the security guard to tell them to leave and to not let anyone enter the PICU.'

'Yes, you did well,' I said to him.

'But sir, they went to the oxygen site and talked to Balwant. They checked the supply system, too.'

Meanwhile, some people had found the central oxygen supply area of the hospital where a huge tank, about

100 feet tall, stood, with a bearing capacity of thousands of tonnes of liquid oxygen. The investigation into the night's events by the local press had begun in earnest.

As for the oxygen situation, during the night, we had arranged around fifty cylinders from local hospitals and another fifty which had arrived on the IGL truck; by 5:30 a.m., the ventilators in the paediatrics wards had started beeping as the oxygen ran out. We had supplied cylinders to other wards in need as well. I decided to check on the IGL driver once more. He was on the way when we called him, but it would take him another three to four hours to reach the city.

Yet again, calculating our options, I called our HOD. This time, she picked up her phone but told me to put the children on ventilators back on Ambu until the IGL cylinders reached us. I was in disbelief.

My mind was being stretched in many different directions. How could I tell a parent whose child was gasping for breath in front of them to perform Ambu on that child? How would they control their emotions while performing medical procedures on their child? Why did these children and their parents' lives appear so unimportant to the conveyers of these cold instructions? Was it because they were poor and powerless?

Shaking off those thoughts, I decided to focus on the circumstances at hand. The solution was simple – we needed more oxygen. We began doing rounds of the nearby hospitals again, from where, after much beseeching and begging, we managed to procure another sixteen cylinders. But I knew it still wouldn't be enough.

The situation at the hospital had been rapidly deteriorating. Ten or twelve women had started wailing loudly in the waiting area of ward 100, and it was clear that nothing could possibly ease their pain.

I was forced to tell the doctors and nurses to restart Ambu, as we had run out of oxygen again. When all the ventilators started beeping together, a collective howl of misery rose from the ward. My hair was standing on end, and I could not bear to think of the parents' grief, of their momentous loss.

A nurse came running to take me to the bedside of a fourteen-year-old who was having seizures. These appeared to be generalized tonic-clonic seizures, for which midazolam had been administered, but the seizures had still not stopped. I told my juniors to give him phenobarbitone on the one hand and a bolus of 10 per cent dextrose and diazepam on the other. After sedation, the child was intubated and started on bag-and-tube ventilation. Eventually his seizures stopped, the oxygen saturation picked up and his vitals stabilized. We breathed a sigh of relief as his pupils began reacting to light.

At the same moment, I noticed that the monitor on another child's bed showed flat ECG waves. I shouted at a junior to start Ambu, examining his chest myself. But there was no heartbeat.

'Sister, inject with atropine and adrenaline!' I yelled, checking for a heartbeat again. His pupils were dilated and unmoving. The child had died.

A loud scream of frustration erupted from my chest, at which everyone in the ward turned to look at me as if I had gone mad. I had shocked myself with the involuntary outburst. The only way I could comprehend it was by coming to terms with the emotional extremes I had experiences within a span of minutes.

An inner voice told me to calm down. I excused myself and walked over to the doctors' room. I sat there for a while with my eyes closed, trying to regain my composure. My chest felt heavy, while my mind was full of anxiety for the remaining critically ill patients on ventilators.

Upon collecting myself, I washed my face and poured some cold water on my head. As I wiped my head dry, a new determination took hold of me. I could not have any more deaths take place under my watch, even though I had no idea how to carry out my mission.

I decided to give the parents the option to take their children to another hospital if they wished to do so. It would lead to chaos, I knew. The people who were already agitated would become angrier and more aggressive. They might get violent with the doctors and nurses too, but if even a few lives could be saved by shifting the critically ill children to a different, why should they not be provided the chance?

On returning, I discovered that one more child, an eight-year-old, had died in cubicle 4.

'Please be very careful while cleaning the body,' I told the nurses who were removing the cannula, the monitoring probes and the nasogastric tube (NG) tube. 'Do not leave even a single spot of blood because that will create a bad impression. It will appear as though we don't care, which will really hurt the parents.' The nurses nodded and continued performing their tasks.

Just then, a nurse sprinted towards me and said breathlessly, 'Sir! They have entered the NICU!'

Leaving the parents with whom I had been speaking, I climbed the stairs two at a time and rushed to the NICU. By the time I reached, ten to twelve people were inside already. I asked them to leave.

We gathered them outside in the waiting hall to explain the same option I had given to the other parents a few minutes ago. I kept talking, without making direct eye contact, scanning everyone's faces as they threw many, many questions at me.

'How are you treating my baby now? Where is your senior?'

'Sir, we are trying our best. You have seen how we have been working through the night ...'

'Yeah, okay, we don't have a problem with you, but why is there no oxygen?' The father's voice was loud, and he was extremely agitated, as he had every reason to be. I did not have any answers for the parents. I simply kept silent until they had released their frustration and then repeated the options, once again.

'We are doing everything we can. We are trying to save every single child, which is the reason I have told my junior residents that if anybody wants to take their child elsewhere, let them. If that is the only way to save a life, we urge you to do it.'

They were not happy to hear this, but nobody argued further at that point, for which I was thankful.

By now, more reporters had collected outside. Some were arguing with the doctors and security staff. 'We need to see what is happening!' I could hear some shouting. 'This is a public hospital – we have to know how people are being treated!'

A few of them had managed to enter the wards and take pictures.

My struggles through the night with Balwant had drawn the attention of many other staff members at the hospital. Anup, an outsourced staffer of the oxygen maintenance department, had shared with me the number of a supplier called Balaji Gas Limited. I called them up immediately.

'Hello, I am Dr Kafeel from BRD. I received your number from Anup. We are facing an acute shortage of oxygen here, due to which we need at least 200 jumbo cylinders. Can you provide these immediately?'

'I can refill your cylinders, but you will have to pay me in cash, at the rate of ₹350 per cylinder.' He paused, letting the amount sink in before continuing, 'As you know, sir, *sarkaari kaam mein paise jaldi milte nahin hain* (when it comes to government work, payments take a long time) ...'

'In that case, I will give you the money. I am sending a man with cash and empty cylinders – please refill them as soon as possible,' I said. I gave a ward boy my ATM card and told him to withdraw ₹20,000 before leaving for the Balaji Gas office.

Around 9:30 a.m., the truck from IGL Faizabad arrived with fifty more jumbo cylinders. I was furious. 'How could you get only fifty when you knew that we need around 250 cylinders per day?' I shouted. What about the medicine ward, the OB-GYN, the trauma centre and emergency wards? Do you think they don't require oxygen? We are all starved, and you have brought us only fifty?'

The driver stood silently in front of me, without offering any explanation, which irked me further. 'This time you won't go back to Faizabad,' I told him. 'We need your truck, and you will have to drive us around so that we can pick up cylinders from local suppliers.'

Alarmed, he mumbled, 'No, no, I have to go, I have to go ...'

Struggling to calm myself, I took a few deep breaths before asking, 'How much do you earn for each round trip?'

'₹2,000.'

'I will pay you the same as well as money for diesel. *Main chai paani ka bhi kharcha de dunga* (I will also give you money for tea and snacks), but you have to help us!'

This seemed to clinch the deal, and he agreed to stay on with his truck.

We called up another supplier, Mayur Gases Limited at Khalilabad, who agreed to refill our cylinders. I immediately sent the truck driver there, accompanied by Anup and around fifty empty cylinders.

I reached out to Dr Khalid Abbasi, the president of the Nursing Home Association of Gorakhpur, and explained our predicament to him to see if he could offer some help. 'I'll try and see what I can I do,' he said.

At 10 a.m., I called the principal, Dr Rajiv K. Mishra, again. To my relief, he picked up his phone. I told him about everything that had happened over the course of the past night. In fact, what we had been through in the paediatrics wards was only part of the story. Apart from the twenty-three deaths in the paediatrics ward, there had been eighteen deaths in the medicine ward. I tried conveying the graveness of the situation to the principal. 'Sir, IGL is sending only fifty cylinders each time, and the local supplier Modi Gas told me that until the principal gives him a contract and cancels the one awarded to IGL, he won't give us any cylinders.'

The principal promised to talk to all parties and to the district magistrate as well.

On hearing his authoritative words, the shock of the events of the night finally took hold of me.

The doctors, ward boys and nurses, who had been working continuously through the traumatic night, wanted to go home. At my request to continue, some agreed, while others went home. Next, I ordered breakfast for everyone; after a quick meal, we returned to the wards. I started doing fresh rounds, moving from one bed to another. A few patients had taken a turn for the worse, so I began advising and consoling their parents.

Some more consultants had appeared now, taking their rounds in the cabins assigned to them. By 1 p.m., the most notable absentee was the HOD, Dr Mahima Mittal.

I decided to call the acting principal, Dr Jaiswal, and the superintendent-in-chief, Dr A. K. Srivastava, to inform them about the situation. Soon, they arrived at the medicine ward, where they told me they would visit the paediatrics wards next. While waiting for them to turn up, I noticed that many more local newspaper journalists had assembled outside the paediatrics wards. They were taking pictures and talking to the parents. As they saw me walking in the corridor, someone called out to me. 'Sir, sir, what is happening?'

'How many kids have died in the night?' another one enquired.

'Is there still a shortage of oxygen?'

'Why is there a shortage? Where are your seniors? Where are the principal and superintendent?'

I wondered why all of them had landed up at the paediatrics wards when the central pipeline oxygen running out must have flung the whole hospital into a crisis. This was a nagging cause of concern, but I had more important things to worry about at the time, so I continued my work, ignoring their questions.

The main issue I had faced in arranging oxygen was the lack of a large-enough vehicle to transport the cylinders. The small truck owned by Balwant's friend could only be used for a maximum of fifteen to twenty of them. I spoke to Dharmendra Kumar, a computer operator, about arranging a larger truck.

'Sir, arranging a truck will be expensive. With that money, we can instead get more cylinders. There is a Sashastra Seema Bal (SSB) containment area near our campus. If we reach out to them, they may help us.'

This was all I needed to hear. We drove immediately to the containment area which was just three kilometres away from the medical college campus.

During my call to the principal to apprise him of the developments, he had told me that he had informed the district magistrate of Gorakhpur. He had also spoken to some nearby hospitals which would give us more cylinders.

Suddenly, I saw that I was getting a call from an unknown number. '*DM sir aap se baat karenge* (DM sir wants to talk to you),' someone said on the line and handed the phone to the district magistrate, Rajeev Rautela.

'Where is your HOD and why is she not picking up the phone?' he asked.

'I don't know, sir,' I replied truthfully.

'Well, what is the situation right now?'

'Sir, around twenty-three kids have died already, and there are several still in a critical condition. I don't know about the other wards in the hospital because I have been busy looking after the paediatrics wards.'

'Okay, I have talked to Modi Gas. They will send over oxygen cylinders. How many do you need?'

'We need at least 250 cylinders per day, sir.'

'Did you ask Pushpa Sales about the oxygen requirements?'

'No, sir, I don't have their number. But I think Principal sir must have spoken to them, or perhaps the superintendent ...'

'Why did this crisis happen?'

'Sir, really, how would I know? I am a paediatrician, the junior-most consultant, who joined only a year ago. I only came to know last night that there is a crisis ...'

'Fine. Keep me updated on everything that happens,' he said.

'Okay, sir,' I said, wondering what exactly I was supposed to report to him.

At the SSB office, we explained the situation to the three or four staff members sitting inside the computer operator's room.

'This is an unprecedented crisis. We need help,' I told them.

Looking at one another meaningfully, they said, 'You need to talk to our deputy inspector general.'

After about a fifteen-minute wait, we were called to the office of the DIG.

I stepped inside the large room to find a uniformed senior official. On the walls hung group photographs of previous and current unit members and photos of border-area landscapes.

'Yes, doctor, tell me,' the DIG said, responding to my greeting.

'Sir, we are faced with a very grave situation at BRD Medical College since the liquid oxygen tank ran out last night and we don't have enough jumbo cylinders left in stock. Children are dying, and we have many critically ill patients at the Nehru Hospital. If you could provide us with one of your trucks, we can get around 100–200 cylinders refilled in a single trip and save lives.'

He listened carefully before gently responding, 'Just write an application and I will arrange for the truck.'

I wrote the application in front of him and signed it. Within ten minutes, a truck was made available to us. I buckled my nerves to ask for a little more.

'Sir, you have a hospital on campus, too – could you provide us with some cylinders?'

'We have a very small hospital, so it won't be possible for us to give you cylinders, but we will send our soldiers to help you load the truck,' he said with a smile.

We returned to the campus, the SSB truck following us through the hospital gates.

5

All Hell Breaks Loose

After the life-and-death struggle for oxygen on the intervening night of 10–11 August, the following day mired us in a different kind of trial. I was waging a war against the indifference, entitlement, arrogance and negligence that seem to come naturally to people in positions of power in our country, even those in the medical profession. We were in a situation that demanded a Herculean effort, both mentally and physically. I did not know it then, but it would be the beginning of how the 'system' would test me.

The cynicism of political actors, who advance their careers on the backs of issues that affect a large section of the public but do little to solve or even address those problems, would also become clear to me.

By the time I returned to ward 100 from the SSB office, the number of reporters outside the building had considerably increased; they now started bombarding me with questions.

'Has the hospital completely run out of oxygen?'

'Yes, the liquid oxygen is over. But we are managing with jumbo oxygen cylinders.'

'How many kids have died? When will you restore the liquid oxygen?' The questions would not stop.

'I am not the right person to answer your questions. Please talk to the principal or the head of our department,' I said.

My reply was met with angry shouts, 'But where are they?'

Without saying anything further, I went inside to examine the children again and make treatment plans based on their clinical status. Since that morning, even though we had spent the day looking for oxygen, five more children had died. It was now Friday afternoon and I had been working since Thursday night when the tank had run dry. I was irritated, frustrated and heartbroken, but my emotions were nothing compared to the parents of the critically ill children. They were growing agitated again, so I tried to reassure a few of them.

Sometime later, Dr Anita Mehta, a professor in our department, called me. 'Where are you?' she asked.

'I am in the ward, ma'am. I have been here since last night. I came to attend to the emergency brought on by the oxygen crisis. Please come here and help us. Nobody else has.'

'What? What crisis?' she enquired, as if I had just reported a bombing.

'The liquid oxygen, ma'am,' I said. It ran out around 7:30 p.m. last night.'

'And nobody told me!' she said, shocked. 'Dr Mahima came to the office in the morning and said she couldn't be on duty because she has the swine flu. She told me she is on leave and left me in charge. Then she went home. She didn't tell me anything!'

My tired brain was doing somersaults.

'Ma'am, the situation here is horrible,' I told her. 'I don't know what HOD ma'am told you, but the truth is that in the past twenty-four hours, twenty-three children have died and the whole hospital is in a crisis because all the wards are struggling due to a shortage of oxygen.'

'Okay, I'll come to the wards soon,' she said, her voice furious.

Meanwhile, we collected empty cylinders from every corner of the hospital and loaded them onto the SSB truck with six or seven soldiers. We were able to gather close to 120 empty jumbo cylinders.

This time, we were to pick up refills from Modi Gas. The DM had told me that he had spoken to the supplier who had agreed to refill our cylinders, so I directed the truck to their office.

Since the situation at the hospital was still out of hand and the casualties were increasing, I had decided to seek help from more people with the power to arrange oxygen supplies. I called the chief medical officer and the chief medical superintendent of the district hospital in Gorakhpur, as well as the additional director of health (Gorakhpur zone) and relayed the grave problem we had been facing.

'Please, sir, send us some jumbo cylinders from the district hospital – it will be a huge favour,' I told them.

What I was unprepared for was how lightly they reacted to my speech.

The CMO asked me to call the CMS, which I did. The CMS, in turn, said, 'I can only provide three to four cylinders.'

The additional director of Health said, 'I am in a meeting; I'll call you back.' But he never called back.

I wondered if I had failed to mention the number of deaths to all of them. Had I been able to convey the graveness of the situation? Was I going crazy, or were they?'

It was now Friday, and my wife had sent me a change of clothes. I made use of the doctors' restroom to wash and clean up and offered my Friday prayers there. My heart was bursting with a single prayer that echoed again and again inside me: *Allah ya Allah*, please, no more deaths. *Rehem kar, mere malik, rehem kar* (Have mercy, my lord, please have mercy).

But the dance of death continued, even during the day.

Every half an hour or so, a small, lifeless body emerged from the PICU or the NICU.

The nurses at BRD normally work three shifts. Night duty begins at 8 p.m. and continues until 8 a.m. However, I had requested the night nurses to continue beyond their shifts on that fateful Friday. A few of them had left, but most were still toiling away. To those nurses who normally finished their duty at 2 p.m., I requested, 'Please don't go home until we find a solution to the oxygen crisis. These are exceptional circumstances. You know that our patients' lives are at stake.'

A senior nurse told me calmly, 'Don't worry, doctor, we know. We are also mothers and sisters.'

I also urged the junior doctors to continue beyond their shifts, and they agreed.

Around 2 p.m., a small group of parents appeared outside, some of them crying and screaming. A lady was holding a baby of about six to eight months. The child was gasping for breath.

I rushed towards them and asked what the problem was. 'The doctor has refused admission, and they are telling us to go to some other hospital. But we have come from very far and my baby is dying. Please, doctor, save my child!' The mother was beside herself with grief and anxiety. The child's grandmother looked at me pleadingly, with folded hands, her eyes full of tears.

As I held the baby in my arms, I saw that though the child was alive, her breathing was shallow, and the body was turning blue. I ran inside the ward, shouting for a nurse to connect the child to a monitor. We found that her oxygen saturation was 60 per cent with a heart rate of fifty-six per minute. I intubated the child, and then put her on a ventilator. Next, after consoling the mother, I inserted the IV cannula and started the fluids and inotropes. Finally, setting the ventilatory parameters to 70% FiO2, PEEP 6, PIP 16, I did an ABG analysis.

We also had to explain to the grandmother what we were doing, and its possible risks, in order to get the consent form signed. I wrote the order for admission and gave a junior resident some instructions, after determining that the child's condition was stabilizing.

Fortunately, that child, Bhumika, survived. She is four years old now, a source of joy for her family. As for me, the life-affirming moment in which I held her filled me with an even greater resolve.

I went to the principal's office and vented my feelings to the principal's secretary, Mrs Shobha, who proved to be a calming influence. I told her how the HOD had suddenly gone on leave, and that the acting principal and the SIC had not turned up at our wards even though they kept saying they were coming.

'How am I to handle all this alone – the crowds of parents and media persons?' I asked her. 'Only the junior resident doctors are with me in the wards. Already more than thirty children have died. Everyone is upset and at their wits' end. Someone senior should be standing alongside me to handle the situation.'

Around 2:30 p.m., the Modi Gas supplier, after making many excuses despite the call from the DM, finally started sending jumbo cylinders to refill the ones we had borrowed earlier. The SSB truck and the soldiers were very helpful, fulfilling a vital function.

I returned to the ward and gave everyone the good news.

The nurses and ward staff, who had been working relentlessly, told me, 'Sir, we are very tired; we have not had lunch. We're really hungry.' Apologizing to them, I immediately arranged for some cold drinks and snacks.

It was an endless runaround for me, from ward 100 to 12 and back to 100, and then to the emergency ward and the NICU.

Whenever I could, I spoke to the junior residents, nurses and ward boys. 'Don't panic. It will lower everybody's morale and spiral the situation further out of control. This is the hour for us to show our humanitarian side. We should try to save every life. Whatever happens next, we will be rewarded. Everybody will get appreciation certificates and awards that will help you in your careers.'

I did not know if my motivational speech had any influence on them, or whether I was addressing them for myself. After all, we were all equally affected by the events of the night. I was also feeling quite disheartened after seeing that despite all our efforts, every half hour another child was dying. I tried not to dwell on my colleagues' lack of response or their body language which conveyed defeat.

Rajini, the nurse in charge of ward 100, had been writing more records and certificates than she had ever written. She helped me inform all the nurses who arrived for their shift at 2 p.m., 'Please tell your family that you may have to work all through the night!'

Meanwhile, I had found another lead to help unravel the mystery of the oxygen crisis. Anup sent me the contact details of the agent at Pushpa Sales, which supplied the liquid oxygen at the hospital. I called him, though this was neither my responsibility nor my jurisdiction. I was desperate to know when the oxygen would arrive. 'Hello, I am speaking from BRD Medical College. Why are you not delivering liquid oxygen?' I asked him straightaway.

He provided an equally straightforward answer, which shocked me to my core and knocked the wind out of my sails. 'Sir, a payment of ₹68 lakh is still due to us. We have sent so many reminders, but nobody is ready to pay our bill. We are not going to resume our supply until our dues have been paid.'

I took a deep breath and tried a new tactic.

'I assure you, after Principal sir comes back from Rishikesh, your payment will be processed. But you must resume the supply right now. Too many kids have died, or I would not be begging to you like this. Please don't let money become a hurdle in a matter of life and death!'

'No, sir. Whatever happens, we are not going to send liquid oxygen, or resume our supply, until the medical college has cleared our dues.' And that was that.

I returned to the wards and spoke to the parents. I cried with some of them and hugged others. It was a deeply emotional moment for the ones offering comfort and certainly those at the receiving end.

Dr Anita Mehta, who had been left in charge by the HOD, took a round of the wards. I heard her calling someone with whom she then had a huge argument. I imagined it was the HOD. I do not know how their argument ended, but suddenly Dr Anita came to me and said, 'The HOD will come soon. I am leaving.'

When the HOD finally arrived, it was 3 p.m. She was accompanied by the chief medical superintendent, Dr Ramashanker Shukla. I briefed her about the events of the previous night and she took down the details. Then she and Dr Shukla went to the seminar room where they had a meeting. They were in the middle of a discussion when I entered the room, but she immediately told me, 'Kafeel, go and see how many cylinders we have right now and how many we have received since last night.'

'Ma'am, I can tell you without leaving the room,' I said. 'The liquid oxygen supply was interrupted at 7:30 p.m. and the reserve cylinders were over by 11:30 p.m. From 11:30 p.m. to 1:30 a.m., there was no oxygen – neither liquid oxygen nor jumbo cylinders, even though we got a few from the nearby hospitals. But that was not enough.' I began to explain to her the difficulties we had with the local suppliers, but she interjected and told me to leave.

Our brief meeting made me realize the need to document all the steps we had taken to procure oxygen. I went to the oxygen supply site. Balwant had gone home, but I found another operator, Kamlesh, on duty. When I asked him to show me the logbook, I was shocked to discover that they did not have any.

'So how do you know which cylinders have arrived and from where?' I shouted.

He showed me a register on the back of which they had written the details of all the cylinders we had collected through the night, along with their numbers. Each jumbo cylinder usually carries a unique number. This brought me some relief, even though it was a matter of grave concern that they did not have a better system of record-keeping.

Back at the hospital, I informed the HOD that all the details were available.

'Sure, yeah,' she responded, sounding preoccupied, before leaving the room altogether.

Two clerks in the paediatrics department, Pandey-ji and Purushottam, told me that the HOD and Dr Shukla had been drafting a letter to send to the principal. This letter, 'No. 1075/BRG/MC/nechi-17 dated 11/08/2017', stated that liquid oxygen was completely over and that the firm responsible for supplying the oxygen had refused to supply it. They requested him to kindly ensure an immediate, uninterrupted supply of oxygen, with the help of the DM and commissioner of Gorakhpur, to save the lives of the critically ill patients admitted at BRD.

'That is great, but what about the immediate need for oxygen? What about managing the patients? When will they apply their mind to that emergency?' I asked.

The clerks looked sheepish and helpless. 'Dr Kafeel, you know how important it is that we should look strong on paper. If something happens afterwards, we will be in trouble.' I left their office. It was pointless to expect proper answers from them.

Now that Modi Gas had begun refilling our jumbo cylinders, the situation had improved.

I called Anup who was at Mayur Gases in Khalilabad.

'What is taking so long, Anup?'

'They are not yet filling our cylinders, sir,' he said. 'They keep making some or the other excuse, so we are waiting.' I told him I would speak to the owner in an attempt to speed things up, but the man refused to talk to me.

A fact that became quite evident during this crisis was that none of the three major local gas suppliers were extending support. Modi Gas had begun supplying only after being reprimanded by the DM. Balaji Gas, after agreeing to give us cylinders, had stopped taking my calls. Now Mayur Gases was refusing us refills, even though we had agreed to pay in cash and our van had been waiting at their location for more than six hours.

I dialled the number from which the DM had called me, which was answered by his personal assistant. He promised to help when I explained the situation to him. Within the next five minutes, I got a call from the office of the DM of Khalilabad, asking what kind of help we required. I told them about our van being stuck at Mayur Gases and needing refills. It was only after they spoke to the owner that we were able to get our cylinders refilled.

Despite that, only seven cylinders could be filled. Their new excuse was that the gas at the plant was over, and it was now closing time. When Anup called to tell me about this new hurdle, a wave of exhaustion washed over me.

'All right, Anup. Come back with the seven at least,' was all I could say.

At six in the evening, at the end of that very long day, following a traumatic night taking rounds of desperate wards and dealing with an oxygen shortage, I suddenly got a call from the acting principal, Dr Jaiswal.

'Kafeel, some reporters are asking me about the details of the oxygen crisis. What should I say?' he asked.

I felt anger coursing through my veins. 'Sir, where are you?' I asked.

'I am at my clinic,' was his astounding reply.

I tried to sound calm, even though my urge was to yell. 'Sir, I have been calling you since last night, but you never showed up at our wards, and now you have gone to your private clinic! Do you realize, sir, that thirty-five kids have died, and eighteen adults, too? *Gardan kategi sabki; thik nahi kar rahe aap* (Heads will roll; what you're doing is not right),' I said and ended the call.

During my years studying medicine at Manipal, I had never faced such a crisis. Even in Gorakhpur, before the night of 10 August 2017, I had no idea who supplied oxygen to the hospital and where the central tank was located.

But now many well-known reporters had arrived on campus – reporters from the *Times of India*, *Hindustan Times*, *Indian Express* and *Dainik Jagran*, among others. And they kept demanding answers.

The nodal officer of encephalitis, who was nowhere to be seen all through the crisis, now appeared at the ward. The HOD was now actively doing her rounds, with a mask on.

Later in the evening, a local member of parliament arrived with a retinue of thirty to forty supporters as well as his bodyguard. He asked the resident doctors to lead him to the paediatrics ward. He walked in, talked to a few parents, some doctors and the HOD, but did not go to the oxygen site.

As a shrewd politician, he let reporters follow him everywhere and even gave them sound bites. He was the first politician to speak to the media about oxygen shortage just outside the PICU in ward 100, and his comments were covered by all the television channels, including Aaj Tak, ABP, NDTV and others. He did not, however, help us with the oxygen cylinder situation or anything else for that matter.

His interview had a huge impact; within an hour, people started arriving out of nowhere. The grounds of the BRD Medical College campus began to resemble a scene out of the 2010 Hindi film *Peepli Live*. There was a long string of outdoor shooting vans from almost every media house in the country.

The Gorakhpur magistrate and the CMO also turned up with a large group of policemen. After they reached, the gates of the medical college were shut.

The DM of Gorakhpur came at around 7:30 p.m. with a few more officers. He was furious. The HOD, the SIC, the CMS and the acting principal were called in for a closed-door meeting. After they had discussed the situation for about fifteen minutes, I was summoned to provide certain details. Everything was now being noted down.

The people from the DM's office took control of the office computers. They called all the consultants and junior residents and instructed them not to issue death certificates without their permission. No one was to be allowed inside the PICU or the NICU, not even parents. No one was to leave the medical college until further orders had been issued. No one was supposed to talk to the media. The BRD campus and the paediatrics department, especially, had become a highly secured area within an hour. I heard someone saying there were news flashes from BRD on all the TV channels. The director general of medical education (DGME), Dr K. K. Gupta, and the additional chief secretary of medical education, Dr Anita Bhatnagar Jain, had also called from Lucknow and spoken to Dr Mittal.

The DM was informed by the HOD that I would be able to explain the crisis better. I told them everything that had happened in the last twenty-four hours. After I finished, he decided to address the media parked at the gates.

Meanwhile, I kept treating the patients.

The media personnel were invited into the seminar room. The DM asked for the data to be gathered – how many oxygen cylinders had been brought and from where, how many children had died, their names, ages, sex, fathers' names and causes of death. We were told not to mention the shortage of oxygen as the cause of death. Now, official administrators would take over.

In his address, the DM said clearly that there was no shortage of oxygen. Whatever deaths had occurred were due to illnesses. He ignored all the questions related to the payment for oxygen supply.

'Yes, the liquid oxygen supply was interrupted but was resumed with jumbo cylinders, and we have arranged for around 250 cylinders in the past twenty-four hours,' he declared. This was completely different from what he had said when he addressed the media at his office in the afternoon. At that point, he had accepted that there was a prolonged shortage of oxygen. 'We have been told that BRD has witnessed a disturbance in the liquid oxygen supply since last night, as the firm has withdrawn the supply owing to non-payment,' he had said earlier.

'At present, there are fifty oxygen cylinders and 100 to 150 more will be reaching soon,' he added.

He also announced that a five-member enquiry committee would be instituted, which would prepare a report within twenty-four hours. The committee would be headed by the sub-divisional magistrate (SDM), and the CMO and the additional director of Health would be a part of it in order to find out the real cause of the deaths and the cause for the interruption in the supply of oxygen.

While interacting with the media, the DM was also fielding calls from Dr Anita Bhatnagar Jain, the additional chief secretary of medical education, and some other officials from Lucknow. He concluded the press meet and spoke to the chief minister. 'We have got enough jumbo cylinders. I have talked to the liquid oxygen supplier and made the payment to them, and soon liquid oxygen will also reach the hospital.'

The commissioner of Gorakhpur told the media that 'there was a shortage of oxygen but was managed through oxygen cylinders from SSB and other resources. No deaths have occurred due to the shortage of oxygen. None of the parents have complained to me or the DM. A committee has been formed to find out the real cause. Twenty-three children died on 10 August and seven until 5 p.m. today.'

Now things suddenly took a turn. Instead of saving lives, all our energies were to be diverted to administrative matters. Now the whole hospital was surrounded by police officers – both men and women. The local police station inspector, the sub-inspector – everybody was present. They did not interfere with the treatment process. Instead, they were in charge of sending the bodies of dead children, wrapped in bedsheets, to their parents – and through the back door. A uniformed police officer accompanied each body.

They had been asked to escort parents to the railway station, bus stop, or to their homes if they lived nearby. But there was no direction to deliver even a single word of sympathy or condolence.

This was not the battle I had been fighting during the last twenty-four hours. Now, with the officials present, I had even more work. I was being called by some official or the other so that I could repeat the same information over and over again. I wanted to go back to the wards to treat our child patients, but each time I went there, I would be called back.

The officials sat in closed rooms, either the seminar room or a consultant doctors' chamber, discussing among themselves and then writing things down. I sensed that everyone was now trying to level the blame on the principal. Why had he left for Rishikesh without informing the DGME? Why had the payments not been made? While the officials were preparing their notes, a few parents refused to leave with the body of their dead children. Crying and screaming, they had begun a dharna on the premises. More and more people were turning up, asking about the number of deaths.

It was the right moment for various politicians, from different political parties, to make their presence felt. NGOs, social workers or *samaj sevis* – everyone had begun to announce how many cylinders they would contribute. That was what began to make headlines. 'Gita Press has announced they will give fifty cylinders!' 'Sarafa Society has announced it will provide thirty cylinders!' Some association or the other announced it would loan twenty cylinders.

The politicians were coming to the PICU mainly to talk to the media. The most surprising fact was that whatever details were being recorded by the officials at BRD were somehow already known to the politicians.

We had made a chart depicting when the oxygen supply was interrupted, and from where we had arranged the cylinders. This went viral by nighttime. The list we had put together of the children who had died was circulating through WhatsApp messages. This could not have been possible without someone from the inside leaking everything to the media.

By the time the long evening faded into the night, we had finally procured enough cylinders. But hypoxia or the deficiency of oxygen causes a breakdown of the body's metabolism, leading to multiple organ failure – the kidney, lung, brain and, finally, failure of the heart. It was only that the duration between these incidents had increased, and now there seemed to be an attempt to show a number far lesser than the actual figure.

Some parents who had lost their children were sent away through the back door. The parents of the children who died signed affidavits, all of which were in the same handwriting, stating there was a shortage of oxygen but the doctors were able to arrange it. If a child had died, it was due to their illness. To a question asking if their child had died due to a shortage of liquid oxygen, the response said: '*Ji nahi. Oxygen ki kami se mrityu nahi hui. Tabiyat atyadhik kharab hone ke karan ilaaj ke hi dauraan ho gayi* (No, the death was not due to a lack of oxygen. The deterioration in their health caused their death while they were being treated).'

I knew that the ventilators would not work properly until the liquid oxygen supply had resumed. The supply came from Rajasthan, and it usually took forty-eight to seventy-two hours to reach.

On Friday night, my brother and a few of his friends brought me food and a change of clothes. We ate dinner with the other consultants and the junior and senior residents.

My family was proud of me now that everybody had started talking about my efforts. I was being given a lot of importance, and the DM and the CMO were calling me personally. Everybody was praising me. Even the HOD and the acting principal were saying that I had done a good job. If I had known then what I found out a few weeks later, I would have recorded each one of those endorsements for my own protection.

Instead, sleep-deprived and completely exhausted, I continued tending to the children in the ICU and answering questions from the officials.

Since I was at the hospital, I remained largely unaware of what was happening on the television news channels and in the world outside. Those around me said there was a huge uproar and that people in Gorakhpur were protesting. Even just outside the medical college, angry groups of people had congregated.

The opposition parties in the state had blamed the government, particularly after the news broke that this tragedy had occurred due to the non-payment of dues to the hospital's oxygen supplier. The public was now driven to a frenzy.

6

The Blame Game Begins

On Friday night, on 11 August, after my brother left, I was resting in the doctors' room, talking to a few of my colleagues. At 10 p.m., the members of the enquiry committee had already gathered in the principal's office. They sent a message calling me and some doctors from other departments as well. The DM's enquiry was to be completed in twenty-four hours, under strict orders from the chief minister.

When I entered and began following the proceedings, I found that many doctors who were said to be the principal's favourites were present. They were trying to protect him by pointing out that he was in Rishikesh on an official visit, had submitted a leave application and had left the acting principal in charge. This was not an irregularity.

As for the glaring issue of the non-payment of dues to Pushpa Sales, this group of doctors said that the budget had lapsed in March 2017 because of an accountant's fault. When this had been detected, one Sudhir Pandey was held accountable and replaced by Uday Pratap Sharma. On 31 March 2017, the budget of ₹2.5 crore that had been allotted to the BRD Medical College had lapsed, unused, and an internal enquiry to look into the matter had been ordered by the principal Dr Rajiv Mishra. Dr Rajkishore Singh and Dr G. C. Maurya had conducted the enquiry and had found the accountants Sudhir Pandey and Sanjay Tripathi and the finance officer or the drawing and disbursing officer (DDO) Dr O. N. Pandey responsible for the lapse.

Another person whose name came up was Dr Satish Kumar, the head of the Department of Anaesthesia, who was in charge of oxygen supply. It was being said that he had been on campus on Thursday morning but had not addressed the crisis, even though the central pipeline operators had informed him in writing about the impending shortage. I noticed that no one was taking the name of the HOD, and the only reason I could think of was that she was present in the room. Dr Kumar, whose name on the other hand had been brought up, was not in attendance.

In fact, Dr Kumar had applied for leave from 11 to 17 August. He had booked a flight on 11 August from Lucknow to Mumbai for himself and his wife. Before leaving, he had put Dr Shahbaz, another professor in the anaesthesia department, in charge. When this was brought up, the DM called Dr Shahbaz and questioned him as well.

Accountants Sudhir Pandey, Sanjay Tripathi and Uday Sharma were called, and they registered their statement. Among the three of them, Sudhir had initially not appeared before the committee. So the DM sent policemen to his house, who escorted him to the DM's enquiry room.

The proceedings took a significant turn when they received the assurance that whoever would sign a statement against the principal's wife would be spared from further harassment or enquiry.

Sudhir took this offer up and wrote a written complaint, blaming the principal's wife for everything. He wrote that she acted as if she was the principal by making all the decisions, and Dr Rajiv Mishra never said anything about it. His complaint made it seem as if the principal's office was actually being run from the principal's home. Hospital files were first sent to the principal's home, where his wife would read them, and only when she had given her approval would the principal sign the documents.

I noticed, bemused and horrified in equal measure, that everyone in the room was writing and typing.

My name was called next, and I was asked to share the details of the events once again. When I finished telling them, they asked me, 'Why was the AC not working in ward 100 on the first floor?'

'I don't know, sir,' I said, wondering why they were fixating on this detail out of all the information I had provided.

Then they asked me to go outside and wait.

The complete report was prepared by around midnight, but it was not made public.

By midnight, Dr K. K. Gupta arrived from Lucknow by car. We re-assembled in order for him to make his assessment as well. Another two hours were spent this way, and I grew quite frustrated. The moment I was free, at 2 a.m., I went to the wards and completed a round with the junior residents. My frustration was owing to the fact that no one in the committee room had appeared concerned about the children. Although the rate of deaths had lessened, children continued to die. We had lost another eleven overnight, between Friday evening and Saturday morning.

At the end of the committee meeting, the people who were held responsible for the tragedy were Dr Rajiv Mishra, the principal, who was blamed for not making payments to Pushpa Sales even though there were enough funds; Dr Satish Kumar, who had gone on leave even though he knew of the impending shortage; and the three accountants. The HOD, Dr Mahima Mittal, was only asked why she had not taken any action, even though the central pipeline operators had told her about the shortage in writing, on the morning of 10 August.

My struggles on that night, and afterwards, finally gave me an understanding of the process by which oxygen supply was maintained at the hospital. When the liquid oxygen pressure dipped below 4,500 MMWC (millimetres of water column), the central pipeline operators were supposed to inform Gajanand Jaiswal, the pharmacist in charge of the supply of jumbo cylinders. It was his duty to inform Dr Satish, so that a fresh order could be placed for liquid oxygen, and any possible tragedy could be averted.

Moreover, piped liquid oxygen was being supplied to BRD Medical College by a private company called Inox Air Products Ltd through Pushpa Sales. It was being dispatched from Inox's facility in Rajasthan, all the way to Gorakhpur, which is at the eastern end of UP, around 800 kilometres away. It took nearly three days for the oxygen to reach Gorakhpur by road.

On the morning of 10 August, the liquid oxygen tank reading had dipped to 900 MMWC. This was well below the limit for a reorder. What had stopped them from placing a reorder or arranging alternative supplies? Even after the committee meeting, there were no clear answers.

At dawn on Saturday, I was still dealing with the dire situation in the wards. It was deteriorating with every passing second.

As I tried, often helplessly, to revive the infants and children, my thoughts returned to my daughter. 'Allah, may I never have to see her in such a state!' I could not help thinking as I worked. The pain of all those parents was affecting me and numerous thoughts were rushing through my mind. I finally lay down to rest in the doctors' room at around 5 a.m.

It seemed as if only moments later I was woken up by a ward boy, who said, 'Sir, HOD madam is calling you!' I looked at my watch and realized that it was 7:30 a.m. After washing my face hurriedly, I changed into the clothes my brother had brought the previous evening, and then ran to the wards.

The HOD greeted me with a grim smile and asked, 'How are you, Kafeel?'

'I am good, ma'am.'

'Listen, the health ministers are coming today, so we have to prepare our notes. Go to the medical records department. You will meet Mr Suleman, the record keeper, there. Ask him to give you the details of mortalities in the past ten years, department-wise, month-wise, as well as the annual figures of encephalitis and non-encephalitis cases in the NICU, the PICU, the general ward ...'

'But, ma'am,' I said, 'we can send D. K. or Pandey-ji [one of the clerks] to collect those records. I need to do my rounds ...'

'No,' she cut me short, 'I need you to do this.'

I had no choice but to leave on this assignment. While I was passing by ward 100, I saw that in the short time that I had been resting, everything had changed. There were new, clean bedsheets, the staff were wearing shoe covers, caps and masks, there was one child per bed, and no parents.

I stopped in my tracks. 'What happened to the other children?' I asked the nurse.

'Sir, some of the stable ones have been shifted to ward 6, and the critical ones to ward 12.'

'How is the situation in ward 12?' I asked, though the nurse's expression confirmed my fears.

I went to ward 12 to see for myself and found that the condition was about the same as on Friday night. It was an ongoing emergency; new admissions had been stopped completely, and more than fifty patients at the hospital had already died.

I was held up in the medical records room until noon. It was a time-consuming and cumbersome task to find all the details and type them out. I found it hard to concentrate, because I was driven by an urge to visit the wards, take rounds and check on patients. The HOD's husband, who was the head of the medicine department, was also in the medical records room at the same time, taking notes.

'Why are we doing this, sir?' I asked him.

'The media is making such an uproar that we need to show how, as in this month, deaths happen every year during a specific period because of encephalitis,' he said.

'But sir, most of the deaths took place in the NICU and newborns don't get encephalitis.'

'Do you think these journalists are so brainy? Ah-ha-ha ...' he laughed.

He then leaned forward and gave me a tip. 'Look, your name has been published in the newspapers, so just be careful, try to document everything and don't talk to the media.'

'Why are you asking me to be careful, sir? I haven't done anything wrong.'

'I am telling you this for your safety,' he replied.

'I have not talked to anyone in the media. Only once, when they were entering the ICU, I told them that the liquid oxygen was over, but we were managing with jumbo cylinders. That is the only time I spoke up about anything,' I said.

'You don't understand politics,' he said, with a look of pity. 'Have you not read how various Muslim personalities are praising you?'

'Who said that?' I asked, surprised.

Soon after, I returned to the wards and made a round of the PICU. That day, all the doctors were present, and they were also taking rounds of the NICU and wards 12 and 6.

At that point, the media had truly descended upon us. Not just the local or national news channels, but foreign media houses like BBC, *New York Times*, *Washington*

Post, too. Everyone was talking about the number of children who had died, the payments for oxygen that had not been made due to corruption and the lack of infrastructure at BRD.

Reporters were milling about the hospital and the college campus – each one looking for an exclusive angle to the story. They began showing the piled-up garbage, cows and dogs inside the wards, the lack of toilets, bathrooms or places to sit for the patients' relatives, the shortage of medicines although there were many private medical shops outside the campus, the CT scan and X-ray machines which were not working, the shortage of doctors, the shortage of nurses – the list went on.

Many stories focused on the hospital's lack of equipment and proper computerized systems even though deaths occurred every year due to the encephalitis menace.

'In the NICU, each warmer has three to four babies and every bed holds two to three kids!' Reporters had begun to reveal the dismal state of our healthcare system. Media houses were now going to the district hospital and the primary health centre and noting down all their deficiencies, too.

On an average, twenty deaths were reported a day at the paediatrics ward of the hospital, since it catered to the entire poverty-stricken belt of Purvanchal, a large chunk of Bihar and a small section of neighbouring Nepal. Unsurprisingly, locals refer to the college as the 'graveyard of Purvanchal'. The peripheral healthcare system in the area, the primary health centres remain in a constant state of collapse, and BRD is always overburdened.

Media houses and the opposition suddenly had the opportunity to dig deeper. Many previously unknown facts were brought to light, and people kept asking what the current chief minister had done as an MP of Gorakhpur. Yogi Adityanath had, in fact, been a five-time member of parliament from Gorakhpur.

While I had been kept busy compiling data from the Medical Records Section, a team of doctors from Delhi, headed by a doctor from Lady Hardinge Medical College, New Delhi, had also come to take note of what had happened. They were guided by the head of NICU and the HOD. The three-member technical team appointed by the central government discovered that eight out of the twelve senior resident posts lay vacant, that only three out of the thirty-one nurses were trained to handle newborns, and that poor parents had been forced to buy disposables and consumables themselves. On the subject of the deaths, however, they were silent, and declared that all the deaths had occurred due to various diseases, and not due to a shortage of oxygen.

Before the health ministers reached the college, a central team of the Congress party, headed by Ghulam Nabi Azad, Raj Babbar and R. P. N. Singh, came to the ward 100. The HOD called for me and told me to show them around the ward. 'Ma'am, I have to go to the principal's office to prepare the presentation for the health minister,' I told her. 'Please could you ask Dr Sharma or any of my seniors?'

'No,' she said. 'You will need to go as you know all the details.'

'Okay, ma'am,' I said, but I wondered why she was giving me such an important role. I was excited to see Raj Babbar, the film star turned politician, but did not know much about the other two congressmen. During the tour around the wards, they stopped at five or six beds and spoke to the children's parents, before praising all the doctors and nurses. 'It's not your fault. Everyone worked very hard,' they said to our staff.

Outside, while addressing the media, they blamed the Yogi Adityanath-led BJP government for everything.

On Saturday at 1 p.m., I was called to the principal's office. The health minister of UP, Siddharth Nath Singh, and the medical education minister, Ashutosh Tandon, had arrived with a team of officials from Lucknow, including Dr Anita Bhatnagar Jain, the additional chief secretary of medical education.

The first piece of news I heard on reaching the principal's office, even before the meeting started, was that Dr Rajiv Mishra, the principal, had resigned. Later, we learned that he had been forced to step down.

Everyone, including the DM, the commissioner of Gorakhpur and other bigwigs were present. The HOD of the medicine department made the presentation. The acting principal, the SIC and other senior doctors stayed silent. From the HOD's presentation, it became clear that due to a lack of funds, the supplier had not been paid and he had thus stopped the supply of oxygen. The reality was that the state government had ignored repeated requests for clearing the supplier's dues, despite being warned that the supply would be cut.

The HOD of Medicine showed a chart of four different occasions on which funds were given to BRD by the state government.

The first time was on the 30th (₹1.5 crore) and 31st of March 2017 (₹1 crore). This allotment of funds had lapsed. Could it have been an accountant's mistake? A technical error? Corruption? Commissions? Or was it because the budget had been released only at 7 p.m. on the last day of the financial year?

The disbursement of funds under any budget had to follow a sequence.

The finance minister allotted the budget to the medical education department.

The principal secretary of medical education sent it to the Director General of Medical Education.

The DGME sent it to the treasury department.

Funds for the BRD Medical College were routed through

the Deen Dayal Upadhyaya Gorakhpur University, which received them from the treasury department.

At BRD, the supplier would submit the bill to the superintendent-in-chief, Dr A. K. Srivastava, who sent it to the pharmacist, Gajanand Jaiswal, to check and verify the details. If he was satisfied, he forwarded it to Dr Satish Kumar, who was the nodal officer for oxygen supply. After Dr Kumar was satisfied with his verification, he sent the bill back to Dr Srivastava. Once the SIC was satisfied with the bill, he forwarded it to the principal.

The principal would scrutinize it further and send it to the accounts department. The accountants would prepare the bill and send it to the DDO, O. N. Pandey, who forwarded it to the UP Treasury Directorate.

When the process was first described to me, I was dumbfounded. How many weeks did it take for a bill to be paid! No wonder I had heard so many times in the last two days that '*Sarkari paise milne mein bahut der lagti hai, sir* (It takes very long to receive money from the government, sir).'

The second allotment of funds was made on 21 April 2017. A sum of ₹121 lakh reached on 6 May 2017, out of which Pushpa Sales was paid ₹33 lakh in two instalments: ₹20,27,024 on 6 May 2017 and ₹13,26,182 on 2 June 2017. The previous dues of ₹13,35,738 had not been cleared since the previous budget had lapsed on 31 March 2017. This payment was not made along with the current sum because the rules stated clearly that no previous payments should be made with the current year's funds, as it would amount to a financial irregularity.

The third allotment of funds was made on 18 May 2017 – this was in the amount of ₹133 lakh. For this sum, it was specifically mentioned that the money was for POCT, a company which supplies equipment, medicine and pathology. The money could be spent only for the stated purpose, as directed by the DGME, otherwise it would amount to a financial irregularity. This condition ensures that the company which paid a commission to the Lucknow office would get its budget passed, otherwise payments would get stuck.

Finally, the payment was made to Pushpa Sales only on 11 August 2017. By that time, the oxygen supply had already been cut off and many children had died. The most crucial question, however, remained unanswered: Who was at fault for not releasing the budget on time?

Moreover, if the first budget had come through with funds for Pushpa Sales on 21 April 2017, why did it take four months to pay Pushpa Sales its remaining dues even though there was a clause in the contract for payments to be made every fifteen days?

Whatever the truth was, the ministers decided not to talk about the budget complication with respect to the payments due to liquid oxygen suppliers. Following this briefing, the health minister addressed a press conference.

As we were entering the college auditorium, the state health minister, Siddharth Nath Singh, asked me just one question, 'You are the same doctor who gave a PowerPoint presentation on encephalitis during my last visit, aren't you?'

'Yes, sir,' I said.

The college auditorium was packed with reporters. Perhaps the health minister was nervous when he began to speak, or he was trying to take charge of the situation with a misguided overconfidence. He said, '*August mein har saal bachhe marte hai* (there are deaths every year in August).' He was trying to point to the annual August mortality rates. In August 2015, the death rate was 16.6 children per day. In August 2016, the daily average was 18.5. In August 2017, we had already crossed these figures and the average deaths per day had climbed to 20.5.

How could we think of the lives of children in pure numbers, I thought, as I listened to his address.

However, his callous statement about deaths being business as usual in the month of August had a great impact on the reporters present, more so than anything else the minister said that day. That statement became a headline and rapidly exacerbated the situation. The media immediately started calling out the state's insensitivity, and political parties began asking for the resignation of both the health minister and the CM.

On TV, it seemed as if nothing but the news of the most unfortunate night of my life was being aired.

When I came back to the wards, more politicians were arriving.

The tragedy had triggered outrage, and the opposition parties of the state – the Samajwadi Party, the Bahujan Samaj Party and the Congress – sought the resignation of Siddharth Nath Singh, as well as compensation of ₹20 lakh to be given to the families of each deceased child.

There was disagreement over the causes of the deaths, but one fact was regarded as indisputable in all the media accounts: Between 10 and 13 August, the hospital's liquid oxygen supply had run out. This had sent doctors, caregivers and parents, whose children were being treated for encephalitis and other critical ailments, into a state of panic.

The liquid oxygen truck reached the hospital around 1:30 a.m. on 13 August 2017 and supply was finally renewed at around 2:15 a.m.

I was so overwhelmed by a sense of relief that I went to the wards and made a final round, congratulating everyone in my path. My juniors and I embraced each other. Every single staff member, from the nurses to the sweepers, the ward boys to the guards, was thrilled at the news.

Parents of the children came and touched my feet or gave me their blessings. I was surrounded by love and gratitude; however, by the time I left for home, I began to have mixed feelings as, despite all our efforts, so many children had died.

When I reached home at 4 a.m., I found everyone awake and waiting for me. My mother kissed my forehead, and I could see her eyes bright with tears.

'Kafeel, today you have made your father proud, even as he rests in *jannat*,' she said.

After a quick bath, I hugged my wife. I could see it in her eyes too, the pride she felt because I had done my duty so diligently. My daughter was sleeping. Slowly, tenderly, I climbed in beside her, careful not to wake her up. Then, cradling her small form with my arm, I plunged into a blissful sleep.

But the arrival of the liquid oxygen was not the end of the crisis for BRD Medical College. The National Human Rights Council (NHRC) issued a notice to the state government, taking suo motu cognizance of the large number of deaths of patients, and sought a report from the state government. The notice said that the incident indicated 'gross callousness' on the part of the hospital and the state administration and asked the government what steps had been taken to compensate the families.

In the meantime, another complaint had been filed by the parents of the children who had died at the hospital.

When a daughter was born at Rajbhar's home in Gopalganj, Bihar, the baby girl was immediately referred to as Gudiya by his family members. But just two days later, the child became sick. Concerned, Rajbhar brought her to BRD, where she was admitted at 3 a.m. on the morning of 10 August 2017. But by 6 p.m. the next day, she was dead.

Rajbhar alleged that his daughter had died due to a shortage of oxygen and the hospital had kept her death hidden from him. However, when the deaths of thirty children and infants at the hospital had created a furore, her body was handed over to him and he was ordered to return to Bihar under police escort.

Ramsakal, another parent of a deceased fifteen-day-old girl, had been told he could collect his daughter's body only after the ministers had left. Ramsakal had come to BRD from Siddharth Nagar, where the local doctors had told him that his child had contracted pneumonia.

Vijay, a jubilant father of a newborn son, had travelled to Gorakhpur from Maharajganj with his ill child and accompanied by his father Mangru. The baby was admitted to the hospital at 7.30 a.m. on the morning of 10 August, but his condition didn't improve. The reports of children and infants dying made Vijay and his father anxious. On the 11th, when the child's condition worsened, they were called by the doctor to pump the baby using an Ambu bag, which they did, but to little avail.

A Gorakhpur resident, Zahid, had lost his five-year-old daughter Khushi. In the reports, he had said, '[My daughter] was alive until the morning and then after half past six I saw her shake and crumble in front of my eyes.' This complaint was covered widely in the media:

> A resident of Bihar's Gopalganj district, whose newborn daughter was among scores of children who died at a state-run hospital here, has approached the police seeking action against UP's health and medical education ministers, an official said today.
>
> However, no FIR has been lodged, the official said.
>
> In his complaint, Mr. Rajbhar claimed that his daughter had died due to shortage of oxygen at the Baba Raghav Das Medical College and alleged that apart from the ministers, the state's principal secretary, health, was responsible for it, according to Akshay Kumar Mishra, the Station Officer (SO), Gularhia police station.

> He said that in the complaint, Rajbhar claimed that he had got his daughter admitted to the hospital on August 10, but due to shortage of oxygen, his child died.

The parents, rightfully outraged, wanted justice for the death of their children. At the upper echelons of the government machinery, however, this would mark the beginning of what seemed to be the hunt for a scapegoat.

7

Hero to Villain

On the morning of 13 August, my phone started ringing at around 7 a.m.

Yet to recover from the trauma and exertion of the past forty-eight hours, I wondered, 'What now?'

My early morning caller was the HOD, Dr Mahima Mittal. 'Come to the medical college immediately,' she said. 'The chief minister and the union health minister are visiting today.'

My sleeping daughter was still in my arms and my wife was also in a deep slumber. I kissed both their foreheads and started getting ready. Not wanting to wake them up, I bathed in a hurry, dressed in formal attire and walked downstairs to find my mother awake. We had tea and breakfast together after she insisted that I have some bread and butter, which I gulped down before leaving for the hospital.

As I was walking out of the house, my brother Adeel, who was also awake and reading the newspaper, showed me the headlines. 'Deaths of 11 More Children' was the main news, along with the fact that the liquid oxygen supply had been resumed. The UP health minister's statement that '*August me har saal bachche marte hai*' had been highlighted by every reporter. And the opposition parties were now baying for blood.

I glanced hurriedly at the stories and found that many were also about me and how I had tried to save the children. I was being called a 'hero', a *masiha* (rescuer), a *farishta* (angel). They had also quoted people present at the scene.

> 'While other doctors gave up hope, Dr Khan managed the situation well by arranging oxygen cylinders from private nursing homes. He saved many lives by his efforts and presence of mind,' said Gaurav Tripathi, an eyewitness.

Another headline was, 'At least 63 kids have died in Gorakhpur hospital in 5 days'. '[Khan] collected as many as 12 oxygen cylinders. The child specialist made four trips to the hospital to ferry these cylinders for children admitted in his ward.'

Srawan Shukla, a correspondent of DNA India, wrote that 'Even as the death of 36 children in Uttar Pradesh's Gorakhpur hospital once again exposed government hospitals' dismal condition and the authorities' colossal apathy, a child specialist at the BRD Medical College where these deaths took place managed to restore people's faith in humanity. Dr Kafeel Khan did exemplary work on the fateful night of August 10 and 11, saving many lives that would otherwise have been lost.'

An article appeared in the *Hindustan Times*, which reported the following:

> Crises brings out the best in some people. At a time when all hell broke loose in Baba Raghav Das (BRD) Medical College following alleged disruption of oxygen supply, one man – Dr Kafil Ahmed – answered the call of duty ...
>
> For several hours, Dr Kafil became a one-man army for the junior doctors and hospital staff ...
>
> Only one, Mayur Gases, agreed to give them the cylinders, provided that the down payment was made strictly in cash.

> With no time to lose, Dr Kafil took out his ATM card and sent one of his office staff to get the cash from the nearest teller machine ...

Even though there was little time to read anything in too much detail, I felt pleased. I had left home in good spirits, after saying bye to my mother, brother and wife. On the way to work, I began to receive many calls of congratulations, as well as calls from the college asking me to reach quickly.

'How much faster can I go?' I wondered. 'I cannot possibly fly!'

I reached the campus by 8:30 a.m. and found that the main gate was closed, and entry was being allowed only to those with ID cards. Hundreds of reporters and thousands of cops swarmed the premises. Many local leaders from the BJP were inside the premises as well as outside, opposition party leaders were shouting slogans asking for the resignation of the chief minister and the health minister. Now all the print and electronic channels were reporting that the supply of oxygen had been stopped by the supplier due to the non-payment of bills.

I went to the wards after showing my ID, glad that the police posted for checking were treating me with great respect. Reporters ran up to me when I got out of the car, but I did not say a word to them. I could hear hundreds of cameras clicking my photos as I walked. I did my rounds, instructed the nurses to change the bedsheets, checked the ventilator tubing and changed the setting according to the ABG. The sweepers were busy cleaning all the wards.

A rehearsal was conducted and one of the visiting politicians chalked out the questions J. P. Nadda could ask the parents and how they should be answered. A few parents who had been spotted talking about the oxygen shortage were shifted to ward 6, so that they would not be able to meet the CM. The commissioner, SDM, CMO,

CMS, additional director of health, DGME and others were present, and multiple meetings took place among the HOD, DGME and SIC. Now that the principal had been suspended, who was going to bear the brunt of the blame? That was the question on all the staffers' minds.

That day, one of the nurses arrived on duty to find only one child in each bed of the PICU. She arranged her notes and went into the first cubicle. She noted the new, tautly stretched sheets, and the child's neatly combed hair on the clean pillow. Her own son had been running a fever, but there was no possibility of calling in with a request for leave on a day when the hospital was under scrutiny by the high and mighty.

Compared to a normal day on the campus, this was a completely different scene. The dumper truck from the Nagar Nigam had already arrived to take out all the garbage. Many hospital sweepers, ward boys and nurses were sent as reinforcements to the paediatrics ward. In the pharmacy, all the medicines were available, and instructions had been given to everyone that if the CM asked about the availability of medicines, they should say that all the medicines have always been freely available. Parents and other visitors who had been identified as a nuisance were asked to leave the premises.

It had been decided that the CM would address the media in an auditorium inside the college building, after completing his round of ward 100. I was told to remain in my cabin and to keep away from the CM, as only the HOD would show him around.

I heard from others that when the CM finally arrived, chaos ensued. The moment he and J. P. Nadda got out of their SUV, reporters jumped at them with their mikes. The CM ignored them and walked towards ward 100, but the reporters continued to run behind them. As soon as the CM and those accompanying him had entered, the doors were shut by the security personnel. Only the CM, J. P. Nadda, Rajya Sabha member Shiv Pratap Shukla, the commissioner, the DM and the DGME were to be allowed inside. But the reporters were hell-bent on following them in. Amidst this chaos, they broke the glass door of the PICU entrance.

The CM turned back and looked at the reporters. First, he shouted at them, then he started lamenting, saying something to this effect: 'For the past thirty years I have been fighting for encephalitis patients, and you are blaming me! It's a conspiracy. I will explain everything to you. *Dhair rakhiye, sabko milwaoonga, parents se, patient dikhaoonga. Pehle hame dekh lene dein* (Please be patient. I will let you meet patients and parents, both. But first, let me see them).'

The DM and the assembled cops took this as a cue to force everyone out. The chief minister entered the first cubicle and talked to the first patient.

'*Kahan se hain?* (Where are you from?) *Kab admission hua tha?* (When were you admitted?) *Koi dikkat toh nahin?* (Hope you haven't had any trouble?) *Medicine mil jati hai?* (Do you get your medicines here?) *Dus ki raat ko kya hua tha?* (What happened on the night of the 10th?) *Oxygen ki kami toh nahin?* (Was there any shortage of oxygen?)'

Then he went to another bed and asked the same set of questions. After talking to three patients, he turned to J. P. Nadda and said, 'See, these patients have been here for the past week. *Agar oxygen ki kami hoti to ye sab bhi mar jate, na?* (If there had been a shortage of oxygen, then these patients would have also died, isn't it?)' Nadda nodded.

He then turned to the HOD and asked out of the blue, '*Dr Kafeel kaun hai?* (Who is Dr Kafeel?')'

I was in another cabin, but I heard the question and, a moment later, a junior doctor appeared, telling me that the HOD was calling for me.

Unsuspecting of what was to come, I entered the cubicle where the VIPs stood and greeted everyone. I had imagined that I would receive a pat on the back, but instead I was met with pin-drop silence. Everyone simply stared at me.

The chief minister stared at me, ignoring my greeting. He was fuming, his face was flushed and angry.

'*Toh tu Dr Kafeel hai?* (So you are Dr Kafeel?)'

'Yes, sir.'

'*Tu ne cylinders ka arrangement kiya tha?* (You had arranged for the cylinders?)'

'Yes, sir,' I acknowledged. I was disturbed by the way he was addressing me with the pronoun '*tu*', indicating disrespect. I could tell something was not right.

The CM then turned to a consultant and asked, '*Ye chaar–paanch cylinders se kitni zindagi bacha li?* (How many lives did he save with these four or five cylinders?)'

No one answered his question.

Inside my head, a voice was screaming, 'Not four or five, we arranged 500 cylinders in fifty-four hours!' But I did not say anything out loud.

'*Toh tu sochta hai cylinders la ke tu hero ban jayega?* (So, you think by getting cylinders you are going to become some kind of hero?)' he asked. I did not know what I could possibly say to this, so I just stood silently.

'*Dekhta hoon tujhe ...* (I will see it).'

Those four sentences are seared in my memory forever because they would very soon turn my life upside down, even though I did not realize it at the time.

And that was it. Somebody put a hand on my shoulder as I was ushered out of the cubicle and instructed to wait in the wards. I felt anxious, horrified, clueless. What was happening and why was I being treated in this manner? Everyone was looking at me sympathetically, but no one came to talk to me. A senior nurse handed me a glass of water. I drank it. I had started sweating, my legs were shaking, I was dumbstruck and racking my brain for the cause of the CM's odd line of questioning, but I could find none.

The CM emerged from the cubicle, but he ignored me.

Next, they went to ward 12. I went with them, but the HOD and Dr Sharma were in charge. I was now being sidelined. After finishing their rounds, they sat in the office of ward 100. The CM, J. P. Nadda and Shiv Pratap Shukla sat, while everyone else stood around them. I was told to wait outside. After fifteen or so minutes, I was called back in.

'So you informed people from the media that the oxygen had been exhausted?' the CM asked me.

'No, sir! They were already at the gates.'

The DM turned to me and told me to keep quiet.

'Who is Dr Satish?' the CM asked. 'Call him. How come he was not present without taking leave?'

Someone called his number and asked Dr Satish to come to the hospital immediately. Meanwhile, the CM said, 'First, remove Dr Kafeel from the post of superintendent of ward no 100.'

What! I wanted to scream loudly, 'I am *not* the superintendent of ward no 100!' But the words would not come out of my mouth.

Now they were discussing who would be the new principal. Dr Reena Srivastava, the head of the OB-GYN department, had already refused to take up the responsibility. Someone recommended Dr K. P. Kushwaha, the retired principal. The CM wanted to speak to him, and when Dr Kushwaha picked up, he asked cordially, 'How are you?'

Then the CM asked him, 'Will you take up the responsibility of the principal's post once again?'

We could glean that Dr Kushwaha had agreed since the CM turned to the others and said: 'He is the right person for this job.'

By this time, Dr Satish had arrived, but the CM had clearly forgotten that he had called for him. Somebody pushed him in front, saying, 'Sir, Dr Satish has arrived.'

'Why did you go on leave without informing anyone when there was a crisis?' he was asked.

'Sir, I had to attend my child's—'

'Shut up! And why was the AC not working?'

Whatever he was about to say remained unsaid, because the DM and the others asked him not to speak and pushed him to the back of the group.

The CM told the HOD to clean up the mess. 'I am going to monitor everything,' he warned.

Then I was told to leave and go wait in a different room.

When the CM and the other VIPs came out, the reporters were asked to go and talk to the parents.

Finally, the CM addressed the media in the college auditorium. All the while, the then union health minister J. P. Nadda did not utter a single word.

On stage, the CM told the reporters that not a single death had taken place due to a shortage of oxygen – they were caused by 'Japanese encephalitis and insanitary conditions'. He said that the crisis was a conspiracy to defame him and his government. He warned the conspirators, saying, '*Itni kadhor karyawahi Pradesh sarkar karegi ki woh manak banegi logon ke anushashan mein rehke karya karne ke bare mein* (The state will take take such strict action that it will become a marker for how to work within discipline).'

The CM then ordered another enquiry committee, headed by the chief secretary, which was supposed to submit its report within a week, by 20 August 2017.

Affirming that we were living in a post-truth age, the government seemed to first want to bury the whole incident by making light of it: 'There are deaths every year in August.' Then they went into denial mode and, when it became apparent that the number of deaths and the scale of the tragedy could no longer be denied, it appeared that rumour-mongers, spin doctors and trolls had spun into action. Out of nowhere, they all came together to sponsor a smear campaign against me on social media, which was quickly picked up by the electronic media without any attempt to verify the facts.

Moments later I got a call at work from my brother who informed me that several reporters had arrived at my wife's hospital.

'A crowd has gathered and is throwing bricks and shouting slogans,' he said. 'They have reached my office as well.' A few minutes after this mob attack, the crowd began looting all the electronics from my brother's showroom – TVs, refrigerators, washing machines, inverter batteries and other valuables.

'We had to run to save our lives,' my brother told me.

He also said that false stories about me were circulating on social media. Some claimed that I stole oxygen cylinders for a clinic, others insinuated that I was in cahoots with the principal's wife or that I was related to gangsters and politicians.

I was stunned by the range of completely baseless accusations and theories. By the afternoon, the same things had started playing on TV as well.

Anchors from big media houses based in Delhi and Mumbai did not come to Gorakhpur to find out about the facts of the story. They picked up the story from social media and suddenly I was made out to be the HOD of Paediatrics, the vice principal and the superintendent all at once. It was as if I was Superman, running the whole medical college alone! On the TV screens, they began shouting and screaming: '*Gorakhpur ke 70 bachho ka kaatil kaun* (who is the murderer of the 70 children from Gorakhpur)?'

Two main narratives were emerging from the crisis that had gripped the BRD Medical College on the night of

10–11 August. First, the deaths due to the oxygen shortage, which had already captured the attention of the public. The other was the corruption and the alleged commission deals in connection with the payments at the college.

But the CM's visit and press conference had changed the entire narrative. The discussion had shifted from the deaths of the children to who were to be made scapegoats. One name which consistently came up throughout the incident was my own, momentarily put on a pedestal, and then labelled as the villain of the entire episode.

The transformation from hero to villain takes place very quickly in the public eye, as I soon found out.

After the CM had left the wards, the nurses, junior residents and ward boys came to me and said, 'We are with you, sir. We have seen you working. If anything happens to you, we will go on strike.'

'No, please don't. If you go on strike, what will happen to the children admitted in the wards?' I told them. 'Please go do your work. Nothing will happen to me. God is watching – He sees everything.'

One of the parents recounted later to a reporter that 'The doctors called in their parents and asked them to quietly take away the bodies from the rear door of the ward as the CM was holding a meeting. The ward boy wrapped the bodies in bed sheets and told the attendants to move out without making any noise. The medical officers did not want any nuisance in the CM's presence.' It seemed that the whole management of the medical college was under the DM and the SSP, and the hospital authorities were just following orders. Masks, shoe covers, caps, gloves, trays – everything looked new and sterilized.

After the CM returned to Lucknow, I was told to go home using a different exit and to not talk to the media or anyone else.

I heard that the CM was very angry and upset but was

told that I could come back to the hospital again in a few days.

'But why is this my fault?' I asked the HOD of Medicine, who was standing next to me.

'Don't worry, he said. 'It's just that right now there is so much media pressure. When things settle down, no one will remember.' But I was unconvinced.

'What about the kids who died?' I asked. 'Their parents will not be able to forget so fast.'

'Don't focus on that,' was his advice. 'You saved so many lives – that's the important thing. Leave the city for a few days – it will be better for you.'

'I am going to Lucknow anyway, as my mother and brother are going for hajj, and their flight, which is on the 16th, leaves from Lucknow,' I told him. He looked relieved. 'Good – you should leave today itself.'

I had no idea then why he was doing all this. It seemed to me he was doing it to save his wife. She was, in fact, the HOD of Paediatrics and had not been questioned about anything. Neither had he faced any interrogation about the eighteen deaths that had taken place on the intervening night of 10–11 August in the ICU of the medicine ward. Between him and the DM, the media blindly believed whatever version was fed to them about the deaths.

This was how the narrative changed so abruptly. I still remember how on 11 and 12 August everyone was asking:

Why was there an oxygen shortage?

Why was the payment not made?

Why had so many children died?

Why did the health minister make that insensitive statement?

The CM and HM should resign, they had said. They had acknowledged that I had helped save lives.

But now only one thing was being repeated everywhere: Dr Kafeel Khan was a murderer.

When the opposition parties and a few Muslim leaders praised me, it made matters worse, painting the incident in communal colours. It became a hot topic across the country as people began dividing themselves on the basis of religion. To some people, it seemed as if my career had reached a dead end; others described it as a tragic nightmare.

When I had gone rushing to get oxygen cylinders that fateful night, I swear to Allah that I never stopped to wonder which of my patients were Hindu and who among them were Muslims, who belonged to which caste, who was poor or rich.

I am a doctor. Such thoughts have never occurred to me in my entire professional career, or ever, for that matter, because in my family we were always taught to respect every religion. For me religion is spirituality, humanity and belief in a higher power. I believe in Allah and consider it my personal choice. I also respect all religions and people, irrespective of their beliefs.

Is heroism today not earned by one's actions or karma, but bestowed and denied on the basis of someone else's beliefs?

When I went home that day, I found my whole family there. My brothers had closed their showroom, my wife had shut down her hospital, and everyone was so scared that no one was talking to anyone. My brothers were trying to contact the CM through some people, but he refused to talk.

Reporters were calling me, but I stayed quiet. Everyone was giving me the same advice: Just don't react for some time, and everything will be okay.

My little Zab, who always brought me so much happiness, was climbing all over me, and I was trying to be my cheerful self with her.

I tried not to think about what had happened. But the moment we switched on the news, or someone logged into social media, there was so much hate that it made me feel ill. I was still wondering what had gone wrong. I had joined BRD as a permanent employee only on 8 August 2016, just a year back, and was still serving my probation. Then how could anyone believe I was the superintendent, or vice principal, or the HOD for crying out loud?

There was another story accusing me of stealing cylinders, which was completely made up. During normal operations, oxygen is supplied to a large central tank from where it is supplied through pipes to the rest of the hospital for patients. Once the liquid oxygen ran out, we got the cylinders refilled during the emergency. The fabrication was similar to saying someone had stolen your neighbourhood's water tank without anyone noticing. I would have laughed if it had not made me cry instead.

But what I still did not know was how the organized fake news machinery, which was spreading rumours on social media, was going to affect my life in ways much worse than if people had just believed the lies about me. Hate news and media trials would soon put me behind bars, deprive me of the ability to practise my profession and rob me of my liberty.

In that maelstrom of hate, lies and false accusations, there were only a few journalists who attempted to report fairly.

Manoj Singh, a local journalist, wrote in the *Wire*:

> On 11 August, when I reached the 100-bed encephalitis ward of BRD Medical College at around 11:30 a.m., I saw a tense Dr Kafeel speaking on his phone, walking back and forth. Meanwhile, jumbo cylinders were being offloaded from a pickup truck outside.
>
> There was a deafening silence inside the ward, while a photographer of a local daily and the stringer of another newspaper waited outside. Soon, a woman arrived at the hospital carrying a child and crying.

> Khan saw the child outside the ward, immediately took him in his arms, and rushed inside the ward. The scene was promptly captured by the photographer.

Later, on speaking to my brother, he added that the charges of '*cylinder chor* (cylinder thief)' did not ring true. 'The oxygen cylinder is very heavy, and it takes four or five people to lift it. Why will Dr Kafeel risk something like that? Moreover, one jumbo oxygen cylinder costs around ₹200. Will a doctor commit a theft of ₹200 and risk his reputation? Most importantly, when it comes to the issue of the shortage of liquid oxygen, Dr Kafeel has become a pawn in some big conspiracy. *Woh sajish ka shikaar ban gaye kyonki woh Muslim hain* (He is victimized because he is a Muslim),' he said.

Others in the medical profession also rejected the charges that were being made against me. Dr R. N. Singh, a convener of the Encephalitis Eradication Campaign, said that the charges of 'cylinder chor' were a lie. 'The allegations that Dr Kafeel is a chor are blatant lies. There is something else for which he has been punished,' he said.

Resident doctors at the All India Institute of Medical Sciences (AIIMS) suggested that I had been made a 'scapegoat'. 'With great pain, we have to say that, once again, a doctor has been made a scapegoat for the infrastructural lapse and failure of the government,' said Dr Harjit Singh Bhatti, president of the Resident Doctors' Association at AIIMS. Their letter accused the Uttar Pradesh government of 'gross neglect of public health'.

The DIG of the Sashastra Seema Bal came forward to talk about how I had addressed the situation with their help. The SSB and the central police force that protects India's borders with Nepal, Bhutan and Bangladesh went on record to say that my efforts and SSB's assistance helped in fighting the crisis.

'It was an unprecedented crisis situation at the BRD Medical College on 11 August. Dr Kafeel Khan came to the DIG, SSB and requested for a truck so that oxygen cylinders could be collected from various locations and be taken to the medical college,' the News18 report quoted SSB's public relations officer O. P. Sahu as saying.

He added, 'The DIG also provided eleven jawans to assist the staff at the BRD Medical College. For hours, our truck collected oxygen cylinders ... from various locations, including a godown in Khalilabad, and ferried them to the medical college where it was a situation of acute crisis.'

In the days that followed, the noise in the media combined with multiple allegations of kickbacks, avoidance of autopsies to establish the cause of the deaths, a chief minister who had been informed of the dues claiming to be unaware of them, and organized trolling and fake news employed to deflect attention, invent scapegoats and to give rise to a deafening cacophony.

PART TWO

Detention

8

Independence Day and Eid

A mere two days after I was being lauded for being a hero, I received a call from the paediatrics ward. I needed to go and meet Dr Mahima Mittal and the nodal officer of the encephalitis ward Dr Bhupendra Sharma, who showed a lot of sympathy and spoke to me in a friendly, caring way. I applied to the HOD for three days' leave, since I was going to accompany my mother, who was leaving for hajj from Lucknow. The HOD signed my leave letter, and I found out from others in the office that the CCTV recording of the entire period of the oxygen tragedy was in the district administration's custody.

After I returned home, I learnt that the media had been told that my resignation as superintendent, which I had neither written nor submitted, had been accepted, and Dr Sharma had taken charge.

I realized now that I was being let down by my own colleagues. I called the HOD, greatly agitated.

'Madam, why are lies being reported about me? How could I be resigning as the superintendent when I have never been one?'

'Calm down, Kafeel,' she said in a soothing tone. 'Don't worry, we have not said these things. The media is making up their own stories. In fact, the DGME has taken charge of the principal's job which he will perform until a replacement can be found.'

But I did not feel satisfied with this explanation. I was sure that someone from the department or administration was not only leaking information to the media, but also giving incorrect feedback to the CM. Some nurses and junior doctors told me that since I had left, they were being telephoned daily, and all my records were being checked to find something to use against me. 'Sir, your leave letters, papers, attendance sheet, records of your previous stint as a contractual employee – everything is being scrutinized,' they told me.

In the midst of this, the DGME released a statement questioning what good I could have done with four cylinders when fifty were already in stock. This made me furious. What was I to do in the face of repeated attacks on my reputation and my work by the print and electronic media, social media, and now this official statement?

So I recorded a video in which I stated clearly, 'No, sir, not four or five, we had arranged 500 cylinders!' I also narrated how I had begged everyone to help us.

At home, my family members were getting more tense with each passing hour. Rumours about an FIR being registered against me were circulating.

Notwithstanding what lay in store for me, the deaths continued at the medical college. Ten to eleven children were dying in the paediatric wards every day, and reporters were having a field day exploring deficiencies in the functioning and administration of the college. They began conducting sting operations, exposing doctors who ran private practices and were involved in other such irregularities.

One of the investigative reporters went to the SSB office, and the DIG confirmed on TV that I had indeed gone to the SSB office on 11 August, and a truck and some soldiers had been provided to assist me in getting the jumbo cylinders filled. Finally, one piece of positive news amidst the storm of lies, false accusations and blame that had been directed at me.

The Indian Medical Association (IMA) also sent a team to enquire about the incident, but Dr K. P. Kushwaha, who was being considered by the administration for the principal's post, was part of this group. They drew a report quickly without consulting me or any other doctors. The report portrayed Dr Mishra and me in a bad light.

Meanwhile, Dr Kushwaha's name cropped up in another controversy. When the liquid oxygen supply contract had been given to Pushpa Sales, even though the firm didn't have the licence to supply medical liquid oxygen, he had been the principal. Now, questions were being asked about why the gas was not being bought directly from Inox Air Products; why a middleman, the Pushpa Sales proprietor, was involved. Dr Kushwaha's re-appointment as principal never took place, even though the chief minister had asked him to take up the role. Instead, Dr P. K. Singh from another medical college was transferred to BRD and appointed as the principal.

Another twist in the story came from a statement released on 14 August by Manish Bhandari, the managing director of Pushpa Sales. It turned out that they had written letters directly to the chief minister's office, multiple times, well in advance. In this statement, Bhandari pointed out that the company never stopped the supply of liquid oxygen despite the outstanding dues. He also said, 'The government must find why there were just around fifty cylinders instead of 400 on that particular day when deaths took place.' An executive of Pushpa sales told *The Telegraph*, 'We personally handed the dues letter to the health minister on August 9th. He and the CM went to the medical college the same afternoon to hold a review meeting. We came to know from hospital authorities that they had told the chief minister about the problem, and he had looked questioningly at Tandon. After that, [the CM] apparently stayed silent.'

It further reported:

> Siddharth Nath tells reporters in Allahabad that the oxygen supply was disrupted because "some people wanted kickbacks". He does not say who they are.
>
> (A health department source had told this newspaper on August 12 that the medical college's account had a balance of Rs 3.86 crore on August 9, and that the vendor had gone unpaid because he had 'failed to oblige some senior members in the government'.
>
> ('No such business operates without kickbacks,' the source said. 'But the principal had recently received orders from Lucknow to stop the payment.')

On 15 August, Independence Day, I had to leave for Lucknow with my mother, my wife, my daughter, my brother Kashif and his wife. We left by car, as my elder brother Adeel and his wife and son stayed back in Gorakhpur. My sister Farro along with her husband and sister-in-law were also scheduled to go on hajj with my mother and brother.

For our family, the day was completely dominated by the events of the previous few days. The news channels were still reporting about the BRD tragedy round the clock. BJP President Amit Shah's statement had also been reported widely: '*Itna bada desh, hadse toh hote hai* ... (In such a big country, tragedies have happened before ...)'

On Independence Day, Prime Minister Narendra Modi made a reference to the Gorakhpur tragedy in his speech from the Red Fort. He expressed sympathy for the affected families, while calling the episode a 'natural calamity'. Other ministers began speaking of a conspiracy. UP Health Minister Siddharth Nath Singh, whose house had been attacked after he had made an insensitive-sounding remark in Gorakhpur, came after me with all guns blazing, giving more statements to several media channels.

There were some reporters from digital media platforms who were showing me support, asking questions and digging deeper to find out the truth.

The Pushpa Sales office had been searched by the police, and their staff had been interrogated.

Beleaguered, Principal Mishra gave a statement 'that he had written several letters to top officials of the Uttar Pradesh government requesting the release of funds to the college, so that it could pay Pushpa Sales.' He had 'even raised the issue in discussions over video-conferencing with officials in Lucknow ... The government finally sanctioned the funds on August 5 and payment was made on August 11'. How could he then be expected to clear dues worth ₹68 lakh? After that, he never spoke to the media again.

Meanwhile, a news article in the *Times of India* reported:

> The government appointed Dr Gupta in June this year despite several allegations of misappropriation during his previous tenure as DGME during the SP government. He was removed in 2015 when complaints against him were made to the Lokayukta. But the BJP government again appointed him. When asked about Mishra's allegations, Gupta said, 'Mishra used to delay files and his working was not at all satisfactory.'

Another described the decline in the medical education budget:

> The budgetary allocation for 14 such medical colleges and their associated teaching hospitals has been pared to less than half from Rs 2,344 crore in 2016–17 to Rs 1,148 crore for 2017–18. The allocation for BRDMC followed the pattern, plunging from Rs 15.9 crore in 2016–17 to Rs 7.8 crore for 2017–18. More specifically, its allocation

for machines/equipment was slashed from Rs 3 crore to just Rs 75 lakh.

On 16 August, I experienced some respite after the release of the DM's report which cleared me of any wrongdoing. My family heaved a small sigh of relief.

The DM's report identified other illnesses, rather than oxygen deprivation, as the reason for the deaths of the children admitted to the encephalitis and neonatal wards between 10 and 11 August and refrained from blaming the UP government for the tragedy. It charged the doctors, paramedical staff and clerks of the medical institution with criminal negligence, while maintaining that the state government was unaware of the situation. It accused the Principal Rajiv Mishra of failing to alert the DGME and health departments to the impending oxygen crisis and demanded strict action against Pushpa Sales for stopping the oxygen supply. Another accusation was against Dr Satish Kumar, the head of the maintenance department, for going on leave from 11 August without taking the principal's permission.

The responsibility for the faulty air conditioner, that had featured in all the questions asked to me about the incident, was laid at Dr Satish Kumar's door, since he was in charge of maintenance and had failed to get the encephalitis ward AC repaired on time. Overwriting in the logbook related to purchase and re-filling of oxygen cylinders was also mentioned in the DM's report.

I was in Lucknow when I got a call from the hospital, telling me that a team from Sanjay Gandhi Post Graduate Institute of Medical Sciences (SG-PGIMS), Lucknow, was in Gorakhpur to record a statement from me. When I told them I was in Lucknow, I was asked to meet them at SG-PGIMS the next day.

The following day was a very emotional one for all

of us. Ammi and Farro's flight was in the afternoon. My mother cried and clung to me.

'I don't want to leave you like this, beta,' she kept saying. 'I am scared of what they can do to you.'

'Nothing will happen to me, Ammi,' I told her, hugging her back. 'You know I have not done anything wrong, so why should anything bad happen to me? Don't worry about me, just go ahead and pray for everyone and come back. I will be here to receive you when you return.'

My sister Farro was also apprehensive. 'Stay in Lucknow for a few more days,' she said. 'Don't go back to Gorakhpur.'

The next day, I went to SG-PGIMS to meet their enquiry team. My wife and daughter waited in the car while I met with the three-member committee. All the members seemed supportive and asked me for a detailed account of the events which I related from the beginning. The meeting lasted an hour, and they told me it was just a formality.

Their report also absolved me of any blame, but I was not happy. According to even this report, 'The alleged oxygen breakdown does not appear to be directly responsible for the deaths ... It was hindrance in supply of liquid oxygen by the manufacturer to the hospital, which resulted in shortfall of liquid oxygen. However, the hospital tried its level best to compensate the shortage of liquid oxygen by jumbo cylinders ... Usage of Bag and Mask was reported to be given during the transition phase...'

From 18 to 20 August, I stayed at home, and what I watched on TV about myself was enough to make me physically sick and mad with rage. I wanted to resume my duties at the hospital, but Dr Mahima Mittal told me not to come back for a few more days. 'I will extend your leave, don't worry,' she said.

'I was just a lecturer,' I reasoned. Besides, I felt that I should have something to fear only if I had done something wrong. When I had not committed any crime, why cower in fear?

Still, sitting at home, watching people on TV spewing venom against me all day and night was the worst experience possible. Every day, local newspapers were printing new fabricated stories about me – how I was close to the principal's wife and that together we used to take money through illicit means, whereas in reality I had met her just once in my life, at the college cultural programme in 2016.

I had never met Manish Bhandari or any agent of Pushpa Sales. In fact, I have no reason to know who was supplying liquid oxygen to the medical college before that night of 10–11 August. Yet, all the news channels were saying that Bhandari had given me money.

I was not acquainted with anyone from the accounts department, except Sanjay Tripathi, whom I had met in relation to my salary. Yet there were accusations being made in the media that I had been taking commissions and was in cahoots with this department.

A late-night message on 21 August from a journalist shocked me and made me wonder what else was in store. 'The chief secretary has accused you in his report. Are you willing to give me an interview about this?'

I immediately mentioned this to my brother Adeel. 'We must read the complete report ourselves and see what it says,' he said, promising me that he would try and get the full text of the document.

On the following morning, the report's contents were splashed in the newspapers. They suggested that the doctors Kafeel Khan and Satish Kumar, the principal and his wife and three accountants were responsible for the crisis on 10–11 August. An allegation was being made against me that I did not inform my seniors about the shortage of oxygen and was conducting a private practice while in government service.

On the same day that the report was published, we all found ourselves suspended and a new departmental enquiry was initiated against us, which was to submit its report within ninety days.

Tensions at my home had reached a peak. I was grateful that my mother was spared this news. But I did not know then that even worse times lay ahead.

The next day, on the 23rd, we received news that an FIR had been lodged against nine people, including the Pushpa Sales owner, Manish Bhandari, and that I could be arrested at any time. It came to light that a committee led by the chief secretary, Rajiv Kumar, had submitted its report to the CM on the 22nd, after which the CM had immediately called for an FIR to be filed.

At the time, it is worth noting that none of the top government officials who also had responsibility for the oxygen supply had been named. This meant that the additional chief secretary in the UP government, Anita Bhatnagar Jain, the DGME, Dr K. K. Gupta, the superintendent-in-chief of BRD Medical College, Dr A. K. Srivastava, the head of the Department of Paediatrics, Dr Mahima Mittal, and the district magistrate, Rajeev Rautela, remained outside the scope of this FIR, even though all of them, and even the chief minister, Yogi Adityanath, and the state minister of medical education, Ashutosh Tandon, had all been informed, months ago, via letters, that they needed to release payments to the oxygen companies. These officials were not even named, while the DGME himself had filed the FIR. However, Anita Bhatnagar Jain was transferred.

The chief secretary's report also claimed that the deaths at the hospital were not related to the snapping of the oxygen supply. The only real way to ascertain the role the oxygen crisis may have played in the death of the children would have been to conduct post-mortems. But the UP government had chosen not to do so.

After feeling certain that I would not be unnecessarily victimized or framed, because I had done nothing wrong, I was surprised to suddenly learn about the FIR. The nine people named in it had been charged under seven different sections of the IPC: 409, 420, 308, 120B, the Anti-Corruption Act 7/13, the Indian Medical Council Act (Section 15), as well as Section 66A of the IT Act.

I learnt that the others accused were Uday Pratap Sharma (junior accountant), Sanjay Tripathi (senior accountant), Sudhir Pandey (the senior-most clerk in the accounts department), Dr Rajiv K. Mishra (suspended principal of the BRD Medical College), Dr Purnima Shukla (Dr Mishra's wife), Gajanand Jaiswal (chief pharmacist), and Dr Satish Kumar (HOD of anaesthesia and the oxygen supply departments).

Although the FIR had been filed at Hazratganj, Lucknow, I found out that the case would now be transferred to Gorakhpur's Gulariha police station for further investigation.

I consulted a local lawyer who suggested that I go to Allahabad and file for anticipatory bail.

My daughter, my beloved Zab, was turning one. Thinking about her had brought me strength and driven me to try even harder to save the babies and children on that disastrous night. We had hoped to celebrate her first birthday, on 24 August, lavishly.

Instead, I was leaving for Allahabad on the morning of her birthday, in search of a lawyer.

For the first time in my life, I sat in an advocate's chamber. It was almost like a test of how people's feelings had been shaped by the media coverage of the last few days. Everyone who came into his chamber recognized me and asked me why I was there. Many of them expressed sympathy and reassured me that nothing would happen, because I had done a good job.

But there was plenty of proof about the effect of the media trial – people were very angry with the principal and his wife – thanks to an image that had been completely fabricated by certain sections of the media. It was sharply evident how dangerous hate-mongering can be. People were cursing the principal and his wife, saying that they should be hanged in public.

After the lawyer arrived, I told him everything. He asked us to put together a range of documents, some of which I had with me and some that I needed to get. In the evening, he took us to a senior advocate. After hearing us out, the advocate told us what was now needed, the first item being his fees of ₹1.5 lakh.

They estimated our total expenditure to be just over ₹2 lakh. My brother returned to Gorakhpur to arrange for the money and the remaining papers, while I stayed behind.

The BRD Medical College refused to hand over any of the papers we asked for. I pulled them from my email and phone scanner, and found some old photocopies lying at home, but we still could not gather all the necessary documents.

While I was in Allahabad, the police had interrogated my wife for four to six hours every day. They conducted multiple raids at my house, my brother's office and my wife's hospital.

On 28 August, we filed a plea for anticipatory bail in the high court and were now waiting for the date of the hearing.

Those days of waiting were made hellish by my daily calls with Shabista, my wife, who would tell me how the police were harassing and mistreating her and my bhabhi, Adeel bhai's wife. I felt an urge to return to Gorakhpur and surrender, but my advocate was confident that he would get me anticipatory bail, so I spent the days clinging on to that slender hope. Besides, everyone advised me to wait and dissuaded me from giving up. But the toll of spending each day like this was so immense that I would frequently break down and cry when alone. Wherever we went for lunch or dinner, people would look at us as if we were terrorists. Some would come over and talk to us and ask the same questions again and again.

Each evening at the senior advocate's office we went through the same routine: he would say that the next day we would get a date for the hearing, but that day just wouldn't come.

The next day, 29 August, we saw reports that the principal and his wife had been arrested by the Special Task Force from his relative's house in Kanpur, brought to Gorakhpur on transit remand, and would be presented in front of the Gorakhpur magistrate the following day. It was awful to watch on TV how advocates tried to hit both of them as they were being led away. People were shouting slogans around them, calling them *hatyare*(murderers).

The day of 30 August proved to be the most painful by far. Shabista cried and cried on the phone, telling me that some fifty policemen had swarmed all over our house through the day and would not even let her feed Zab; our nephew was so scared that he had locked himself inside a bathroom, and my bhabhi was not eating at all. The policemen camped at our house had told my family members that if I did not return that day, they would arrest my whole family.

On 31 August, I got up with the firm resolve to return home and told my brother as much. 'I will address a press conference in Delhi and let the whole world know what really happened, and then surrender,' I said, before leaving Allahabad. I was halfway to Delhi when I got a call from my advocate that my hearing was scheduled to take place on 4 September, so I should wait for four more days.

Meanwhile, my brother said he would go to Lucknow, try to meet the chief minister and explain everything to him in the hope that he would understand.

But the first day of September brought fresh horrors as the local policemen pasted a notice on the door of my home. It announced that my home and offices – in short, all my property – would be confiscated by the government if I did not surrender within a week.

The police reached and raided my sister's house in Lucknow and remained there for about ten hours. Someone had tipped them off that I had been staying with her. Finally, when they could not find me, they arrested my brother and kept him at the STF's office in Lucknow. After my sister told me what had happened, I dropped the plan to address the media but made a few videos instead, so that in case something was to happen to me, my family could use the video to tell the world the real story.

My brother called at night, sounding panicked and scared, to say that if I did not surrender by the next day, they would arrest my sister and brother-in-law as well. 'But you wait till the 4th, Kafeel,' he told me.

'No, I am coming,' I said. At around 1:30 a.m., I left Delhi in my car.

On the way, whenever I saw a police car, I could not help but think it was out looking for me. But no one stopped me on the way. At all the highway toll plazas, the people just stared at me blankly. I did not stop to even have tea, making do with just some bananas.

I reached Lucknow at around 8:30 a.m. on the morning of 2 September and was told to wait near the Harley-Davidson office. An STF official arrived and took me straight to their office. I was quite surprised when everyone ran up to me to welcome me like a hero. They took selfies with me and offered me tea, samosas and sandwiches. They were nice and hospitable, introducing me to many people who came into the office.

'Sir, one selfie with me too. My wife will be very proud; she is a huge fan of yours,' someone said.

'And you?' I asked.

'Yes, yes, we are also fans, sir,' was the reply. 'You are a true *deshbhakt*, a true soldier, a masiha.'

Even the DIG, who arrived with a few other officials, praised me. I requested him to let my brother go, as it was Eid-ul-Adha and he needed to offer namaz. They let him go soon after.

'We need only you, sir. We know you are not a criminal, and it is just politics and circumstances, but our hands are also tied. We know how you saved so many children's lives – the whole country is proud of you,' they said.

I was not asked any questions, nor made to write or sign on any paper. They behaved very politely, always addressing me as 'sir', or 'doctor sahab'.

Around 10 a.m., we left in a police jeep for Gorakhpur.

On the way, they stopped near Faizabad for tea. I requested them several times to allow me to offer my Eid namaz at any of the mosques along the way, but they expressed their helplessness, saying they had received strict orders to take me to Gorakhpur as soon as possible.

'It will take just five to ten minutes,' I pleaded. 'I won't run away! After all, I have surrendered.' Still, they refused.

When we were about to reach Shahjanwa near Gorakhpur, they called the circle officer. He arrived with two plainclothes constables and, from there, they took me to a guest house belonging to the hydel department. I asked why I was not being presented before a magistrate. Somehow, I still had some hope that maybe when a magistrate heard my story, he would not send me to prison.

I was in that guest house for the next six to eight hours. I was put in a room where they brought me lunch and dinner, of which I ate little. The circle officer was friendly with me, giving me the impression that he was not happy with my arrest and that what was happening was wrong. He listened to me as I recounted my experience of the last few days, expressed sympathy over the whole event and the children's deaths, and told me his parents were huge fans of my work and wanted to meet me.

But I saw his true colours only in the evening when we sat before the TV and reports were being shown of JNU students protesting my arrest at Jantar Mantar in New Delhi.

He made unpleasant remarks about some of the well-known student activists. Then he suddenly turned towards me. '*Tum logo ko baba ji ka CM banana digest nahi hua na? Isi liye ye sab kiya?* (You people have just not been able to digest the fact that Babaji [Yogi Adityanath] has become CM, isn't it? That's why you did this?)'

I was stunned.

Many police officers in plainclothes came and asked me questions. But this was all a formality. They asked me to sign a paper stating that they had caught me at the bus stop in Shahjanwa, trying to leave the city after someone had tipped off the police about me, and that was how I had come to be arrested. Later, the newspapers reported the police as saying that I 'was arrested just before [I] was allegedly trying to flee to Nepal'.

I initially refused to sign, but they threatened to beat me up. I told them I would expose them to the media but then, feeling helpless and powerless, I finally signed the paper.

Every time I begged them to let me talk to my family, they promised they would, but I was never given the chance.

Around 8:30 p.m. they took me to the hospital at the Shahjanwa Community Centre for a medical checkup and warned me against trying to speak to the media. They did not inform my family I was with them.

It was a small hospital with hundreds of policemen and reporters milling around.

After covering my face, they took me to an emergency room and shut the door. The doctor who examined me addressed me as 'sir' and treated me nicely. They did not really check anything; instead, they just asked if the police had used physical force, to which I replied in the negative.

It was yet another official procedure. I was asked to make a thumb impression on many papers.

The circle officer and the inspector had taken complete charge. The people from the STF's office who had brought me here were nowhere to be seen.

Next, they hurriedly took me to the jeep. I tried to talk to the media, but I was hushed and taken away. As the vehicle started moving, I gazed outside and thought how, just a few days back, I was a free man, driving my car, listening to music, happy. Today, I was sitting in a jeep with five cops and my hands tied like I was a criminal.

It was night by the time we neared the Gorakhpur city area. I was looking out, trying to spot someone I knew. Even though there were few vehicles on the road, I was searching for someone I could scream to so I could ask them to tell my family that I had reached Gorakhpur.

I was expecting some advocate to come to my rescue, because they were talking about taking me to the magistrate's home, and then to prison.

We reached the magistrate's house at around 10 p.m. Reporters had been calling the circle officer who had told them that they would go to the court complex where the magistrate was expected. I was preparing for what I would say in front of the magistrate and hoping that an advocate would be there to represent me.

The police took my papers directly up to the first-floor flat where the magistrate lived in the judges' compound, and got it signed. They had not asked for my police custody, but directly for judicial custody for fourteen days.

I felt betrayed and angry. 'I want to meet the magistrate!' I shouted. They shouted back, '*Chup chaap baitha reh*! (Shut up and sit quictly!)'

Then they drove to the jila prison in Gorakhpur – the district jail. It was on the way to the BRD Medical College but I had never been there.

The vehicle followed the same route I used to take to work each morning in my doctor's suit, listening to loud music in my car. It felt strange and surreal. Now I was certain that I was going to jail, and all my hopes were fading. The truth was painful. I wanted to see my wife and my daughter one last time. I wanted to talk to my brother. My mother was away on hajj. How would she react when she found out?

Soon a storm of questions drowned out all other thoughts in my head.

What would happen in jail? What would the other prisoners do to me? What work would I have to do there? When would I be free? Would I have to stay there for fourteen whole days? Was there any chance that I would be released earlier?

My brother and those STF cops had told me that I would be released within three days at the maximum. But all the movies I had seen about prison life were making me feel quite worried.

Now, with every second that I drew nearer to the prison, my fears grew worse from uncertainty – I just wanted to reach and find out what would happen to me. I wanted to fly to the end of the story. A voice inside me kept repeating, 'Kafeel, you are going to jail. Kafeel, you are going to jail ...'

When we reached the prison gates at around 10:30 p.m., again there were many policemen and reporters present.

My photo was taken with the circle officer and the police inspectors who were holding up my hand proudly, as if I was their trophy. I shouted '*Maine kya kiya hai? Mujhe kyon jail bheja ja raha hai?* (What have I done? Why am I being sent to jail?) This is wrong.' Before I could say anything else, they covered my face and took me inside the prison.

The moment I entered the huge gate, my heart sank.

Ya Allah, why are you punishing me like this? Have I done anything wrong? I thought to myself.

Tears rolled down my cheeks, but I wiped them immediately.

Zab's image kept flashing before my eyes again and again.

And Shabista? She and I had been together for just two years and ...?

Adeel bhai? Abaan? Rid? Zara? Jasir? What were they all thinking?

I saw those huge, scary walls of the prison and wondered when I would ever leave them.

There are no words that can describe how utterly helpless I felt in that moment.

My entire life was in front of me, and I was struggling to think of what I could have possibly done to deserve this punishment. At that late hour of the night, it seemed as if my whole world was sinking into a deep darkness.

9

Counting Days and Nights

First they made me squat on the floor. A guard took down all my details and entered them in a big register: my name, father's name, my age, address, and then he took my thumb impression. The investigating officer, Abhishek Singh, handed over the court papers to the jail staff and left.

The outside world had now faded away and I was at the mercy of the jail authorities – the jail superintendent, Suresh Dhani, the jailor, Shukla, and the deputy jailor, Ashish Singh. I was frisked and asked to remove my clothes. My belt and shoes had already been removed before I entered through the big gate, though I had no idea who had taken them.

I stood before them, barefoot and without my clothes, but they insisted I take off even my underwear and vest. Feeling very exposed, I asked, 'Why are you asking me to be naked?'

'To search for two identification marks,' was their reply.

'But I could have told you where they are!' I protested.

'We have to confirm their authenticity,' they said.

It was noted that I have a mole on the left side of my abdomen and a cut on my left index finger – the spot where I had accidentally cut myself with a knife as a child.

Embarrassed, I closed my eyes, wanting the humiliation to be over as quickly as possible. When they had finished noting everything down, I asked if I could put my clothes back on, but they said I could do so only after the medical examination.

I went through a second big gate, parallel to the first one, and entered a large open area. This was the *hawalat* office. Here, my weight and height were recorded: 68 kilograms, 5 feet 8 inches. The medical examination takes place in the prison hospital, but since new inmates usually arrive by 6 p.m., it was closed at that late hour.

My medical examination was being conducted at night because, they said, I was a VIP prisoner. When I saw the junior jail surgeon who was to examine me, I realized it was Dr Verma, who had obtained his MBBS from BRD Medical College and lived in the same locality as me. We greeted each other and he treated me with respect. He was fully aware of the situation in the medical college.

Dr Verma's examination was more of a formality. He wrote the word 'normal' inside many boxes, and I signed and put down my thumb impression. Now that I was allowed to put my clothes back on, I finally felt a bit relaxed.

The jailor and his deputies began talking to me about the incidents of 10 and 11 August. I described the events in chronological order, after which they asked some follow-up questions. The conversation was amicable, and they even displayed sympathy for my plight. During a pause in the conversation, the jailor asked his colleagues, 'Where do we lodge him?'

The superintendent responded, 'The Nehru barrack has been opened for them. Send him there.'

'Have you eaten dinner?' asked the jailor.

'Yes, sir,' I said.

'All right, otherwise your food awaits you in the barrack.'

At around midnight, I entered the Nehru barrack. It was a huge hall that could accommodate thirty people. There were blankets on the floor and four people were lying on one side of the room. All of them looked elderly.

On the other side was the principal Dr Mishra, next to whom were two of the 'writers'. I found out very soon that the writers' job was similar to that of a class representative or monitor. The two that I had seen as soon as I came to Nehru barrack were Dadhi Kaka, who was known as the *mulakat* writer because he facilitated meetings between prisoners and their visitors, and Bala, the writer of this barrack.

In disuse for a long time, the Nehru barrack had been opened for only the eight people expected by the jail authorities in our 'high-profile' case. We were to be lodged together in this barrack, and four other prisoners had been moved here to keep an eye on us. The jail policemen stood outside in the corridor.

There was a lawn just outside the barrack, whose main gate could be seen in the distance. There was also a Nehru library, which remained closed at night. I learnt that Dr Mishra's wife was in the *mahila* barrack.

Everyone at the Nehru barrack was awake and waiting for me.

I greeted the principal. 'Good evening, sir.'

'Kafeel, if I had not gone to Rishikesh, this incident would not have happened,' he said to me ruefully.

All I could do was nod. What was there to say at that point? I had just entered a prison – the last place I thought I would find myself in after the events of the previous month.

Bala gave me two blankets – one to sleep on and the other to use as a cover. As I lay down, the same questions exploded in my head once again.

I couldn't sleep a wink that entire night, which I spent just staring at the roof.

At 6 a.m. the barrack door opened, and everyone had to stand in a queue for the counting. *Ginti*, or counting, became a much-heard word for me in the days that followed. That first day, everyone was scrambling to return to the queue after going to the toilet – where they had also stood in queue because there was only one foul-smelling toilet with a broken door. I was thankful for not needing to use it too urgently, as I had hardly eaten anything the previous day.

Around 6:30 a.m., I was taken once again to the mulakat office where entries for the new prisoners were recorded. The process for making these entries was called '*mulahija*'. Almost twenty new prisoners were waiting, mostly for petty crimes. I had to undergo the process of stripping and showing my identification marks once again.

They began noting my name and details in a huge prison register. Name, father's name, address, qualifications – MBBS, MD (this was the first time during the whole process that I felt a moment of pride). But then they asked, 'Married? Wife's name? How many children? Child's name and age?'

My beloved Zab's name in a prison register. It felt so strange and incredibly upsetting.

The deputy jailor I had met the previous night was sitting there, monitoring the whole process. There were also other writers present besides the ones from Nehru barrack. All of them were prisoners who would be imprisoned for a long period of time – a few were educated, some were MBA holders convicted in cases of dowry, murder, or under the POCSO Act. They were the ones who had been handling the computers and paperwork.

The new prisoners had to make their thumb impressions with black ink. Someone would hold the prisoner's hand and press it on the charcoal stamp pad, and then push it down hard on the register press. Then they would ask the prisoner to wipe off the ink on the hair at the back of their head. I asked for paper to wipe my thumb, at which they stared at me as though I had demanded gold.

Then it was time for the photograph: from the front, left lateral, right lateral and, finally, the thumb impression. My mind was racing – did digital India now mean my record would be available all over the country? What if I wanted to travel abroad? Would my passport be impounded?

I was taken back to the barrack. The bathroom, which included a toilet, came attached, but the door to the toilet was broken. When I went to relieve myself, I felt like vomiting because of the intense stench. I had to pinch my nose, and focus somehow.

I did not have toothpaste or a toothbrush. The principal gave me some toothpaste, and I cleaned my teeth using my fingers. I wanted to have a bath but did not have a change of clothes, so I just splashed some water on my face and head.

Then it was time for breakfast, which turned out to be *dalia* and watery tea – my first breakfast and tea in jail. I didn't know if I wanted to laugh or cry.

There were strict rules for meeting visitors. That first day, Dadhi Kaka came to me at 10:30 a.m. with a *mulakat parchi* (meeting paper). He told me that my elder brother Adeel had come to see me. Then he recited the rules.

'Three meetings are allowed in a week for approximately one hour. You can meet a maximum of three people at a time. Visitors have to register before 8 a.m. for the first meeting and 11 a.m. for the second meeting. The first meeting starts by 11:30 a.m. and the second by 1 p.m. Saturdays and gazetted holidays are no-meeting days. The writer will take you and bring you back, accompanied by prison policemen. You have to carry your bed sheet to sit on. Your visitors can bring you fruits and clothes, but no homemade food is allowed. You have to pay ₹50 at the registration desk and ₹50 to ₹100 inside, which will be divided between jailors, and, out of that, I will get ₹10. This is an informal payment.'

I just nodded in agreement. I did not feel like talking to anyone and kept myself isolated, even though the principal would console me occasionally. My throat felt tight, as if I would cry a lot if only I could cry openly. But I firmly restrained myself.

Around noon, the writer took me outside the barrack towards a common meeting point. It was just outside the hawalat office, in a large open field. The total capacity of the jail was 800 inmates, but there were 1,897 inmates that day. In the open area, there were around 100 inmates and 200 visitors, some advocates, and twenty prison policemen. It was an animated view – people chatted, cried, drank tea.

My control vanished the moment I saw Adeel bhai. I ran towards him and started crying the second we hugged. He held me for a long time. For ten minutes we did not speak at all and just held each other tightly.

He finally told me that he would have me freed within ten days. I asked him what the procedure would be like.

'First we have to apply for bail in the lower court. Our advocate will make an argument, the judge will grant bail, and then you will be released,' he said.

'But why bail? Why not have the whole FIR quashed when I have not done anything wrong?'

'That's the procedure we have to follow, Kafeel.'

'A magistrate gave me fourteen days' judicial custody even though at the time I was not represented by an advocate. How can we apply for bail – wouldn't that be acknowledging that I have committed some crime?'

'Kafeel, the government is putting so much pressure that every officer is scared. It's only because of the media and government pressure that you have come here. Once things have settled down, everything will be okay – don't worry. Think of it this way – there was so much public outrage over the children's deaths that the government needed a scapegoat to save themselves. It's not at all your fault. Outside, everyone is saying the same thing.'

'The principal and his wife are here, and they keep saying it's a conspiracy,' I said.

'Perhaps it is. But you don't worry,' said Adeel bhai. 'Shabista, Ab and Zab are all okay. They will come visit you soon. We have not told Ammijan or Kashif yet.'

He handed me my clothes, some soap, a toothbrush, toothpaste and other daily necessities.

After forty-five minutes the bell rang, and he had to leave.

They took me back to the barrack after the counting.

I was upset again. Lunch arrived – watery dal, a half-cooked roti, rice and a reddish cabbage sabji. I did not eat any of it, having just the bananas that my brother had brought for me. The barrack doors were closed again for three hours and were to open at 4 p.m. I lay down on my *otta* (blanket), sensing that the other inmates were all trying to console me, but I was not in a mood to talk. My mind was on another plane, so much so that those people's voices sounded like echoes in the barrack.

I sat in a corner of the barrack, thinking, thinking, thinking. Nothing in my childhood or early life had prepared me for this kind of a situation. In our student days, justice is not a concept which we spend a lot of time thinking about. Courts and jails are not places we ever enter. To think that I could face such rank injustice, in my own birthplace and hometown, hurt me deeply.

I was a prisoner in this jail for having practised my profession as a doctor, and for doing everything I could to save the lives of critically ill children during an unprecedented crisis.

Whichever way I thought about it, this fact just did not make any sense to me.

It was around 6 p.m. The sun was setting and mosquitoes had begun their evening drill. The barrack gates closed once again and we were now locked inside the hall. My fellow prisoners were sympathetic and kept trying to console me. But I was like a hurt animal in a cage and could not respond to them. Instead, I lay on my floor-bed and looked up at the roof.

Dadhi Kaka came in late, washed his clothes and had a bath before eating his dinner. Then the lights were switched off. I was once again plunged into darkness, alone with my tortured thoughts.

It seemed as if I had been asleep for only a few minutes when I had a bad dream in which someone was shaking my shoulder and saying, '*Chalo, chalo ginti ke liye* (Come, come for the counting).'

I slowly realized this was no dream but my new reality. We all went out and stood in a queue for the day's counting. After that, I came back and lay down again. I had not been assigned any work yet.

At around 10 a.m., Bala came to inform me that the STF had picked up Adeel bhai from outside the prison the previous day, when he was about to leave after meeting me.

This news was agonizing. Initially, I felt very scared and thought, *Why him? What did he do?* Then, the more I pondered over it, the angrier I got.

No one else came to meet me, and I spent the hours alone, sitting in a corner or lying down. No lunch, no dinner, no bath, but I had to go and use that foul-smelling toilet. I spent the entire day praying for my brother. I had stopped focusing on the fact that I was myself in prison. All I wanted was for my brother to be safe. If he was in danger for having visited me, I did not want him to come again.

There was absolutely no news of him all day.

That evening, when the principal came over to console me, I broke down. 'What did I do wrong, sir? I asked him. 'I called you that night to inform you of the shortage. I was the junior-most doctor; I didn't even know where the oxygen supply came from!'

By the third night, I was an absolute mess. Every sound triggered me into remembering afresh that they had got my brother. I despaired over what they could be doing with him for two days. I prayed and prayed to Allah to show some mercy and leave my brother out of the mess in which I had landed him. There was no chance of getting any sleep – all my thoughts were about Adeel bhai. I worried about the other members of my family – Shabista, Zab, Ab, Bhabhi – had they also been arrested? Zeenat and Samar lived in Lucknow – were they now in Lucknow Jail? Had Ammijan been told about my imprisonment? How would it affect her hajj? What would her reaction be? What about Shabista's family? They must be so ashamed of me …

I thought, then, of my colleagues in the medical college. The junior residents, nurses and ward boys. Did I still have their support, or had things changed? Were the police still going to my home? What were my neighbours making of it all? Was anyone helping us at all, or were they just watching the circus?

I worried about the impact of my imprisonment on my nephew and niece. After all, children only knew about police and robbers, or the good guy and the bad guy. Is that how they were going to think of me now, as a bad guy, having been sent to prison by the cops? In my head, I was saying, 'No, beta Ab, your chachujaan has not done anything wrong.'

My sweet Zab would not even understand where her father had gone. 'I swear to Allah, my dearest, I have not done anything wrong …' As I thought of my loved ones, my eyes filled up with tears. And there was still no news of my brother.

But I was learning very fast that in prison, waiting for time to pass is a skill one needs to learn quickly, otherwise one can go mad. Waiting in queue to use the toilet, waiting in queue for a bath, waiting in queue for breakfast, waiting for mulakat, waiting for the next day, waiting in queue for lunch, waiting to wash your hands, waiting, waiting, waiting …

I realized that perhaps this is why there is a second hand in watches. Every second counts. In an hour, I would look at the wall clock ten to twenty times.

I ran to the deputy jailor when he visited the barrack in the morning.

'Is there any news from my home?' I asked him in desperation.

'No,' he snubbed me rudely, and left.

But a while later, Dadhi Kaka came bearing good news. 'Your brother Adeel has come to meet you.' It is hard to describe how satisfying that moment had felt.

For the first time in that prison, I smiled. Actually, when I thought about it some more, maybe it was the first time I had smiled since the tragedy.

This was another lesson I learned in prison. Small moments of happiness are essential to one's survival. It gives you hope to overcome the next hurdle. I was ready to smile and sing because Adeel bhai had not been arrested or sent to jail.

The next two hours were again spent waiting. Looking at the wall clock, walking, sitting, going to the toilet, washing my hands, going again, feeling anxious, then relaxed, although not without a nagging feeling of nervousness.

Bala came and saw that I had been wearing the same kurta and jeans for five days now. 'Take a bath and change your clothes before your mulakat with your brother,' he told me. But I was in no mood to do anything, I just wanted the clock to strike 12:30.

When I saw Adeel bhai, I did not say anything, just hugged him for a long time, and broke down for the third time in five days.

'The STF picked me up and put me in their car, which drove around the city for two or three hours. Then they took me home, searched every corner of the house, and confiscated all the papers and everyone's laptops and mobiles,' he told me.

'Why did they take Bhabhi and Shabista's laptops?'

'I don't know. They were very rude, treating us like terrorists. I gave them whatever they wanted because we have nothing to hide. They left around 11 p.m. It was probably more of a scare tactic because the very next day they returned all the mobiles and laptops,' he said, and I felt relieved.

'But since then, everyone has been very afraid. The kids are so terrified they have stopped playing or watching TV. They just confine themselves to a corner of the house and don't do much. No one cooks, no one feels like eating. First the UP police, now the STF. Everyone is completely shaken and worried about what will happen next.' It hurt to hear his words.

'We thought that once you'd surrendered, everything would go back to normal, but it's becoming much worse. I think they are trying to convey a message to us,' he said, looking at me with a serious expression. 'Don't speak about the oxygen tragedy to anyone in prison – not at all. No one should come to meet you here. Even in court, it's best if you don't say anything, otherwise it is not just you but your whole family might suffer the consequences.'

We looked at each other. The message from the police and the government was clear: 'Keep your mouth shut.'

I thought of the young children in my family who had been terrorized by the actions of the police and the STF. Zab would be okay, perhaps, because she was too young to understand what was happening. But Ab and Rid, and my younger brother's children, Zara and Jasir, who were in Lucknow, were frightened. Zara and Jasir all the more so, as their parents were away on hajj with my mother, and they were at their maternal grandparents' home. I was glad that at least everyone was safe and not in jail.

'All right, we will be careful, but we can't afford to keep quiet in the court out of fear due to their dirty tricks,' I said. 'I know, and my Allah knows, that I have not done anything wrong.'

I asked him about our advocate and the status of my bail application. He looked at me blankly and I realized that this was another mistake.

'The STF guys kept us busy when I got the time to hire an advocate,' he said, explaining that there had been no progress with the bail application.

Then he broke the news that Manish Bhandari's application for anticipatory bail had been rejected by the high court. The judge had said, 'The court is inclined to accept the submission that custodial interrogation of the accused may still be warranted and it would not be appropriate to grant him bail at this stage.' Clearly, our application did not stand a good chance.

He had brought fruits, which I ate while still with him. Our eldest aunt had come to stay with the women in our family, he told me, and I was happy that they would have some moral support.

'I am going to Allahabad,' Adeel bhai told me. 'I may not be able to visit again too soon.'

Oh! I could feel the disappointment in my stomach. 'So how will I get any news?' I asked him. He shrugged and said, 'I don't know. Let me think of something.'

I was also struck by a thought – did this mean that I was going to be in prison for a long time?

He left, and I could only stand there, watching him helplessly. He turned around to give me a parting look.

I was brought back to the barrack by the writer and the prison police, along with other inmates and the principal.

I noticed that the principal was looking very upset. For the next few hours, until sunset, he did pooja. Usually, his routine included prayers every morning for an hour after his bath, then again, every evening from around 6 to 7 p.m., and finally at night before he went to sleep. But today he was looking worried, so I asked him what had happened.

He said, 'Kafeel, everything we have been doing in prison has appeared in the newspapers. "The principal was very happy to see Dr Kafeel", "The principal gave Dr Kafeel his blanket", "They had dinner together", "They are talking in English", "They are good friends", "The real culprits of the BRD deaths are planning another conspiracy", "They are planning something big", "The government is keeping an eye on them", "The DM and the commissioner are in direct contact with the jail authorities" – these are going to be the daily headlines.'

I was feeling tired and, once the lights were switched off and the gates were closed, I slept – it had been six days and nights since I had slept properly.

But I woke up a couple of hours later after having a bad dream in which I was shot and my body was left to rot.

After that, I was wide awake the whole night, tossing and turning on my otta. It was hard and I felt cold. I had never slept on the floor like that. The fan overhead turned very slowly, and there was a light that was left on for the policemen on duty to monitor the inmates. They had a duty change every four hours.

Once sleep had deserted me, every sound, every chink of light, the stony floor and the fact that my life seemed to be in a shambles came together to ensure that my weary soul would not get any rest.

10

A World within the Walls

The principal's suspicions of the previous evening turned out to be true. On the morning of 6 September, the deputy jailor, Surya Pandey, came and told me to pack my stuff, as I was being moved from the Nehru barrack.

'Why?' I asked him.

'I don't know – it's an order from the DM. The media is printing too many stories about the bonhomie between you and the BRD college's principal.' His words knocked me speechless for a moment. Bonhomie? I barely knew the man and he was my superior at the college; I had certainly not been on chatting terms with him. But since it was a direct order from the DM, there was no use protesting any further. I would have to comply. Another lesson I had learned quickly was that it was best to just follow the orders and not ask too many questions.

'The DM has asked the superintendent to separate the two of you,' Pandey offered by way of explanation. Gathering my towel and one bed sheet, I followed Pandey out. On the way to my new lodgings, upon sensing my agitation, he told me a story. Once, after a cat scratched an officer's wife, the officer ordered that all the cats in the city should be arrested. The cops were bundling all the cats together when they saw a camel running around. They asked the camel, 'Where are you going?

The camel replied, 'If I go to prison, it will take me years to prove that I am a camel and not a cat.' Saying this, he went on his way, laughing.

Soon we arrived at the Shatabdi barrack, also known as the Millennium barrack, so called because it was inaugurated in the year 2000. Some people also called it the Mulaihaija barrack. Compared to the rest of the buildings, which had been either built during under British rule, or in the years immediately after Independence, this was a newly built structure, supposedly the cleanest barrack, with a cement floor and a roof that did not leak during the rainy season. It was also better painted, and the toilets outside it were the cleanest, compared to the rest. The whole complex had two sub-barracks, each sixty feet long and twenty feet wide, that one entered through a huge iron door.

This complex is supposed to cater to sixty inmates in each barrack at a time, but I found out that at the time one was occupied by an ex-minister who had been convicted for life in a murder case, and the other was catering to about 160 to 200 inmates. Each barrack had just one toilet, so once you were locked up inside, it was nearly impossible to use the toilet. Each inmate was given a space of six feet by two feet on which to spread their otta. There were several large windows with iron bars, called *argada* or *jangala*. To be allotted space near one of the windows, you had to pay up or use your sources. The extra space made it easy to keep your possessions as you could make use of the windowsill as a shelf and the grills for hanging bags from it and the breeze from the window kept you from feeling suffocated, as there were only seven fans that didn't circulate the air properly.

Outside the barrack, there were six toilets and six taps in the open to be used for baths and washing clothes.

All inmates were kept locked inside from 6 p.m. to 6 a.m. and from noon to 3 p.m. The only exceptions were if you were a writer or worked as a cook in the *bhandara*, or if it was meeting day. All new prisoners initially spent their first week here, and then every Saturday they were distributed to other barracks. Unless of course you paid *pakki baithaki* – a monthly amount to stay there for as long as it took you to get bail.

In this isolated barrack, inmates are trained to follow orders. Essentially, they learn to stop using their brains and mouths, whether or not they like it, it is ethical, legal or a violation of human rights. This barrack prepares a prisoner for anything that may happen next. It is in the Millennium barrack that you are marked as either a VIP (those who pay pakki baithaki of ₹1,500 to ₹2,000 or *kacchi baithaki* of ₹200 per day for not doing any work) or a prison worker who cleans toilets, makes food, or does the gardening and sweeping. The writer's post is costly and whether you can get the job depends on your crime, your caste, religion, sources, influence and how much money you can pay to land the job. Undertrials are not eligible to become writers. This is because once you become a writer, you are free to roam all over the prison, can talk to the jail authority, and most importantly, can torture fellow prisoners and earn money.

As he escorted me to this barrack, Pandey advised me not to talk to anyone or become friendly with them, as most of the prisoners were hardcore criminals who, if they came to know that I was from a well-to-do family, would start demanding money or threaten my family members, using their external sources, in an attempt to extort them. 'If you have any problem, tell the writer Shailesh Singh, or a prison cop,' he suggested.

The first person I met in the barrack was D. Ram, a retired PWD employee who was under trial in a forgery case under IPC 419/420 and a respected person in the barrack. D. Ram was a committed admirer of the present state government. He had created a small pooja corner near his sleeping area where everyone came and prayed. He was very particular about his possessions. No one could touch them, use his utensils, or sit on his bed. Even his bucket and mug were kept separately. He was a proud and devout Thakur, a distant relative of the writer, who was himself a Thakur. He had special privileges that allowed him to use the toilet or the bathing tap before anyone else; he freely used other people's possessions. In the days that followed, I saw that while other people paid for items at the canteen and shared them with each other, his lunch and dinner arrived from the canteen for free – specially made sabji and dal – but he never shared it with anyone, always eating by himself.

Shailesh did not like D. Ram much but treated him with respect because of his caste and age. D. Ram was an old, grumpy, short-tempered man who often abused other prisoners with the choicest Hindi swear words. He never allowed anyone to wear slippers inside the barrack, but wore a pair himself, and even went to the toilet with his slippers on. He could even hit a person if he found them putting their feet on his otta.

He read the newspaper line by line and he had a pile of newspapers with him but never had to pay for a single one. Every day he lit two mosquito coils, but I never saw him buy any. He always asked the other inmates for the coils. On Saturdays, when *jalebi* with curd was on sale, he always ate some without having to pay for it. From him, I learnt how to hide newspapers under my blanket.

D. Ram gave me a spot near his, offered me bhujia and water, and newspapers to read. I was grateful to him. At long last I read all the news that was painting me as a villain, even one month after the tragedy and despite me being behind bars.

When I had been busy with D. Ram, all the other prisoners were giving me strange looks and murmuring,

'*Haan, yehi Dr Kafeel hai* (Yes, this is the same Dr Kafeel), *BRD Medical College wala*.' Gradually this murmur became louder, and the whole barrack wanted to talk about my case. Another lesson I learned about prison life was that prisoners pass the time by complaining and gossiping about others, because there is little else to do. In jail, the walls are high but they also have sharp ears – whatever you say will be relayed to every last person within moments of your saying it.

D. Ram extended friendship by telling me his story – how he was a victim of politics, falsely framed in a forgery case, and would be out soon. I noted how everyone in jail said they would get bail soon, or that by the next hearing they would be set free, but in 99 per cent of the cases, that never happens. One goes from one hearing to the next without any progress, sometimes passing months and years in this way. Perhaps this has been best immortalized by Sunny Deol's dialogue in the Hindi film *Damini* which questions the lack of justice even after '*Tareekh pe tareekh pe tarikh* (date after date after date)'. Sometimes it takes months and years just to get a hearing. Only those who are powerful and can throw money around can get out in two or three months. I noticed that whenever people spoke like this, they were, in fact, falsely assuring themselves. When you tell someone that you will be leaving soon, you are trying to convince yourself that you will get out soon. D. Ram had been in jail for a year when I first met him.

People started coming up to me to try and have a conversation. Someone brought bananas, another got a guava, and someone else brought biscuits. '*Aap hi Dr Kafeel hain*? (You are Dr Kafeel?)', 'We have seen you on TV!', 'Every day we read about you in the newspaper!'

Soon they started saying, '*Kya kya dharaayein lagi hai* (Which sections of the IPC have you been charged under?)', '*Uss din kya hua tha*? (What happened on that day?)', '*Hamein pata hai aap ko fasaya gaya hai* (We know you have been framed)', '*Aap ne bahut bachchon ko bachaya hai* (You saved many children).'

As I began answering their queries, they became more curious. '*Kitne bachche mare the us raat*? (How many children died that night?)', '*Oxygen kyun khatam hui*? (Why did the oxygen run out?)', '*Baki saathi kahan hain*? (Where are your co-accused?)' They also wanted to know who all were at my home, where it was, what kind of doctor I was, and a hundred other things. I felt relieved when D. Ram reprimanded the curious prisoners, asking them to leave me alone when he felt that things were getting out of hand. Then he took me outside the barrack to sit in the sunshine and started telling me his story.

Through D. Ram I met V. Singh, a retired soldier from Barabanki, charged under the Narcotics Act. He was very nice to me and helped me throughout my stay. He introduced me to several other prisoners, including a man named Dilip from Bihar who had been arrested on charges of extortion and kidnapping a well-known psychiatrist – it was supposedly a very high-profile case.

The person who familiarized me with all the rules I had to follow in the barrack was Fauji sahab. He was a CRPF soldier who had murdered someone from his village during a property dispute. Now, he was the co-writer or the helper to Shailesh Singh. As he narrated the rules, I thought to myself, 'It is one thing to watch and hear about criminals in movies, but an altogether different experience to meet and talk to them face to face. It's scary.'

These were the rules Fauji listed:

- Get up at 5:55 a.m. sharp and stand in the queue for the counting. If you do not leave the otta the moment the door opens, you will be beaten with a stick.

- Make sure you have finished using the toilet, eating, bathing, etc. by 5:45 p.m. because you have to be in the queue by 5:55 p.m.
- From noon to 3 p.m., you will be locked in the barrack unless it is your meeting day. No one should have to call you back to the barrack. You should come inside by yourself, otherwise you are to blame for your torture.
- Never complain about a writer or a *sipahi* (prison officer), no matter how much he harasses you. If another prisoner is harassing you, complain to me or to Shailesh Singh, the writer.
- Whatever money you get from home, you cannot keep it with you.
- Remember you are not a doctor here anymore. You have to do whatever work we tell you to do. As a routine, clean the inner toilet and sweep the barrack every morning after it opens and in the evening before it closes.

He was about to walk away and gave me a look that said, 'We will tell you the rest later,' but then thought better of it and added:

- No mobile, no homemade food and no non-vegetarian food.
- You will fill our water bottles three times a day.
- Every day, before you sleep, you have to massage my whole body.

Immediately I said in reply, 'Everything is acceptable, except this last one.'

Irritated, he said, '*Tujhe Shailesh Singh hi aa kar sikhayenge* (Shailesh Singh himself will have to come and teach you a lesson).'

He continued:

- You have to help me maintain the registers. There are five or six registers to maintain: one is for the details of new prisoners, another for the details of *rihai* (acquitted prisoners), a third one for *chhatni* or distribution, a fourth for *pakki* payment and a fifth that records *kachchi* payment. We also have a register for *pehradari* or night duty.
- Just like the *sipahi* night duty of four hours at night, even prisoners have to wake up and check on other prisoners, in two-hour shifts. The batch of prisoners on night duty changes every fifteen days. If you do not want to be on night duty, you have to pay a fee.
- Most importantly, you will not leave your place without permission.

The jail routine was punctuated by breakfast, lunch, dinner and tea which were all served at fixed times: breakfast at 7 a.m., lunch at 11 a.m., tea at 4 p.m. and dinner at 5 p.m. The tea we got here had little resemblance to what we were used to at home – one big drum of hot water, lots of sugar, a few tea leaves and milk dumped in. To drink it, we had to bring a cup, which was usually a Bisleri bottle cut in half. Or we would slurp it out of our plates.

Lunch and dinner usually consisted of watery dal, uncooked rotis and sometimes rice and boiled vegetables – mostly radish or potatoes. The prisoners would begin to run the moment they saw two people carrying a big bucket of dal and another two carrying a big aluminum thali of roti. They ran to get plates which were limited in number – about eighty or so – and those who ran the fastest would get a plate, stand in the queue and get to eat quickly. Another way to get priority was if you were a bigger criminal, with murders, rape cases or robberies to your name. Caste and class played a part as well – the rich, the Thakurs and the Pandit-jis could bypass the queue.

Mealtimes felt like a contest from the way people ran and competed for food. There would be a separate queue for vegetables, brought in an old oil container by a couple of food bearers who were also prisoners, both tall and well built. A writer and a prison policeman accompanied them, so that they could not go anywhere else. They were on bhandara duty, but only as distributors, making sure that no more than four or six rotis, one bowl of dal and one bowl of watery vegetables were allowed per person. Those who managed to get their portion ate in the open field, while others – not as lucky – looked on and waited their turn. It was embarrassing, and I usually got a plate right at the end. In fact, in the early days, I could not even bring myself to eat this food and tried to satisfy my hunger with fruits instead.

Of course, prisoners would still want to have tea at times that were not part of the timetable. Every hour or two, a prisoner would come around with a kettle, and one could buy tea from him for ₹5. 'Chai, chai,' he would announce, just like they do at railway stations. Often, these tea-bearing prisoners were also the ones who brought marijuana for those who wanted it.

Becoming a co-writer or occupying any of the positions that gave you authority over the other prisoners generally meant you had been given a life-imprisonment sentence, and often, ironically, that you could not read or write. Every convicted prisoner who worked earned ₹20 per day and the total amount they would earn was usually given to them after a year or so. This was a pitiful sum, all the more so as they had to give away a portion of it to the jail authorities. Currency notes were not supposed to be in use in the jail, and you had to instead make do with jail tokens – each prisoner was allowed tokens worth about ₹1,600 every month.

But all that was merely on paper. In real life, I never once saw that jail token. Currency notes flowed everywhere, and every rupee spent within the jail went into the pockets of the jail officials. There was an established code as well as commission rates.

Doctors were not left out of the earning machinery. The jail doctors received commissions based on how they certified healthy and resourceful prisoners at the time of admission, as well as from the sales of drugs such as alprax, clonazepam, diazepam, tramadol and cough syrup.

The worst, most powerful criminals paid lakhs of rupees for better facilities and a bigger space inside the jail, or a stay at the hospital. This was a well-oiled system, and no one from outside ever interfered in these arrangements. It did not matter who was in power, which party was ruling at the central or state level, or who the chief minister was. The prison system operated under its own esoteric rules.

There were so many sources of income and the cuts to be given to specific people, from the writer to the jail minister, were also fixed. It was a machinery that worked without glitches or interruptions, even when a new jailor, superintendent, deputy, minister or chief minister took charge. I could gather that this was how every jail operated, at least in UP.

You don't want to work? Pay the kachchi baithaki of ₹200 per day, or the pakki baithaki of ₹2,000 per month.

You want to run the canteen? Pay ₹5 lakh per year.

You want to meet your family or friends? Pay the mulakat fee of ₹50, or the pakki mulakat amount of ₹2,000 which allows you to meet your girl behind the walls of the meeting area.

Homesick? Pay ₹50 to call your family or get access to a mobile phone.

Pay ₹2,000 to get the barrack of your choice.

Want to have more vegetables? Pay ₹50 for a bowl and ₹20 for eggs.

Feel like a smoke? Pay ₹150 for a packet of Capstan cigarettes, ₹50 for a pack of bidis and ₹200 for a small pack of Gold Flake. You could pay to get marijuana or charas as well.

You paid a heavy amount to keep and use a mobile phone (though it is strictly not allowed in the Mulaihaija barrack).

You paid to meet your family six days a week during both the meeting hours.

You could pay ₹25 for a water bottle, ₹30 for curd, ₹30 for a sweet and ₹15 for a paratha.

If you fancied a long stay in the hospital barrack, it was available for ₹5,000 to ₹10,000 per month.

You could pay to get other prisoners' help for your personal chores – they would wash your clothes, clean the toilet before you went to use it. They would also give you a massage, if you so wished. In other words, you could buy yourself a cheap slave.

Everything depended on your paying capacity. The Millennium barrack writer would mark your ticket, which would serve as an indication to everyone about your status. If you belonged to a rich family, or were a politician, or a criminal with a record of extortion, bank robbery or big thefts, you could live well inside the prison by paying ₹50,000 to ₹1 lakh per month.

Another norm was that the moment any decent-looking man in nice clothes, supposedly from a 'respectable' background, arrived as an inmate, there would be competition among the others to decide who would be able to stay close to him and get to be his friend – so that he could bear their daily necessities such as bidis, cigarettes and snacks. Most prisoners who were living out long sentences came from the poor socio-economic stratum. Habitual offenders and those from other cities hardly had visitors, so they depended on other prisoners for their daily needs.

If you had money, life inside the prison could be easier. But I knew the moment I entered that all these roads were blocked for me.

The Millennium barrack compound is separated from the main prison compound. It has a large, open space that is as large as four badminton fields put together. Half this space was used by the prisoners to grow vegetables. On the other side was the toilet complex, containing six toilets with half doors. The bathing space was just opposite, with six taps for prisoners to take a bath in the open. There was also a hand pump in case the overhead tank overfilled.

The toilet was dirty and extremely stinky. Some people behaved as if they were shitting in a train – they did not use water to wash down the excreta or even wash their hands after going to the toilet. I usually had to clean the toilet every time before using it.

After coming to the prison, I did not take a bath for ten days. I had never bathed in the open before, so I was a little hesitant. Moreover, it was a huge mental adjustment for me, trying to make sense of the changes to my life and my living situation.

Shailesh Singh came in just before the closing of the gates. He came up to me the moment he saw me.

'Doctor sahab, I am a big fan of yours. You saved the lives of so many children – I really admire you,' he said. Everyone looked up at us, surprised. He was usually very strict with the other prisoners and was one of the favourites of the jail authorities because he was their biggest earner.

After the counting, he took my otta from D. Ram and placed it near his. He was really friendly, but I was still not in the mood to talk. Thankfully, he was saying enough for the both of us. While having his dinner, he even asked me if I had eaten. I lied and said that I had.

Although I did not offer much by way of conversation, his friendly gestures towards me were a source of some comfort.

He said, 'Today you can take some time to settle down. Tomorrow you have to smile and laugh!' He was trying to cheer me up, but I just took my blanket, covered my face and pretended to sleep. But sleep was far, far away. I was very hungry, so much so that I remembered that evening's dal and roti and regretted not accepting Shailesh's offer to eat dinner with him.

Night fell over the barrack. Around 2 or 3 a.m., I felt so ravenous that I picked up a dry roti from the food kept for the new prisoners and tried to somehow gulp it down with water. All the while, I looked around myself, worried that someone was watching me. It was suffocating – 180 people crammed inside that hall, which seemed quite small at night.

These people were snoring, chatting, coughing, scratching, sneezing, laughing, crying, arguing, farting, going to the toilet and returning to their little spaces. Someone sleeping beside you might put his legs on your body, another person lying in the next row might put his hands on your head. The fans overhead revolved ever so slowly. The large windows which made cross-ventilation possible provided some respite from the intense suffocation.

Finding myself unable to breathe properly, I stayed awake, hoping that the sun would come out soon. After a while, I got up and looked around. The lights were on and most of the people were sleeping, but some were smoking and chatting, or just looking at me. Every two hours, prison officers would come and shout, '*Pehredaar, pehredaar*!' It was extremely irritating. They would take the thumbprints of the prisoners who were the designated night sentries or pehredaars. Sometimes they chatted loudly, asking for water, something to eat or a smoke.

I was inside a world that a mere few weeks ago I had never known existed. Neither did I know that I was going to be a part of it for a long time.

11

Inmates and Insights

Everything I came to understand about the prison currencies, and how prisons operate in general, became clear to me over time. I am writing about my experience here, in a single condensed account, but my time in prison constituted some of the most agonizing, humiliating – and what I considered senseless – experiences of my life.

Separated from my family and prevented from practising the profession for which I had trained and worked for so many years, it seemed I had become the victim of a process that promised to deliver justice. Instead, everyone told me it was not a just process – but it would be over soon, after things had 'settled down'. But what was this 'settling down' and how would it happen? How could anything settle down when the media frenzy around me was daily being fed by further falsehoods? What was my antidote against the anchors who thundered from the safety of their TV studios day and night, assaulting my character?

I would have been willing to clean the toilets and do all the prison-assigned tasks if I thought that in some way I had done some wrong, that I had committed a crime against my family, society and country. Instead, I felt like I had drawn the worst punishment only for doing the right thing in the most difficult circumstances, and then, for speaking the truth.

On 7 September, I woke up for the counting and joined the toilet queue. My turn came only after an hour, but when it did, I took a broom and an old oil container, and began one of my assigned tasks. The stench was so terrible that I vomited while cleaning the toilet, but I still cleaned it properly. I swept the barrack with two more prisoners, brushed my teeth, had my tea and waited for the mulakat. Dadhi Kaka came at around 11 o'clock, but he brought disappointing news. I had no visitors. So Adeel bhai may have gone to Allahabad, but couldn't Shabista have paid me a visit? What had happened to them? My mind collapsed once again into an ocean of questions and worries. I sat by myself in a corner until the noon bell rang, instructing us to go inside, after which I went into the barrack.

But how long could I continue my self-imposed isolation? Gradually, I began interacting with my fellow prisoners. One could say that I was finally able to absorb the trauma and shock of being in a jail, and I started noticing the different personalities around me.

Azad was a nineteen-year-old with grave charges levied against him under the POCSO Act. His story was similar to many who are charged under this act by hostile families. He was seventeen when he had a love affair with a teenage girl who was then fifteen. They wanted to marry each other and ran away from home to Mumbai until her family found them. The girl changed her statement under pressure from her family and an FIR was registered. The fast-track court sentenced him to seven years of rigorous imprisonment, which he was now serving.

I found him to be a very cheerful person who took care of Mantri-ji, as one of the inmates was called. Azad made Mantri-ji's bed, served him tea, fruits and snacks, coloured his hair and washed his clothes. Most of the time, Mantri-ji was reprimanding or swearing at him, but Azad ignored it all and continued his work in the spirit of '*jail me samay katna hai* (one has to pass the time in jail somehow)'.

Another young man I met was Rohu, a twenty-five-year-old charged under Section 376 which includes the charge of rape. He claimed that he had got married as a child in his village. When he went to Mumbai for work, he had met and married another woman there. Later, the people of the village learnt of this fact and his first wife filed a rape case against him, even though he had been taking care of both the wives. Rohu was a hard worker who worked as a supervisor for Shailesh. He would monitor the other inmates who had not paid the pakki baithaki and saw to it that they completed their duties of cleaning the barrack, the toilet, gardening and garbage disposal. This last one was done by bringing in a dustbin – a huge drum into which people threw leftover food, paper cups and other trash. It was filled twice a day and four inmates carried it out of the barrack to the dumping ground.

I could never get used to the lack of concern most inmates displayed about basic personal hygiene. On the other side of the barrack, waste from the toilet used to flow out into the open through the cracks in a broken pipe, attracting millions of flies. Just the thought of going there made me feel like retching. But it was a place that inmates habitually visited in order to take a leak under the open sky. I never figured out if this was because the toilets were very dirty, or they were just used to peeing in the open.

For me, having access to water and washing my hands with soap was so important that after a few days I got myself some paper soap that I could always keep on my person.

Viswa, a young policeman and fellow inmate, was also very helpful and friendly. He had been charged under the Dowry Act, since his wife had died by suicide within a year of their marriage. He said that they used to have fights over small issues, and one day she locked the room and hanged herself. Listening to him, I started thinking about the first year of my marriage, which were some of the most beautiful days of my life. Viswa's parents had also been convicted, and his mother was in prison, too, although his father had received bail. His brothers' names had been excluded by the police after Viswa had paid them a hefty amount. To top it all off, although both families wanted to reach a compromise and get him out of jail, the girl's family was asking for ₹10 lakh to withdraw the case. Viswa was an irritable man and often had fights with other prisoners because he thought of himself as a police officer. Other prison cops were also friendly with him, but Shailesh did not like him, and they had frequent arguments. As far as I was concerned, I liked this young prisoner only because he conducted our physical training or PT sessions in the morning and taught us about Babasaheb Ambedkar.

On the other hand, meeting and interacting with Mantri-ji furthered my education in another direction.

Mantri-ji was a *bahubali* politician from Maharajganj in Gorakhpur. He was counted in the league of former well-known bahubalis of Purvanchal. His clout was immense, and he had been a minister in many UP governments, including those of the Congress, Bahujan Samaj Party (BSP) and Samajwadi Party (SP).

Mantri-ji's fortunes turned after he allegedly had an affair with twenty-four-year-old poet and political aspirant, who, after getting pregnant, was found dead in her apartment. Both Mantri-ji and his wife were found guilty of conspiring to murder the girl, and were sentenced to life imprisonment, of which they had served sixteen years when I reached Gorakhpur Jail. I had heard of him even when I was working at BRD, because he spent a lot of time at the college roaming around freely. He had returned to prison only after the change of government in 2017, and his barrack had been reserved for him.

He was known to help other prisoners, but his habit of

then insulting that person in front of everyone took away from his image of a generous man.

I also faced my share of taunts from Mantri-ji. He would tell me, 'You claim that *you* got the cylinders, and that's why you are here. Once you stop talking about that day and stop asking "Why am I here?" you will be freed. If you keep repeating "What was my fault? So many kids died!" you will rot in this jail. Or, even if you get released, you will come back again.'

I was silent when this insight was revealed to me. What was there to say?

One day, Mantri-ji told me the story of Yogi Adityanath's stint in prison in 2007, when he had been arrested under the charge of rioting.

'He was an MP from the BJP when a communal riot broke out and an outfit torched many buses and public property. Even a rail compartment carrying handicapped students had been targeted. His supporters and he were jailed on charges of disturbing the peace and violating prohibitory orders. He spent fifteen days here, in the same Millennium barrack in which you are lodged – and he would ask people who would come to meet him, saying, "Go do something about my situation – don't just come visiting!"'

Other prisoners who had been present at the time substantiated Mantri-ji's story. How strange, I thought, that he was once a resident of the same jail barrack I was in.

Another prisoner who stood out from the rest was Akash, a young man in his thirties, who was in jail on the charges of double murder. His brother was also in jail in another barrack. Akash had bipolar disorder and used to suffer violent psychotic episodes. He wanted to talk to me, but I always maintained some distance from him not because of his illness, but because of his dependence on drugs and other such substances. Everyone was either scared of him or avoided him. Sometimes he barked like a dog for hours. Sometimes he fought with other inmates and, when teenage boys were brought in, he forced them to sleep near him. His wife had left him and he hardly received visitors.

Another unspoken truth of the prison was the sexual abuse that took place within its walls.

The abusers would target youngsters by either paying them off or forcing themselves on the boys, which became routine, even though the barrack for children was a separate one. Everyone in prison knew of this but averted their eyes from the reality. But if someone got caught, they would be beaten up badly and sent to a high-security barrack for some time.

During my time, I only heard stories of such events as they were rare in our barrack. However, one day in the toilet, a sixteen-year-old boy suddenly grabbed my leg and pleaded for help. He told me that two men had switched off the back lights near the toilet and tried to attack him. I asked if he could name his assailants, but the terrified boy kept crying.

I took him along to Shailesh and told him the story. Shailesh advised him to sleep near us.

In the morning when I asked him again if he could identify his attackers in front of the jailor, he refused, saying they would kill him if he revealed anything. After that, Shailesh sent him to the children's barrack, and I didn't see him again.

On 9 September, I met Sudhir Pandey, the senior-most clerk in the BRD Medical College's accounts department, who had been named responsible in the enquiry report about the lapsed budget of March 2017. Sudhir had virtually grown up at BRD and knew everyone, from the grade-four employees to the doctors. His father had also worked in the college, so he had spent his childhood playing with other officers' children. Most of them later joined the medical department, so he had relations with officers from Gorakhpur to the Lucknow secretariat.

I was meeting Sudhir only for the second time in my life. The first time was when he had come to ward 100 on 11 August and told me he would arrange cylinders from Modi Gas.

Sudhir was a typical sarkari babu who maintained good relationships with everybody. He spoke in very familiar terms about Mantri-ji and informed me that he had visited the Millennium barrack when it was being built. But I took his claims of being thus acquainted with Mantri-ji with a pinch of salt.

Talking to Sudhir enlightened me about the power equations and allegations of corruption within BRD Medical College, just as talking to the principal in the Nehru barrack had done. It was clear that they belonged to two different camps.

The principal had alleged that Sudhir Pandey and the SIC were in cahoots, selling hospital medicines outside the hospital and taking commissions when clearing each bill. He mentioned that his wife had pointed out Sudhir's proximity to Modi Gas. She claimed that the supplier had defrauded the medical college in the past, during Principal Kushwaha's tenure, by charging for empty cylinders. In fact, he went on to tell me that this was what had led to the principal awarding the medical oxygen contract to IGL. He also cited various instances of lobbyists, who wanted Kushwaha back as principal, creating a media hype around various incidents in his absence. These included a broken-down lift, a ruckus raised by the patients' relatives, a workers' strike, missing medicines and, finally, an incident on Dhanteras on 28 October 2016, when the liquid oxygen tank valve ran into some issues and the oxygen supply had stopped briefly.

On the other hand, Sudhir spoke extensively about how the principal Rajiv Mishra's wife was running the whole show from their home, which was like a camp office. All the tenders, contracts, payments and order files would first be read by her, after which she would influence decisions as to who would be paid and who were to be given contracts.

I listened to both parties without offering any theories or conjectures of my own. All the charges and counter charges that both camps were levying meant nothing to the children who had perished in August 2017, or to their parents. While corruption was being alleged by both parties at many levels, from the clerks in the accounts department to the office of the DGME and the principal secretary, of what use was it to me, serving a prison sentence for having committed no crime whatsoever?

In reality, a single genuine investigation could have uncovered the facts, drawn out the truth, and helped punish the culprits. But no one had carried out a proper investigation. Since the beginning, every officer involved, or even those unconnected to the case, wanted to bury the facts. No one cared about the children who had died, or their parents, who had lost their precious babies.

Was it because all the children who had died had one thing in common – that they were children from poor families?

In spite of the insights into the BRD Medical College's politics and corruption that I had been given by the principal and Sudhir, and even the advice proffered by Mantri-ji that I should not claim credit for arranging oxygen cylinders or proclaim my innocence – my mind was still bursting with questions. If there was ever a proper investigation, it should have addressed all these points:

When both Dr Rajiv Mishra and Dr Satish Kumar, who was in charge of oxygen supply, were on leave, who took their place and why was their role not investigated?

On the intervening night of 10–11 August, how many adults had died in the wards of other departments – such as surgery, trauma, medicine, gynaecology – where the oxygen supply had also been affected?

Why was the role of other doctors in the paediatrics ward not investigated, especially the head of the department and the head of encephalitis? What had doctors from other departments done about the oxygen shortage that night? Who would investigate the role of top officials like the DM, the DGME and the principal secretary, particularly since they were heading the enquiry – all the letters written by Pushpa Sales about the non-payment of dues had been addressed to them. Why were the health minister and the minister for education not questioned by the police even once during their investigation? How did a company like IGL get the contract for supplying jumbo oxygen cylinders when it was located so far from Gorakhpur city? Who would investigate the central pipeline operators on account of their having informed the hospital administration about the imminent crisis after the level had dipped below 900 MMCW, when they were supposed to do so at 4,000 MMCW? Why did they provide this information only after the principal had left town? When even the Allahabad High Court had questioned the tripartite agreement between Pushpa Sales, BRD and Inox, why was it not investigated? Under whose orders was the investigation stopped all of a sudden? What was the role of the ex-principal and why was this not investigated further, even though notices were served to him and several others?

There was no getting away from all these questions, and yet no answers were available.

12

Visitors and Other Arrivals

On Sunday, 10 September, Dadhi Kaka brought me the news that my wife Shabista was coming to meet me. My heart started singing. I took a long bath and cleaned up well in anticipation of the visit. In the prison, soap doubled up as shampoo, which I used to clean myself thoroughly. I got dressed, ate my breakfast and waited for Shailesh to send someone with my *parchi*.

Visitors needed to arrive early in the morning to register their names for the visit. Registration took place between 6 and 7 a.m. for the first visit, between 8 and 10 a.m. for the second. At this time, they would be given a slip of paper – a parchi. Then Dadhi Kaka would come and show the computerized slip to the inmate who had visitors and ask him if he wanted to meet them.

When the inmate's assent had been registered, Dadhi Kaka would pick up the inmate's card from the prison office and check whether it was his turn to be visited or not, as per the quota of visits allowed each week. After that the jailor would sign the visitor slip.

Slips for the first meeting would then be sent around to those who were to receive visitors during the first meeting slot at around 11:30 a.m., while slips for the second meeting slot were sent out after the visits during the first slot had been concluded, which was around 1 p.m.

The worst situation was when the slip came as late as noon because the jailor was not present, or the writer who was supposed to bring the slip forgot to deliver it and was relaxing somewhere with a friend and a cigarette. On those occasions, every minute and every hour felt horrible and the waiting period was unbearable. At such times, you felt like begging the circle officer, a prison officer or the writer to bring your slip and take you to the waiting area.

Sometimes, even when the slips arrived, out of the fifteen people with registered visitors, some would be eating, taking a bath, or were not prepared for the visit yet. This would make certain people (like me), who were ready by 11 a.m. impatient. The same feelings surfaced when one had to wait for the second meeting slot, and the ones who had gone to meet their visitors during the first slot were taking a long time to return.

Finally, the writer called out our names and our fathers' names, we were counted and made to walk in pairs towards the visiting area.

The people who came to visit the inmates also had to follow a long procedure. First, they stood in a queue to have their name and address verified, submitted a copy of their Aadhaar card, gave their thumbprint and got a stamp put on their hand which said 'VISITOR'.

Next, they joined a queue to get their belongings checked – bags, purses and so on.

The third queue was to enter the prison, but once they had done so, their bags would be checked again in yet another queue.

In the fourth queue since they arrived, the visitors would have to get their stamps checked by the deputy jailor or writer, and that person would sign under the stamp with a red pen. It could take two to three hours for a visitor just to get inside.

I was feeling very restless that morning – how would my

poor wife and daughter withstand such a long process in the scorching heat?

The moment I saw Shabista, I wanted to run and hug her, but we were not allowed to leave the area where we were asked to wait.

She was wearing a blue salwar suit and sports shoes. Zab was in a pink dress. They both looked so lovely.

Shabista began walking towards me, holding Zab in one arm, and in the other, a bag with my clothes, and a plastic bag with fruits, snacks and biscuits. Zab was hugging her tightly.

As soon as our eyes met, they filled with tears. That moment in which I met my wife while in jail, after not having seen her for fifteen days, was so painful. Our whole world had come apart in that period. I called out to my daughter. 'Zab! Zab!' I said loudly, and people started turning to stare at me. But I did not care.

Zab turned around and saw me. She gave me a strange look, perhaps because of my beard. I had not shaved since the day I had been arrested. But once I held out my arms, she smiled in excitement and began to wriggle in her mother's arms. Shabista let her go, and she started toddling towards me. Barely able to walk, she fell down. I ran and took her in my arms and started kissing her like a mad man. I hugged my wife and started crying. But she was stronger than I was.

'Kafeel, people are looking at us,' she said gently. Reluctantly, I let go of her with a heavy heart. We sat on the floor atop the bed sheet she had brought. Zab began playing with my beard and head hair. For a few minutes, no one spoke. We just looked at each other quietly.

'How are you?' she asked.

'How are *you*?' I replied.

'You tell me first.'

'I am fine. I am sorry that all of you have gone through so much because of me, jaan. How badly our whole family is suffering.'

'No, don't say that. It's not your fault. We are with you. Everyone around us knows it's not your fault and they are praising you and cursing the government.'

Her words were like a balm to my heart.

'And don't worry – you will be out before you know it. Adeel bhai is going to file your bail application soon,' she continued.

Her next words were worrying. 'The police are still coming, every day. They ask all kinds of weird questions, like why did you go that night when no one else went to the hospital? Why did you talk to the media? They are looking at your documents – IT returns, your car, bike and house papers. I think they are expecting money.'

'No!' I exploded. 'Don't give them a single paisa! For what? When I have not done anything wrong, why should I have to pay?'

She gave me a grave look. 'They are saying if you pay the money, it will be easier for you to come back.'

'No way,' I repeated. 'Let them do whatever they want, but we are not going to pay them anything.'

Shabista told me she had tried to meet the DM three times, at his home as well as his office, but he had refused to grant her audience. 'Once I even ran after his car with Zab in my arms; he finally stopped and agreed to listen,' she said. 'But the commissioner and SSP were very rude to me. I waited for hours at their office, I knew they were inside, but they refused to meet me.'

The DM and commissioner used to praise me for my hard work when they visited the BRD Medical College, but they stopped after the tragedy. Even a few months ago, the DM and SSP had praised me at an IMA programme. At the ICMR meeting in June 2017, the commissioner had said that we need doctors like Kafeel Khan to fight this encephalitis menace. I shook my head, unable to come to grips with the things worked in high office.

'The reporters are asking why he didn't pay them when Pushpa Sales had written letters to the DM reminding him about the dues. The DM has enormous power and crores of rupees in funds. He could have stepped in and saved lives. Questions are also being raised about how they had no inkling of the mounting dues even though the DM and the commissioner visited the medical college many times before the incident.' I listened to Shabista and realized that questions surrounding that night's crisis had not faded away, especially not in the minds of the public.

'Anyway, we have decided to meet the chief minister. I will tell him that my husband is innocent, he has not done anything wrong, and beg him to show us some mercy,' she said.

I looked at her, impressed at her strength in the face of hardship. She had gone to meet the DM and the other officials for me, with no fear.

And there was more.

'I told the investigating officer: Don't come to our house after 6 p.m., otherwise I will complain to the DGP. After that, he started visiting only during the day,' she said, smiling. She looked composed. I wondered how Allah had blessed me with a wife as brave as her!

I asked her about all our other family members and how they had been affected.

'Ammi doesn't know because we did not want to disturb her while she's at hajj. But Farro and Kashif bhai both know everything. They are all praying for you. Besides, after so many sting operations conducted by the journalists, it has now become public knowledge that the crisis happened due to the non-payment of dues, and you were the junior-most doctor.'

She sighed and I saw a shadow cloud her face as she continued. 'The most painful thing is that no one comes to our house now. Relatives have stopped picking up our phone calls. Everyone is keeping a distance. Adeel bhai's showroom has been completely destroyed. Even on Bakrid, the day you got arrested, we were really scared, but no one came to ask how we were doing, to offer some sevai or find out if we needed any food. *Chulha nahi jala aur hum sab bhuke rahe din bhar* (The stove never got lit and we all stayed hungry the whole day), and still not even close relatives, or our neighbours, your friends or Adeel bhai's friends – no one came.'

I was absorbing what she said, and the hurt was slowly seeping into my body.

'Every year, when we had made the sacrifice, people came to collect meat – those people have also disappeared,' she said. 'Life teaches us so many lessons.'

I asked about her parents. 'Mummy and Papa have assured us of all the help they can give and said that they will pay for the cases. Don't worry, you will soon be with us again.' I felt greatly relieved. '*Par aap vada kijiye aap medical college se resign kar denge* (But promise me that you will resign from the medical college),' she said.

'We will discuss that later,' I said. 'Let me first get released from the prison!'

The tea seller came with his five-rupee tea for the inmates.

Zab had become irritable and nodded off to sleep after Shabista fed her. I took her in my arms, cherishing each moment we had together. In an instant, the call began, '*Chaliye, chaliye* (Come on, come on).'

'Does Zab miss me? Will she ask for me after you go home?' I asked.

'No, usually she doesn't remember, but the moment she saw you, she did. Sometimes she does look for you. "Papa, Papa," she mumbles,' Shabista replied.

Now there were only seconds left. 'How are you?' I asked once again, unable to look anywhere except at her. I was drinking in her face and her presence with an unquenchable thirst.

'I am okay,' she said, and we both knew it did not even begin to describe what was going on in both our minds and hearts.

I held her hand tightly but she did not say anything. She just looked at me, her eyes full of love. I wanted to hug her, to kiss her. I also wanted my beloved Zab to sleep in my arms once more.

Instead, I had to watch her walk away with tear-filled eyes.

My heart plummeted like a stone as I watched them walk out of the gate which shut me inside in the next instant. The outside world had never felt more different from the one I was in at that moment.

I stood in the queue for the counting and then walked back to the barrack. I paid my ₹50 and handed over my fruits, namkeen and biscuits to the prison cops. I had no will left to oppose such practices. After meeting my family members, I was even more depressed, and it took me at least two days to recover from this pain.

News from the courts gets relayed even faster in prison than by local journalists. On Monday, 11 September, Dadhi Kaka came and told me Dr Satish Kumar would be arriving at the jail that day.

A gentle and polite person, Dr Satish was the HOD of Anaesthesia. While Sudhir knew him well, I remembered meeting him once or twice in regards to room allotment, as he was the maintenance head and hostel warden.

That evening, we were locked in by 6 p.m. I was sitting idly on my otta when Dr Satish arrived. I went and wished him, to which he responded warmly. He had shaved off his moustache and was looking a bit strange without it. 'Moustache?' I said. He answered with a sad laugh.

It was to hide from the media and the public, he said. He had shaved his head and his moustache, donned saffron clothing and ridden his bike to court to surrender at exactly the moment the magistrate called his name.

The police officers had wanted to play out the same exercise they did with Sudhir and me – that they had caught us as we were planning to leave the city, on receiving a tip off. But Dr Satish had acted on his advocate's counsel.

He told me his part of the story. Yes, he was the head of Maintenance, but his work started when he received the liquid oxygen; he did not have anything to do with its procurement or payment. His job was to deliver the oxygen to each bed from the central tank. The principal had a different take on this; he had told me that Dr Satish was the head of oxygen supply and that all the central pipeline operators, as well as Gajanand Jaiswal, were working with him. That he was the one who was supposed to place an order when the liquid oxygen level went below 4,500 MMCW, something he hadn't done on the night of 10 August.

'When you called me on the morning of the 11th, I was on the way to Lucknow to catch my flight. I reached Mumbai by evening. My wife and I had dinner and were resting in a hotel room when I got a call and came to know about the incident,' he told me. 'By this time, of course, the news was also flashing on national TV.'

Dr Satish did not attend his son's convocation and returned on the 13th, the day the CM visited. The HOD of Medicine had called and congratulated him, saying, 'Come and start your new job!'

So, on his return, he was optimistic about becoming the principal. His wife was also very happy, though they were both disturbed by the news of so many children's deaths. When they reached Gorakhpur, everyone congratulated him at the office, and he was collecting all his papers and working with the DGME in the principal's office when he got a call from Dr U. C. Srivastava telling him that the CM had summoned him to ward 100 immediately.

Dr Satish was delighted that he would receive the news about the job from the CM himself.

'Sir, Dr Satish Kumar is here,' someone announced.

Everyone turned around to look at the entrance as the CM fixed his gaze on Dr Satish. There was pin-drop silence in the room.

The chief minister asked, 'Why did you go on leave without informing anyone?'

'Sir, I had informed the principal and taken official leave – here is the documentation,' said Dr Satish. But the CM was not at all satisfied.

'Why was the AC not working?' was his next question.

'Sir, I had instructed ...' began Dr Satish.

'Shut up!' said the CM. And that was it. Dr Satish was promptly led out of the room.

What had happened to me happened to Dr Satish as well. Everyone told him to leave the city for a few days and to stay away from the media. So he stayed at his brother's house in Lucknow. But as they say, the real faces of your so-called relatives will be revealed when you are in trouble. When the police started raiding various places in search of him, his brother told him to leave. He had also received assurance from his lawyers in Allahabad that he would get anticipatory bail, until which time he needed to hide somewhere.

He returned to Gorakhpur and stayed at his friend's house while his wife went back and forth from the local police station to Allahabad. He confined himself to his room, but one day, when his friend hinted that he and his family were scared, he decided not to wait for the Allahabad order and to surrender instead.

On the way to the jail, in the inmates' van, he overheard some criminals discussing him and saying, '... he has earned so much through corruption – he has to pay.' They asked him to give them his wife's number, making him feel very uneasy.

He was upset and depressed. Sudhir consoled him and told him not to worry. 'No one will touch you in jail while I am here,' he assured Dr Satish. Shailesh gave him a place to lie down. I offered him a blanket and some food. He ate and tried to rest. But sleep eluded both of us.

13

More Links in the Chain

After Dr Satish Kumar's arrival, I gained some measure of peace in prison. He was fifty-six years old and I was thirty-six, but at least now there was someone with whom I could share my feelings and my thoughts about what had happened at BRD. Every time I asked aloud, 'Why am I here?' Dr Satish answered simply, 'Because it became public knowledge. Otherwise, nothing would have happened.'

In prison, I was coming to terms with my destiny in new ways.

Irfan and Rizwan were two brothers who had been charged under the Dowry Act. Irfan was an AC mechanic and Rizwan a medical representative. One day, when I was sitting under a tree, Irfan came and told me that this was where inmates came to do pooja, so it was better we sat elsewhere. We recognized each other – I realized I had seen him a few times when he had come to the wards at BRD to repair ACs. We began talking. He told me he knew it was not my fault that things had panned out the way they had.

After that conversation, Irfan and Rizwan both became friendly with me, and began taking care of me in small ways, by bringing me tea, for instance. It was nice to not feel so isolated anymore. They also relayed the jail chatter to me.

One fellow I really felt sympathetic towards was a nineteen-year-old youth imprisoned on charges of theft. He was called Thapa by other inmates as he was from Darjeeling. Even though he was Indian, his fellow prisoners treated him as an outsider because of his features.

The young guy did not know Hindi, and no one knew his native tongue Nepali either. He was generally treated very badly by other prisoners who made him do a lot of odd chores; if he said 'no' to anything, he got beaten up badly. His family did not know that he was in Gorakhpur Jail, and he did not have an advocate to help him. After giving him a few of my clothes and some money, I wrote a letter to his family. When he was finally let go, I felt relieved.

Just as I was getting used to interacting with people from such disparate spheres of life, I was also adjusting to the environment. I could not help my discomfort from being in such close proximity to so many people all the time, but I slowly adapted to the sights, sounds and smells. Snoring, coughing, farting, the clapping of hands as people mixed powdered tobacco and lime in their palms, all of it gradually became background noise.

The snores of my fellow barrackers were a real menace. A few of them sounded like train engines! Shailesh tried getting the snorers to sleep in the corners, but he liked to keep a few people close to him and they all snored very loudly. So he gave me cotton to plug into my ears at night. This was a true blessing, as the cotton protected my ears from the snores as well as insects, which would otherwise crawl into our ears at night and die there. After a few days, this produced a foul-smelling discharge and a severe earache.

During the rainy season, rats, centipedes, millipedes and snakes were some of the other creatures with whom we had to share space. The ever-present mosquitoes, combined with the hum of people talking and clapping for *surti*, or going repeatedly to the washroom at night, made it tough to get uninterrupted sleep.

To make matters worse, the night guards would shout at random, some of the drug addicts would occasionally have a seizure, a person sleeping next to you would suddenly put his arm or leg on your face – there was always some kind of disturbance.

Finally, the most important question keeping me awake – whether depressed, angry, or frustrated – was: 'Why am I here among criminals?'

On 13 September, there were new arrivals from the BRD oxygen tragedy case: Sanjay Tripathi, senior accounts clerk, and Gajanand Jaiswal, chief pharmacist and the person in charge of the oxygen cylinders. They told me they had surrendered, but the police narrated the same story of having caught them based on an informant's tip. The newspapers carried stories thus: 'Clerk Sanjay Tripathi has been arrested from Cantonment police station area. He will be later produced in the anti-corruption court,' said SSP, Gorakhpur, Anirudh Sidhartha Pankaj. Also, 'Former chief pharmacist of the medical college, Gajanand Jaiswal, had surrendered in a city court and was sent to judicial custody.'

For me, this confirmed a pattern – the police were not asking for remand, and all the accused were sent directly to judicial custody. It was almost as if nobody wanted to investigate why the oxygen tragedy had transpired. To me, it seemed as if the arrests were made to satisfy the media and appease the angry public.

I did not make any attempt to talk to Sanjay or Gajanand, because I did not know them at all. I had seen Sanjay perhaps once or twice at the hospital office, when I went to collect my salary, while I was meeting Gajanand for the first time ever. Sudhir knew them both, so he showed them where to keep their possessions and helped them settle in, after which Shailesh came and made more arrangements for them. Dr Satish knew them both as well, but since both of them had given statements against the other, Gajanand and Sanjay were polite yet wary with each other, and not particularly friendly.

When we finally spoke, Gajanand revealed to me, 'We usually kept fifty-two reserve cylinders, and there were as many that night.'

After what we had been through, I wondered: When you need 250 to 300 cylinders in a day, and it is also known that liquid gas takes two or three days to arrive after an order is placed, why were at least 500 to 600 cylinders not reserved for an emergency?

I had not had any visitors for four days, and was desperate for some news from home. On the morning of 14 September, I was relieved to get a slip from Dadhi Kaka informing me that Adeel bhai was coming to meet me. I had a bath and got in the queue early.

But no one called for me for the first meeting slot. After waiting for a long time, I finally asked Dadhi Kaka what was going on. '*Pata nahi, bachcha* (I don't know, son),' he said. I was upset and asked him to find out if I would be called for the second slot, which he promised to do.

At noon, the barrack doors closed and there was still no sign of him. I waited and waited, feeling frustrated as the minutes ticked from 12:00 to 12:30. People kept coming over to ask me why I was being so quiet or if something had happened to upset me. Some tried to reassure me by saying everything would be okay.

I was screaming inside: Everything was *not* all right!

Had Adeel bhai gone to Allahabad? Was he busy in court? If so, why did he register for a meeting? Was there any bad news?

When Dadhi Kaka came to return my card after the second meeting period got over, I ran after him to ask if he knew anything.

'Your brother came, bachcha, but the jailor didn't allow the meeting.'

'But why?' I asked, completely stunned.

'I don't know, bachcha,' he said, turning away.

This brief exchange was enough to unleash a hundred new questions in my mind.

Why had the jailor not allowed my brother to meet me? Did he want some money? Had the DM or anyone else threatened him? Did this mean I could no longer meet my family?

But there was no one who could give me an answer.

The eighth arrest in the case was that of Uday Pratap Sharma, who arrived a day after Gajanand Jaiswal and Sanjay Tripathi. He was the youngest of us all. He had got his job at the BRD Medical College after his father expired and had joined the accounts department only in May 2017, after the principal had made Sanjay the senior accountant and Uday the junior accountant.

Both Sanjay and Uday had a similar story to tell: 'We just followed orders. If the principal said, "Pay the bill," who were we to refuse? We did not have the power to question anything. After March 2017, whenever the budget arrived, it came with specific instructions about who was to be paid. We never knew anything else.'

Most importantly, they said, the money train would run when there was fuel. When the money had not even been sanctioned from Lucknow, how could they, mere clerks, have made payments?

That night, as if to give the new arrivals an idea of what lay in store for them in jail, one of the alcoholics started showing withdrawal symptoms. First, he screamed, fought and demanded alcohol. Then he started hallucinating.

'I have told the SSP to send me a box full of whiskey bottles!' he shouted. 'Behave properly with me, or else I will tell the DM and have you all suspended!' he threatened. 'Open the gate – I want to have my bath! Where is my chicken biryani?'

As thus he railed, sprinting from one end of the barrack to another, stumbling and running into other inmates and the prison officers. At first, amused by his antics, people made fun of him. But once he went completely out of control, they held him down and gave him a rough beating.

These incidents were not unusual in the Mulaihaija barrack – the new prison where all new inmates were first brought. While I had witnessed a few such episodes already, the rest of the people from BRD were only just learning about the suffocating prison life that was now theirs as well.

14

Thick Skin and a Doctor's Profession

On Friday, 15 September, I felt a nagging premonition after my bath. The '*chhatni*' or redistribution of inmates took place every Saturday. From the Millennium barrack, new arrivals were dispatched to other complexes that lay further inside. I had heard a great deal about the inside barracks – old and dilapidated, dominated by bullies and bahubalis, a place where you could face torture, extortion or worse at the hands of hardened criminals.

I was now used to this barrack and, most importantly, I had Shailesh for company and had grown fond of him. Going elsewhere and facing frightening, unknown inmates filled me with dread. I decided to ask whichever member of my family who came to meet me next for money, so I could pay the pakki baithaki and remain where I was.

But my plans were short-lived. At noon on Friday, Shailesh brought news that the jailor had specifically asked for the people from BRD to be distributed across different barracks. No two people from BRD should be together.

I spent all night wondering what was to happen to me, and finally told myself, 'Jail is jail. How does it matter which barrack is assigned to you?'

On Saturday morning, I was prepared to be sent to an old barrack in the interiors of the prison, but Sudhir had asked Mantri-ji to speak to the jailor and prevent it. So, for the time being, we continued to stay together. Now, at last, we sat down and discussed the tragedy amongst ourselves, day in and day out – the different views, the various conspiracy theories, how some people had been spared while others seemed to have been framed.

I was about to complete my fourteen days of custody so my '*pesi* (presenting)' date had come up. At the pesi, I would be presented in front of a magistrate who would decide whether my custody was to be extended for another fourteen days or until the next court hearing.

Theoretically, the pesi is a means for the judicial magistrate to make sure the person in prison is not an imposter, that they are getting food, have not developed any medical issues and their human rights have not been violated. In reality, it is a mere formality. No one ever asks how you are doing, if you're having any trouble or wish to make a complaint. The laws may have been framed by people with foresight, but they are executed very differently.

Until your chargesheet is submitted in court by the investigating officer, these appointments are conducted through videoconferencing, commonly referred to as VC. After that, you have to go to the court and sign.

Inmates are supposed to remember their court dates, but usually no one did. Around 2 p.m., a slip reached each barrack from the VC office containing a list of names whose pesi was on that day. After that, you were taken to the VC office at around 2:30 or 3 p.m. This was a separate building containing two fully air-conditioned rooms. It was near the area in which we had our meetings with visitors, and other spaces such as the storeroom, the hawalat and jail offices. Every day, at least ten or twenty people from each barrack would have their pesi. So, even though the process of being presented before the magistrate took two seconds, there was a long wait before your name and number were called.

I stood in a queue until the writer screamed my name: 'Dr Kafeel Khan, son of late engineer Shakeel Khan.' Then, as I used to do in school, I raised my hand and said 'Present, sir,' to the magistrate. The person in front of me was, however, not the magistrate but a court clerk. I was given my next date and promptly the pesi was over.

The court needed to know that I was alive, that is all.

I waited for everyone from my barrack to finish their turn, and then we were back inside by 4:30 p.m. The next date I had been given was 3 October, since Dussehra was on 30 September that year, Muharram on 1 October and Gandhi Jayanti on 2 October. I had learnt that once everyone accused in the case had been arrested, we would all be given the same date.

My equation with Shailesh, the Millennium barrack writer, played an important role in making me feel more at ease in prison. An undertrial charged under the Narcotics Act, Shailesh was a good cricketer – a batsman who had played at the Ranji Trophy level. He was born in Kolkata to a poor family, studied till class twelve and always dreamt of playing for India, but could not progress beyond the state level. His desire to earn money quickly had led him to the world of drug trafficking.

He was a very strict monitor for our barrack, who also knew how to extract money from new inmates. Shailesh would focus on hardcore criminals, politicians and government servants who could afford to pay. He made the rest of the inmates work hard and herded them by acting tough. Sometimes, he would beat the inmates, particularly the drug addicts, because he was very clear about two things – under his charge, no one could smoke, consume drugs or use mobile phones. If anyone wanted to do any of these things, they would need to move to another barrack.

But I also saw his thoughtful, protective and helpful side. If I ever needed anything, he tried to arrange it for me – newspapers, books, diaries, pens and, at times, the rare paratha and curd from the kitchen.

He talked to me about his case and made me read his chargesheet some twenty times. It was in English, and he listened carefully as I would read it aloud and explain it to him. He looked out for me, advising me about whom I could talk to and whom I should keep at arm's length. When my family members visited, he would tell them not to worry, as he was there to take care of me. If anyone in Gorakhpur Jail could be called a friend, it was Shailesh.

Nevertheless, sometimes I was still forced to navigate difficult situations in spite of being on good terms with him. One night, an addict started running around the barrack screaming and fighting with other inmates. Whenever such an inmate showed withdrawal symptoms, Shailesh usually sent him to the hospital, since there was a risk that the person might turn suicidal. But it was late at night, so he tied this man to the gate with the help of a few fellow prisoners.

The addict was hallucinating, looking at the roof and talking to an imaginary person. 'Okay, send me charas, I will give you 2,000. Fine, 3,000, all right? No, I want it now! Don't tell my wife, you bastard. Ha ha ha, I am coming, we will smoke up together, no one will find out. If you don't give it to me now, I'll beat you up! I'll burn your house. I'll burn *you*! I'll *kill* you!' He paused for a few minutes before resuming the cries and threats.

The night guard began beating him with a stick, so he pleaded, 'No, no, don't beat me – I'll give it to you too! I won't take any money from you! You will enjoy it, I promise.' Every few minutes, he would become quiet, but the screaming would start again soon.

At around 3 a.m., I woke up, but not because of the noise he was making. In fact, the other inmates were giving him a beating. I went up to the man and said, 'I will give you what you want tomorrow. All right?' He looked at me with the resigned desperation of an addict and said hoarsely, 'Okay, but give me some whiskey now, at least.'

I handed him a bottle of water. He took a long gulp and finally fell asleep.

It became clear to me that a quarter of the new inmates that came in every day to this barrack were young drug addicts who had been caught for petty crimes – pickpocketing, stealing, chain snatching, gambling and fighting. They would get desperate when they could not obtain cigarettes, bidis or drugs. They had no money and no one came to visit them. They begged from the other inmates and did whatever work required of them in exchange for a cigarette, bidi or gutkha. They rarely bathed or changed their clothes, hardly slept and had very poor personal hygiene – wandering around with dusty hair and bare feet, giving off a foul smell and lying down wherever they wanted to sleep, usually without a blanket. Sometimes, when these inmates would lie down near you, inevitably they would put an arm or leg on your face and shake you awake from your sleep.

Many of them had withdrawal-related seizures within two or three days of arriving at the prison. They would fall in the toilet, outside the barrack or in a corner. The other inmates would come rushing to me or Dr Satish, saying, '*Doctor sahab, jaldi aaiye* (Doctor, please come fast).' After reaching the scene, I would place the person in the left lateral position, wipe off any blood or saliva, take care of the falling tongue, which could block their airway until the seizure stopped, and then have the inmate transferred to the hospital. Most of the time, when they fell down, they got injured and bled. Sometimes, the people around them tried to arrest their seizure by holding their shoes to their noses.

I taught a few of the inmates what to do in case their fellow prisoners suffered a seizure. Gradually, I started keeping a few medicines with me for fever, vomiting, abdominal pain, headaches, diarrhoea, itching, fungal infection, scabies and deworming. All these medicines were essential because someone or the other would approach me every day with health-related complaints. I would hand out medicines to a number of them, and for others, I would write a prescription so that they could get their medicines from outside through a family member or friend.

On Sunday, 17 September, the news broke that Manish Bhandari, the owner of Pushpa Sales, had been caught. Television channels had been giving the impression that he had fled to the US and would never be arrested, but that was as false as the news that I had flown to Dubai via Nepal. In the afternoon, Adeel bhai confirmed the news in person when he came to visit me. Manish had also been arrested while on his way to surrender at the Gorakhpur court, because his car had a number plate from outside the state. Two days earlier, he had been declared an absconder by the anti-corruption court, which had issued orders for the state to attach his properties.

I complained to Adeel bhai, 'It's been fifteen days since I came here. You had promised I would be out in ten.'

He nodded but did not answer. I was relieved to learn that at least everyone at home was okay.

'What happened on that day? Your name was on the visitors' list, and I waited for you a long time,' I pressed further.

'The jailor didn't allow me to enter, saying he was under a lot of pressure from higher authorities,' he told me.

'But today I brought my advocate who argued with him, so they permitted the meeting.'

'What does the advocate have to say about my bail?' I asked.

'He says we should not file for bail now. First, let the others apply and get bail. The principal's wife has applied – let's see what happens. The media is cooking up more stories insinuating that you colluded with the principal's wife.'

'But how? What proof do they have?' I asked in frustration.

'No proof. They just write that they have received information from various sources, that you were part of the tender committee, or that you took lots of money from Manish Bhandari ...'

'I have never met Manish Bhandari in my life!'

'Yes, we know,' said my brother. 'But when has the truth ever stopped them?'

At around 7 p.m., I finally got my chance to meet the infamous owner of Pushpa Sales. I was talking to Tika, the younger brother of a notorious shooter, who was accused of murdering three people. I usually tried to avoid him because he used to ask me for my home address, but he always enjoyed a good chat. He told me that they had a plan to beat up Manish Bhandari that night. This sort of beating was known as *kambal pitai*, executed by literally wrapping the inmate in a blanket after which everyone had a go at him. This plan had been made because there was a general perception that the principal's wife and Manish Bhandari were the real culprits in the BRD tragedy.

'No, don't do that. How will we hear his side of the story if we beat him up like that?' I tried to change his mind – the idea of violence always repelled me.

When Manish arrived, Shailesh gave him a blanket and a place to sleep. He treated Manish like a VIP because, as

1

The central liquid oxygen tank which supplied piped medical oxygen across Nehru Hospital at the BRD Medical College.

B. R. D. Medical College Gorakhpur 2
Liquid Oxygen Tank

Plan of Connection to Manifold (6 Manifold)

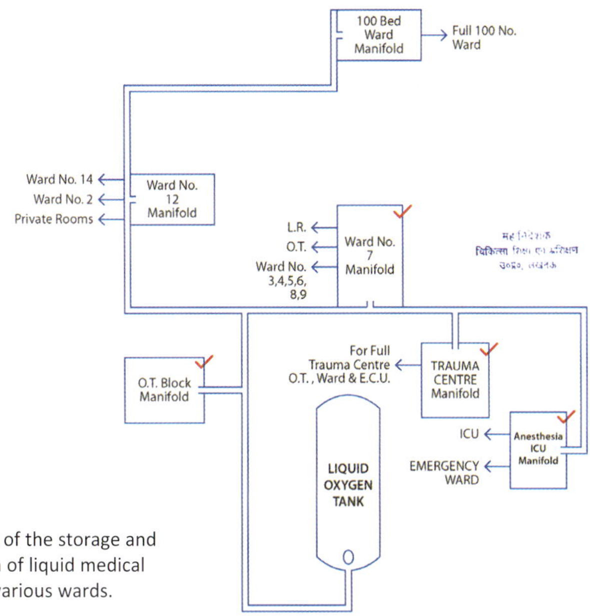

A blueprint of the storage and distribution of liquid medical oxygen to various wards.

3

The alarms of the oxygen delivery system buzzing on the intervening night of 10–11 August 2017 after the supply of liquid oxygen had run out.

4

The liquid oxygen meter displaying a reading of zero at 10:39 a.m. on 11 August 2017.

5

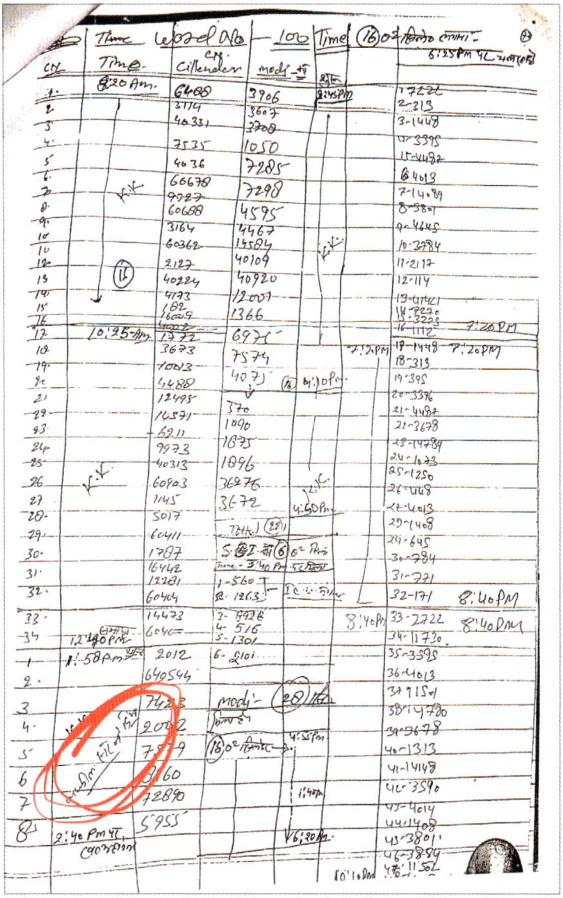

The logbook of the central pipeline operators with records of the jumbo oxygen cylinders.

Below: The fifty jumbo cylinders delivered by IGL at around 2 a.m. on 11 August 2017.

6

7

Jumbo cylinders arrive in a pickup truck outside the hospital on 11 August 201

Below: A letter from the cł medical superintendent to the principal of BRD Medic College on 11 August 2017 stating that oxygen had completely run out at the hospital.

8

कार्यालय मुख्य चिकित्सा अधीक्षक,नेहरू चिकित्सालय मेडिकल कालेज,गोरखपुर।

संख्या 1675/बीआरजी/एमसी/नेचि–17 दिनांक 11 अगस्त,2017

सेवा में,

प्रधानाचार्य,
बी0आर0डी0 मेडिकल कालेज,
गोरखपुर।

महोदय,

आपको सूचित करना है कि चिकित्सालय में लगे लिक्वीड आक्सीजन गैस पूर्ण रूप से समाप्त हो गया है तथा आक्सीजन गैस की आपूर्ति करने वाली फर्म द्वारा मॉग पत्र के अनुसार गैस आपूर्ति नही कर रही हैं। उक्त के सम्बन्ध में आज दिनांक 11.08.2017 को वार्ड संख्या 12 के सेमिनार कक्ष में विभागाध्यक्ष बाल रोग/ डा0 बी0एन0शंक्ला,वरिष्ठ परामर्शदाता बाल रोग/उपाधिक्षक आदि की बैठक सम्पन्न हुई जिसमें सर्व सम्मति से यह निर्णय लिया गया कि वस्तुस्थिति से प्रधानाचार्य महोदय को अवगत कराया जाय तथा उनके द्वारा वैकल्पिक रूप से मेडिकल आक्सीजन की व्यवस्था कराये तथा साथ ही साथ मंडलायुक्त महोदय एवं जिला प्रशासन से भी वार्ताकर आक्सीजन गैस की उपलब्धता सुनिश्चित कराये।

अतः आप से अनुरोध है कि बैठक में सर्व सम्मति से हुए निर्णय के कम में जनहित/संस्थाहित में जीवन रक्षक मेडिकल आक्सीजन गैस की आपूर्ति शीघ्रातिशीघ्र कराने की कृपा करें जिससे चिकित्सालय में भर्ती गम्भीर मरीजों की जान बचाई जा सके तथा निर्वाध रूप से अनका निदान किया जा सके।

भवदीय,

11-8-17

मुख्य चिकित्सा अधीक्षक

9

An enquiry report by the chief medical superintendent containing details of the cylinders that were arranged between 10 and 12 August 2017. According to the document, at 7:30 p.m. on 10 August, after the beeping alarms indicated that the pressure of liquid medical oxygen had severely reduced to 150 MMCW, oxygen was supplied using jumbo cylinders. Piped liquid oxygen was eventually restored at 2:15 a.m. on 13 August.

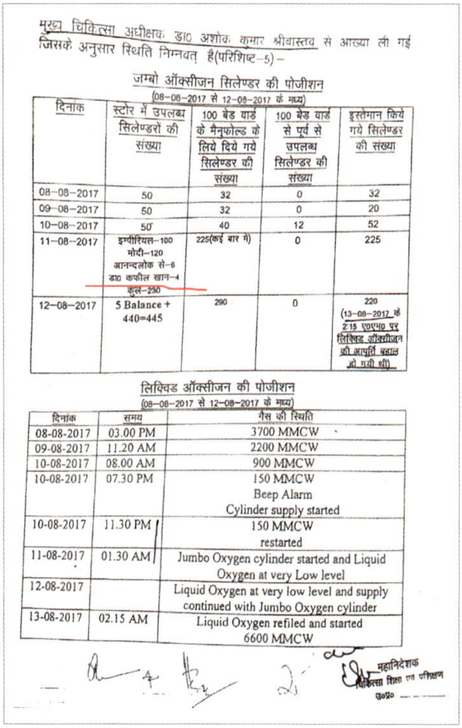

मुख्य चिकित्सा अधीक्षक डा0 अशोक कुमार श्रीवास्तव से आख्या ली गई जिसके अनुसार स्थिति निम्नवत् है(परिशिष्ट–5) –

जम्बो ऑक्सीजन सिलेण्डर की पोजीशन

(08–08–2017 से 12–08–2017 के मध्य)

दिनांक	स्टोर में उपलब्ध सिलेण्डरों की संख्या	100 बेड वार्ड के मैनुफोल्ड के लिये दिये गये सिलेण्डर की संख्या	100 बेड वार्ड से पूर्व से उपलब्ध सिलेण्डर की संख्या	इस्तेमान किये गये सिलेण्डर की संख्या
08–08–2017	50	32	0	32
09–08–2017	50	32	0	20
10–08–2017	50	40	12	52
11–08–2017	इम्पीरियल–100 मोदी–120 आनन्दलोक से–6 डा0 कफील खान–4 कुल–230	225(कई बार मे)	0	225
12–08–2017	5 Balance + 440=445	290	0	220 (13–08–2017 के 2:15 एएम0 पर लिक्विड ऑक्सीजन की आपूर्ति बहाल हो गयी थी)

लिक्विड ऑक्सीजन की पोजीशन

(08–08–2017 से 12–08–2017 के मध्य)

दिनांक	समय	गैस की स्थिति
08-08-2017	03.00 PM	3700 MMCW
09-08-2017	11.20 AM	2200 MMCW
10-08-2017	08.00 AM	900 MMCW
10-08-2017	07.30 PM	150 MMCW Beep Alarm Cylinder supply started
10-08-2017	11.30 PM	150 MMCW restarted
11-08-2017	01.30 AM	Jumbo Oxygen cylinder started and Liquid Oxygen at very Low level
12-08-2017		Liquid Oxygen at very low level and supply continued with Jumbo Oxygen cylinder
13-08-2017	02.15 AM	Liquid Oxygen refiled and started 6600 MMCW

महानिदेशक चिकित्सा शिक्षा एवं प्रशिक्षण उ0प्र0

10

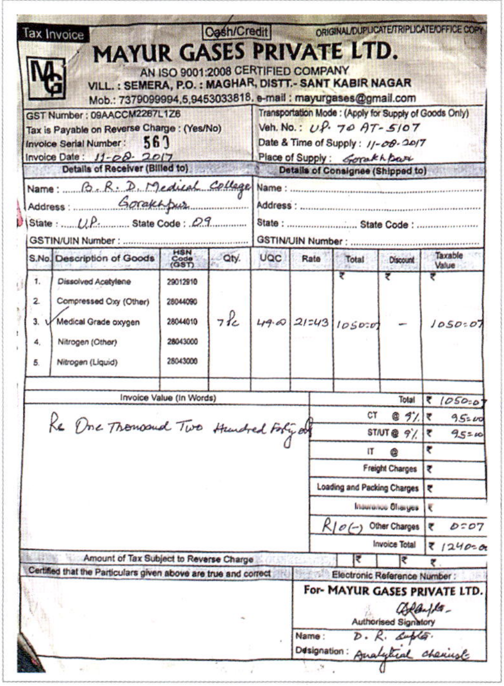

Tax Invoice Cash/Credit ORIGINAL/DUPLICATE/TRIPLICATE/OFFICE COPY

MAYUR GASES PRIVATE LTD.

AN ISO 9001:2008 CERTIFIED COMPANY

VILL. : SEMERA, P.O. : MAGHAR, DISTT.- SANT KABIR NAGAR

Mob.: 7379099994,5,9453033818, e-mail : mayurgases@gmail.com

GST Number : 09AACCM2267L1Z6

Tax is Payable on Reverse Charge : (Yes/No)

Invoice Serial Number : 563

Invoice Date : 11-08-2017

Transportation Mode : (Apply for Supply of Goods Only)

Veh. No. : UP. 70 AT-5107

Date & Time of Supply : 11-08-2017

Place of Supply : Gorakhpur

Details of Receiver (Billed to)

Name : B. R. D. Medical College

Address : Gorakhpur

State : U.P. State Code : 09

GSTIN/UIN Number :

Details of Consignee (Shipped to)

Name :

Address :

State : State Code :

GSTIN/UIN Number :

S.No.	Description of Goods	HSN Code (GST)	Qty.	UQC	Rate	Total ₹	Discount ₹	Taxable Value ₹
1.	Dissolved Acetylene	29012910						
2.	Compressed Oxy (Other)	28044090						
3.	Medical Grade oxygen	28044010	7 Pc	49.0	21=43	1050=07	–	1050=07
4.	Nitrogen (Other)	28043000						
5.	Nitrogen (Liquid)	28043000						

Invoice Value (In Words): Rs One Thousand Two Hundred Forty only

Total	₹ 1050=07
CT @ 9%	₹ 95=00
ST/UT @ 9%	₹ 95=00
IT @	₹
Freight Charges	₹
Loading and Packing Charges	₹
Insurance Charges	₹
R/o(-) Other Charges	₹ 0=07
Invoice Total	₹ 1240=00

Amount of Tax Subject to Reverse Charge ₹ ₹ ₹

Certified that the Particulars given above are true and correct

Electronic Reference Number :

For- MAYUR GASES PRIVATE LTD.

Authorised Signatory

Name : D. R. Gupta

Designation : Analytical chemist

A receipt from Mayur Gases Private Ltd dated 11 August 2017 against the supply of seven oxygen cylinders for the sum of ₹1,240 paid by me.

11

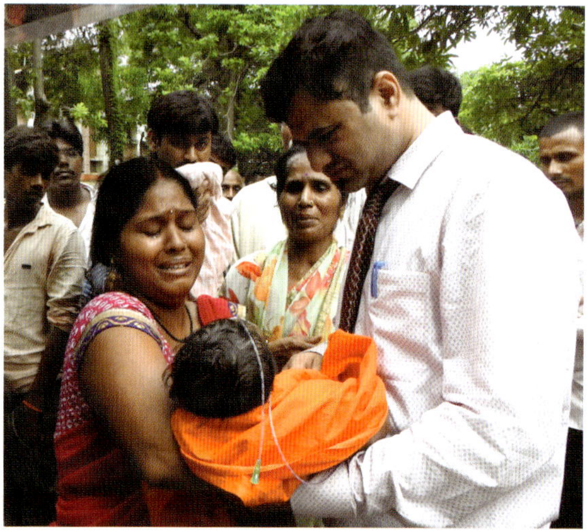

Me holding Bhumika, one of the infants with encephalitis who was in critical condition on 11 August 2017 at the hospital but survived.

12

दम तोड़ रहे मासूम को बचाने के लिए जूझते रहे डॉ. कफील

गोरखपुर | कार्यालय संवाददाता

गुरुवार रात के दो बज रहे थे। इंसेफेलाइटिस वार्ड के कर्मचारियों ने प्रभारी व बाल रोग विशेषज्ञ डॉ. कफील अहमद को सूचना दी कि अगले एक घंटे बाद ऑक्सीजन खत्म हो जाएगी। इस सूचना के बाद ही डॉक्टर की नींद उड़ गई। वह अपने कार से मित्र डॉक्टर के अस्पताल गए और वहां से ऑक्सीजन का तीन जंबो सिलेंडर लेकर शुक्रवार के तीन बजे सीधे बीआरडी पहुंचे। तीन सिलेंडरों से बालरोग विभाग में करीब 15 मिनट ऑक्सीजन सप्लाई हो सकी।

सुबह साढ़े सात बजे ऑक्सीजन खत्म होने पर एक बार फिर वार्ड में हालात बेकाबू होने लगे। मरीज तड़प रहे थे, तीमारदार व्याकुल होने लगे, वार्ड में तैनात डॉक्टर और कर्मचारी परेशान होने लगे। उधर, ऑक्सीजन सिलेंडर की खेप आने में करीब दो घंटे देर थी। ऐसे में डॉ. कफील ही हर मोर्चे पर जूझते रहे। वार्ड में घूम-घूम कर बेहद ऐसे मरीजों का इलाज किया जिनके दिल की धड़कन मंद हो रही थी। साथ में जूनियर डॉक्टरों को एम्बु बैग चलाने को निर्देशित भी किया।

ऑक्सीजन सिलेंडर मंगाने के लिए जूझते रहे डॉक्टर : डॉक्टर कफील को यह समझते देर न लगी ऑक्सीजन सिलेंडर मिले बगैर उनका यह प्रयास सफल न होगा। उन्होंने जिले में आधा दर्जन ऑक्सीजन सप्लायरों से फोन पर बात की। मयूर गैसेज ऑक्सीजन सिलेंडरों को नकद भुगतान मिलने पर रिफिल करने को तैयार हो गया। डॉ. कफील तुरंत एक कर्मचारी को एटीएम कार्ड देकर रुपये निकालने को भेजा। फैजाबाद से आए इम्पीरियल गैसेज कंपनी के ट्रक चालक को डीजल और दूसरे खर्च की रकम जेब से देकर खलीलाबाद भेजा।

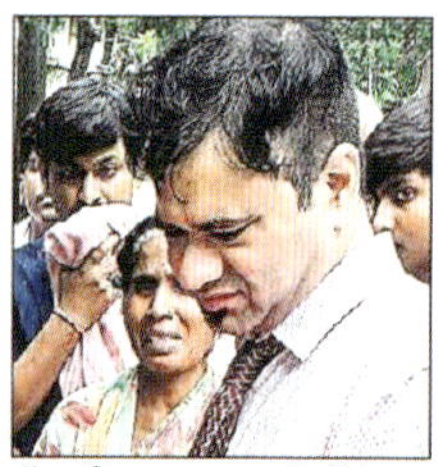

डॉ. कफील अहमद, बाल रोग विशेषज्ञ

अधिकारियों से मांगी मदद : मयूर गैसेज संचालक जब सिलेंडरों को रिफिल करने से मुकरने लगे तब एक बार फिर डॉ. कफील सामने आए। उन्होंने पूरे मामले की जानकारी प्रशासन के आला अधिकारियों को देकर मदद की गुहार लगाई। हालांकि तब तक काफी देर हो गई थी।

नाम को सार्थक कर गए डॉ. कफील: कफील का मतलब मददगार होता है। शुक्रवार को डॉ. कफील ने अपने नाम के अर्थ को सार्थक कर दिया।

An excerpt from an article dated 12 August 2017 in *Hindustan*, a Hindi-language newspaper, which mentions the oxygen cylinders I had arranged during the crisis.

13

1. पुष्पा सेल्स का लिक्विड अक्सिजन टैकंर खलीलाबाद गोरखपुर बार्डर पार कर रहा है, लगभग दो घण्टों में मेडिकल कालेज गोरखपुर पहुच जायेगा।
2. मोदी कैमिकल ने आज सुबह से छः रात नौ बजे तक 250 सिलेण्डर की अपूर्ति 12.08.2017 को किया।
3. आई0जी0एल फैजाबाद ने 130 सिलेण्डर की अपूर्ति 12.08.17 को किया।
4. वर्तमान समय में हमारे पास 233 सिलेण्डर मौजूद है।
5. मोदी कैमिकल ने 10.30 रात्री दिनांक 12.08.2017 100 सिलेण्डर तथा सुबह 2.30 दिनांक 13.08.17 को 100 सिलेडण्र अपूर्ति करने को कहा है।

The notes made on 12 August 2017 by the authorities about the oxygen crisis of 10–11 August.

14

NEWS18.COM GET STOCK QUOTES

Speaking to the media, DG Medical Education KK Gupta said: "The role of Dr Kafeel Khan is under the scanner over how he managed the oxygen cylinders and from which sources." The DG also hinted at Dr Khan's private practice.

News18 now has enough proof to question the government's action against Dr Khan. This proof has come from the Sashastra Seema Bal, the central police force.

According to SSB's Public Relations Officer OP Sahu, "It was an unprecedented crisis situation at the BRD Medical College on 10th of August. Dr Khan came to DIG SSB and requested for a truck, so that oxygen cylinders could be collected from various locations and be taken to the medical college."

An article in News18 that quotes Sashastra Seema Bal's public relations officer who confirmed that I had arrived at their office requesting for a truck to collect oxygen cylinders from other locations.

15

The Inox Air Products Ltd truck that reached the hospital at around 1:30 a.m. on 13 August 2017 to renew the supply of liquid oxygen.

16

आरोपियों पर इन धाराओं में दाखिल हुई चार्जशीट

डा. राजीव मिश्र : 409 , 308, 120 बी और 7/13 भ्रष्टाचार निवारण अधिनियम
डा. कफील खान : 409, 308, 120 बी
डॉ. सतीश कुमार: 120 बी, 466, 468, 469, 471 , 308 व 7/13 भ्रष्टाचार निवारण अधिनियम
डा. पूर्णिमा : 120 बी व भ्रष्टाचार निवारण अधिनियम की धारा 7/13, (8) (9)
मनीष भण्डारी : 120 बी और 406
उदय प्रताप शर्मा : 120 बी, 7/13 भ्रष्टाचार निवारण अधिनियम
संजय कुमार त्रिपाठी : 120 बी, 7/13 भ्रष्टाचार निवारण अधिनियम
सुधीर कुमार पाण्डेय : 120 बी, 7/13 भ्रष्टाचार निवारण अधिनियम
गजानन जायसवाल : 120 बी, 466, 468,469,471, 7/13 भ्रष्टाचार निवारण अधिनियम

डॉ. कफील से तीन धाराएं हटाई

पुलिस की विवेचना में डा. कफील खान को बड़ी राहत मिली है। उनके ऊपर से तीन धाराएं हटाई गई है। भ्रष्टाचार की धारा के अलावा 420 यानी धोखाधड़ी, इंडियन मेडिकल काउंसिल एक्ट 1956 का सेक्सन 15 और आईटी एक्ट 2000 के सेक्शन 66 की धारा में पुलिस को डॉ. कफील के खिलाफ कोई सबूत नहीं मिला। लिहाजा पुलिस ने तीनों धाराओं से डॉक्टर कफील को क्लीनचिट दे दी है। जिस हिसाब से पुलिस डॉ. कफील को मुख्य आरोपी मान रही थी उस हिसाब से इन धाराओं से क्लीनचिट डा. कफील के लिए बड़ी राहत है।

बीआरडी का इंसेफेलाइटिस वार्ड • फाइल फोटो

A news clipping carrying details of the charges filed against the nine people named in the chargesheet: Dr Rajiv Mishra (principal), me, Dr Satish Kumar (head of the anaesthesia department), Dr Poornima Shukla (the principal's wife), Manish Bhandari (managing director of Pushpa Sales), Uday Pratap Sharma (junior accountant), Sanjay Tripathi (senior accountant), Sudhir Pandey (the senior-most clerk in the accounts department) and Gajanand Jaiswal (chief pharmacist).

17

प्रभार प्रमाण-पत्र

प्रमाणित किया जाता है कि प्रवक्ता पिडियाट्रिक्स विभाग बी० आर० डी० मेडिकल कालेज गोरखपुर का पदाधिकार उत्तर प्रदेश शासन, चिकित्सा शिक्षा अनुभाग–1 के शासनादेश संख्या–168/2016/2080/71–1–2016–जी–131/2015 लखनऊ दिनांक 03 अगस्त ,2016 के के अधीन जैसा कि व्यक्त किया गया है । दिनांक 08–08–2016 को पूर्वान्ह/अपरान्ह में जैसा कि यहाँ व्यक्त किया गया हैं हस्तान्तरित किया गया।

मोचक अधिकारी
[signature]
डा० कफील अहमद खान

प्रतिहस्ताक्षर
[signature]
प्रधानाचार्य
मेडिकल कालेज,
गोरखपुर।

कार्यालय प्रधानाचार्य, बी० आर० डी० मेडिकल कालेज, गोरखपुर।

संख्या 1516/बीआरजी/एमसी–16/ईसी–1 दिनांक: 08 अगस्त, 2016

प्रतिलिपि निम्नलिखित को सूचनार्थ एवं आवश्यक कार्यवाही हेतु प्रेषित।

1. प्रमुख सचिव चिकित्सा शिक्षा अनुभाग–1 उ0प्र0 शासन, लखनऊ।
2. महानिदेशक, चिकित्सा शिक्षा एवं प्रशिक्षण उ0प्र0 लखनऊ।
3. महालेखाकार उ0प्र0 इलाहाबाद।
4. मुख्य कोषाधिकारी, गोरखपुर।
5. विभागाध्यक्ष, पिडियाट्रिक्स , विभाग, मेडिकल कालेज, गोरखपुर।
6. वरिष्ठ प्रभारी अधिकाकरी, मेडिकल कालेज, गोरखपुर।
7. प्रमुख चिकित्सा अधीक्षक, नेहरू चिकित्सालय, मेडिकल कालेज, गोरखपुर।
8. संबंधित चिकित्सक ।
9. लेखानुभाग, मेडिकल कालेज, गोरखपुर ।

[signature]
(आर० के० मिश्रा)
प्रधानाचार्य

My appointment letter from the BRD Medical College, dated 8 August 2016.

118

Pushpa Sales Pvt.
(Healthcare
Luckno
551 Jha/148, Ram Nagar, A
Lucknow
Ph. / Fax: 0522 - 4042458, 9935222999, 97
E-mail : manish@pushpaser
TIN : 099

PUSHPA

सेवा में,

प्रधानाचार्य

बी0आर0डी0 मेडिकल कालेज REMINDER 1

गोरखपुर। दिनांक–06.04.2017

पत्रांक सं0–PSPL/2017-18/006

विषयः– लिक्विड मेडिकल आक्सीजन पिछले छः माह के बकाया भुगतान लगभग 5234774.00 रू0 एवं सप्लाई के संबंध में।

महोदय,

सादर अवगत कराना है, कि लिक्विड मेडिकल आक्सीजन की आपूर्ति के उपरान्त दिनांक 03.04.2017 तक बकाया धनराशि 5234774.00 रू0 हो गया है। जबकि बिल प्रस्तुति के 15 से 20 दिन के अन्दर बकाया भुगतान होना था, जो कि अभी तक नही हुआ आप के संज्ञान में लाना है कि आप द्वारा पत्र संख्या 3331/बीआरजी/एमसी-17आडिट दिनांक 22.12.2016 में हमको अवगत कराया गया था। कि बजट के अभाव के कारण बकाया भुगतान नहीं हो पा रहा है जैसे ही बजट प्राप्त होगा हमको प्राथमिकता के आधार पर बकाया भुगतान करेगे। परन्तु 23.11.2016 से 03.04.2017 तक 5234774.00 रू0 बकाया हो गया है जो अभी तक हमें प्राप्त नही हुआ है। हमारे द्वारा पत्र संख्या PSPL/2016-17/208 दिनाँक 28.02.2017 में अवगत कराया गया है। जिसकी छायाप्रति संलग्न है आप से निवेदन है कि अविलम्ब बकाया भुगतान करने का कष्ट करें। जिससे हम INOX कम्पनी को समय पर भुगतान कर सके विलम्ब से भुगतान होने की स्थिति में हमें सप्लाई नहीं मिल पायेगी जिसकी पूरी जिम्मेदारी बी आर डी मेडिकल कॉलेज गोरखपुर की होगी।

अतः आपसे निवदेन है कि कृपया उपरोक्त संबंधित बकाया भुगतान शीघ्रातिशीघ्र करने का कष्ट करें। जिससे हमारी संस्था आगे भी समय पर सप्लाई जारी रख सके।

Pushpa Sales Pvt. Health Care Division

दीपांकर शर्मा
मो0– 9839511238

प्रतिलिपि – निम्नलिखित का सूचनार्थ एवं आवश्यक कार्यवाही हेतु प्रेषित।

1. मुख्य मंत्री उ0 प्र0 शासन,लखनऊ।
2. स्वास्थ्य मंत्री, उ0 प्र0 शासन,लखनऊ।
3. प्रमुख सचिव मेडिकल एजुकेशन उत्तर प्रदेश लखनऊ
4. महानिदेशक चिकित्सा एवं स्वास्थ सेवायें, उत्तर प्रदेश लखनऊ।
5. एस0आई0सी0, बी0आर0डी0 मेडिकल कालेज गोरखपुर।
6. विभागाध्यक्ष, बाल रोग विशेषज्ञ, बी0आर0डी0 मेडिकल कालेज गोरखपुर।

Delhi Office : Pushpa Sales Pvt. Ltd.
B 231, Basement Greater Kailash-I, New Delhi-110048
Mobile: 9810269435 Ph:011-29232190, 46132516. E mail:aman@pushpaservices.com

Pushpa Sales Pvt. Ltd. Health Care Division

Official letter sent by Pushpa Sales to the principal of BRD Medical College on 6 April 2017, asking for payment against outstanding dues of ₹52,34,774 that accrued between 23 November 2016 and 3 April 2017. Copies of the letter were marked to the chief minister and the health minister of Uttar Pradesh.

19

Pushpa Sales Pvt. Ltd.
(Healthcare Division)
Lucknow Office :
551 Jha/148, Ram Nagar, Alambagh,
Lucknow - 226 005
Ph 0522 - 6556677, 6556686, 9935222999
E-mail : manish@pushpaservices.com
TIN : 09952003060

136

माननीय मंत्रीजी — दिनांक; 09/08/2017

चिकित्सा शिक्षा एव प्रशिक्षण

उत्तर-प्रदेश लखनऊ

सविनय आपको अवगत कराना है कि मै मनीष भण्डारी पुष्पा सेल्स प्रा0 लि0 (हेल्थ केयर डिवीज़न में डायरेक्टर) हू । आपके गोरखपुर मंडल BRD MEDICAL COLLEGE गोरखपुर में लिक्विड ऑक्सीजन गैस कि सप्लाई हमारी फर्म द्वारा करायी जाती है
आपके संज्ञान में यह लाना है कि पिछले छ: माह से BRD MEDICAL COLLEGE गोरखपुर द्वारा लिक्विड ऑक्सीजन गैस का भुगतान जो कि आज दिनाक 08.08.2017को 6865702. 00 रूपये है अभी तक भुगतान नही किया गया है इसके लिए हमारे द्वारा BRD MEDICAL COLLEGE गोरखपुर में प्रधानाचार्य को कई बार पत्राचार,मोखिक,टेलीफोनिक,ई-मेल तथा लीगल नोटिस द्वारा भेजने पर भी कोई प्रतिक्रिया उनके तरफ से नही आई है ।

आपके संज्ञान में यह भी लाना है कि परिसर मे स्थित सवप नेहरु चिकित्सालय100 वार्ड में AIS/ मस्तिक ज्वर तथा अन्य गंभीर मरीजों के चिकित्सीय उपचार मे प्रयोग होने वाली सेन्ट्रल ऑक्सीजन पाइप लाइन के 24 घंटे संचालन में मरीजों के लिये अत्याधिक महत्वपुर्ण है ।
अत: आपसे विनम्र निवेदन है कि उक्त विषय को संज्ञान मे लेते BRD MEDICAL COLLEGE गोरखपुर को निर्देशित करने का कष्ट करे जिससे कि हमारी बकाया धनराशि का भुगतान हो एवं भविष्य में सप्लाई करने में कोई बाधा न हो ।

आपकी अति कृपा होगी ।

संलग्नक :- छायाप्रति : -प्राप्तांक संख्या :- 01.PSPL /2017-18 /79 DATED 08/08/17
02. PSPL /2017-18 /78 DATED 31/07/17
03.PSPL /2017-18 /77 DATED 18/07/17
04.PSPL /2017-18 /73 DATED 06/07/17
05.PSPL /2017-18 /61 DATED 13/06/17
06.PSPL /2017-18 /55 DATED 02/05/17
07.PSPL /2017-18 /40 DATED 16/05/17
08.PSPL/2017-18/30 DATED 02/05/17
09.PSPL/2017-18/25 DATED 17/04/17

छायाप्रति : -लीगल नोटिस प्रष्ठ संख्या 1 से 3

मनीष भण्डारी

(डायरेक्टर, पुष्पा सेल्स प्राइवेट लिमिटेड)

Delhi Office : Pushpa Sales Pvt. Ltd.
B 231, Basement Greater Kailash-1, New Delhi-110048
Mobile: 9810269435 Ph 011-29232190, 46132516 E mail:aman@pushpaservices.com

Another letter from Pushpa Sales, dated 9 August 2017, addressed to the state minister of medical education, Ashutosh Tandon, declaring the outstanding amount due to them from BRD Medical College as ₹68,65,702. The letter also mentions that despite repeated oral and written reminders, telephonic communication, emails and legal notices, no payment had been released from the hospital to Pushpa Sales for the supply of liquid oxygen.

An excerpt from a ten-page letter I wrote while in prison, describing the details of all the events that transpired at the BRD Medical College during 10–13 August 2017.

Below: A newspaper clipping of a report in *Hindustan Times*, dated 11 April 2018, which carried the Indian Medical Association's official statement that I had been made a 'scapegoat to let go the big fishes'.

20

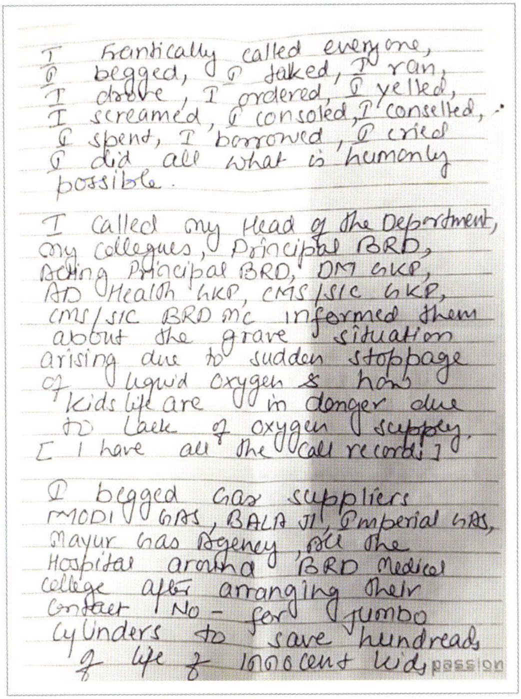

I frantically called everyone, I begged, I talked, I ran, I drove, I ordered, I yelled, I screamed, I consoled, I conselled, I spent, I borrowed, I cried, I did all what is humanly possible.

I called my Head of the Department, my collegues, Principal BRD, Acting Principal BRD, DM GKP, AD Health GKP, CMS/SIC GKP, CMS/SIC BRD MC informed them about the grave situation arising due to sudden stoppage of liquid oxygen & how kids life are in danger due to lack of oxygen supply. [I have all the call records.]

I begged Gas suppliers MODI GAS, BALA JI, Imperial GAS, Mayur Gas Agency, all the Hospital around BRD Medical college after arranging their contact No - for jumbo cylinders to save hundreads of life of innocent kids

21

BRD HOSPITAL TRAGEDY

Doctors made scapegoat to let off big fishes: IMA

HT Correspondent
letters@htlive.com

GORAKHPUR: Almost eight months after the death of 30 children in BRD hospital on August 10 rocked the country, doctors from Indian Medical Associations (IMA) have come out in support of their jailed colleagues, claiming doctors, including ex BRD principal Dr Rajeev Mishra, Dr Sateesh and Dr Kafeel, had been made scapegoat to let go the real culprits.

"On the one hand, the government maintained that deaths were not caused due to disruption in oxygen supply, on the other hand, it sent three doctors to jail. This smacks of a conspiracy to make doctors scapegoat to let go the big fishes," said Dr RP Shukla, secretary IMA Gorakhpur, while addressing a press conference with other office-bearers of Gorakhpur IMA on Monday.

The IMA has questioned why the ministers and officials in Lucknow and Gorakhpur failed to act on repeated reminders by oxygen supplier to pay the dues despite having the sole power and authority to do so.

"This has raised suspicion that such incidents could reoccur in future if the real culprits are not sent behind bars by conducting a time bound fresh probe into the incident," it said adding, "The failure to bring real culprit to justice and framing innocent doctors, against whom not even a single criminal case was registered, raise serious question over the judicial system and the government."

The IMA officials expressed deep concern over deteriorating health of jailed doctors, denial of bail to them and improper medical treatment provided to them.

They spoke about poor health of Dr Rajeev Mishra whose condition deteriorated twice in recent days.

"He is under treatment in Lucknow for liver cirrhosis, blockage in arteries and overgrown heart," they said.

The association in its 11-point demand letter to the governments has asked it to constitute a fresh time-bound probe to identify and punish the real culprits responsible for the BRD tragedy besides allowing the jailed doctors to re-serve the society by providing them bail.

Women consoling each other in the wake of BRD hospital tragedy in Gorakhpur last year. HT FILE PHOTO

SC GRANTS BAIL TO OXYGEN SUPPLIER

Press Trust of India
letters@hindustantimes.com

NEW DELHI: The Supreme Court on Monday granted bail to the proprietor of a firm which supplied oxygen to Baba Raghav Das (BRD) Medical College and Hospital in Gorakhpur where scores of children had died last year.

The court noted that he had spent seven months in jail for an offence which entailed maximum punishment of three years imprisonment and a charge sheet had already been filed in the case.

Manish Bhandari had moved the Supreme Court against the Allahabad High Court order rejecting his bail plea.

22

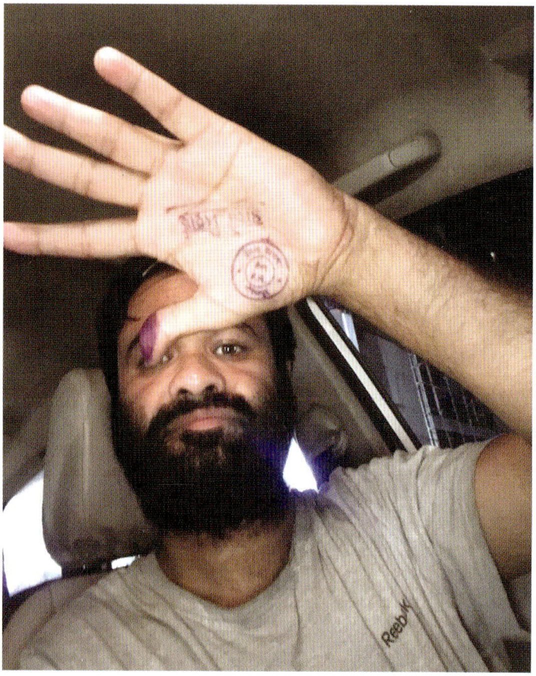

The round stamp on my arm, which reads 'WASTE REHAI', signed by the deputy jailor on 28 April 2018, the day of my release from Gorakhpur Jail.

23

Reunited with my wife Shabista and daughter Zab outside the prison.

 24

At home with my family on the night of 28 April 2018.
From left to right: Shabista holding Zab, me hugging
my mother and my brother-in-law Samar.

25

No proof of med negligence by BRD doctor Kafeel: HC

Rohan.Dua@timesgroup.com

Lucknow: The Allahabad high court, while granting bail last week to hero-turned villain Dr Kafeel Khan in Gorakhpur's BRD Hospital tragedy, came down heavily on prosecution and said there was no evidence on record to suggest medical negligence by the doctor.

Khan was nodal officer at state-run Baba Raghav Das Medical College where 32 children had died on August 10-11 last year allegedly due to the shortage of liquid oxygen in the wards.

The court had granted bail on a plea by Khan, who was charged with criminal conspiracy and negligence while on duty at. Khan had shot to fame after it was found that he had arranged a batch of medical oxygen cylinders from a private vendor from his own money on August 10-11 night. He was suspended a day later.

> **Having considered the submissions advanced, the court notes that there is no material on record, which may establish medical negligence against the applicant individually**
>
> **JUSTICE YASHWANT VARMA**

The court also said that the Uttar Pradesh government, in its affidavit, never 'attributed the deaths to 'shortage of oxygen'. The state government and the UP police have maintained that the kids' death was natural and unrelated to shortage of oxygen, yet it booked doctors and BRD hospital staff for medical negligence.

"Having considered the submissions advanced, the court notes that there is no material on record, which may establish medical negligence against the applicant individually," Justice Yashwant Varma said in his order.

Khan was released from Gorakhpur jail on Saturday and was greeted by his family members and a crowd of local patients. Images of Khan weeping inconsolably and hugging his wife, mother and daughter went viral online. The court further pointed out that Khan 'is a medical practitioner, a government employee with no criminal history'.

The HC also observed that though UP police, in its FIR and chargesheet, showed Khan as head of the ward where the kids allegedly died, he was nowhere involved in the tendering process of medical oxygen.

On 30 April 2018, the *Times of India* published this article, which reported the Allahabad High Court as stating that 'there was no material on record, which may establish medical negligence' against me.

26

To,

The Principal ,BRD Medical college ,Gorakhpur,UP — Dated -

From-

Dr KAFEEL AHMAD KHAN

Suspended Lecturer ,Dept Of Pediatrics ,BRD Medical college, Gorakhpur, UP

Subject -Request to revoke suspension order

Respected sir/madam,

With all due respect it is stated that i Dr Kafeel AHMAD KHAN has been suspended on 22/08/2018 (2017) (ref letter no-2372/71-1-2017-G-220/2017) and was languishing in prison since 02 sept 2017.During investigation **charges of corruption 7/13 , Indian medical council act ,420,66 IT act ,have been dropped due to lack of evidence against me**.

H"ble High court in his bail order dated 25 /04/2018 (no 5727 of 2018 court no 59) **noted that there is no material on record ,which may establish medical negligence** and **Dr Kafeel Khan was not slated to be part of the tendering process** that resulted in the enlistment of the entry ,which was charged with the supply of medical oxygen.

So therefore it is requested to forward my request letter to the concerned authority to revoke my suspension and allow me to continue my service as Lecturer, Department of Paediatric,BRD Medical college ,Gorakhpur. Thus enable me to serve poor sick children specially affected with encephalitis.

Thanking you.I would be grateful to you.

(DR KAFEEL AHMAD KHAN)

ATTACHED-

19.05.18

27

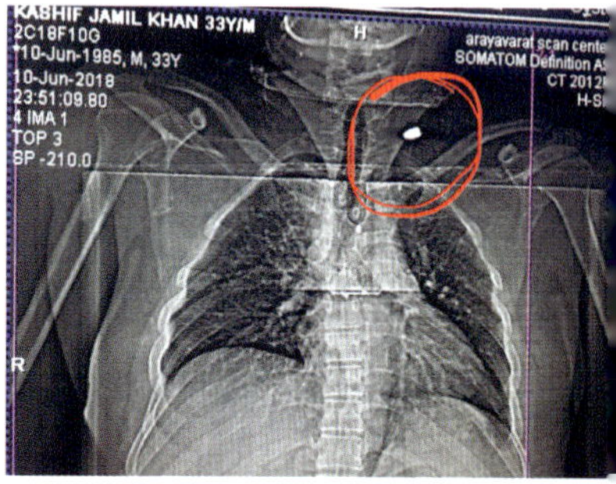

Left: My letter dated 19 May 2018, written after my release from prison, requesting the principal of BRD Medical College to revoke my suspension.

Right: A CT scan of my brother Kashif's torso showing a bullet lodged near his carotid artery after he was shot at on 10 June 2018.

28

An RTI report evidencing there was no vice principal at the BRD Medical College, despite claims made by News Nation and various sections of the public that I held that position in August 2017.

सेवा में,

नोडल अधिकारी,
जन सूचना अधिनियम--2005,
बी0आर0डी0 मेडिकल कोलज,
गोरखपुर।

महोदय,

डा0 कफील अहमद खान, पता 172, बसन्तपुर, गोरखपुर के पत्र दिनांक 04/09/2018 के द्वारा मांगी गई सूचना के सम्बन्ध में बिन्दु संख्या 03 एवं 04 की आख्या निम्नवत है।

बिन्दुसं0 3	बी0आर0डी0 मेडिकल कालेज, गोरखपुर में उप प्रधानाचार्य (**Vice Principal**) का पद शासन द्वारा स्वीकृत किया गया अथवा नहीं।	संस्था में उप प्रधानाचार्य का कोई पद सृजित नहीं है।
बिन्दुसं0 4	बी0आर0डी0 मेडिकल कालेज, गोरखपुर मे अगस्त, 2017 में (**Vice Principal**) के पद पर कार्यरत व्यक्ति का नाम एवं अन्य विवरण उपलब्ध कराने की कृपा करें।	संस्था में उप प्रधानाचार्य का कोई पद सृजित नहीं है।

दिनांक 05, सितम्बर, 2018

पी0ए0
प्रधानाचार्य कार्यालय,
बी0आर0डी0 मेडिकल कोलज,
गोरखपुर।

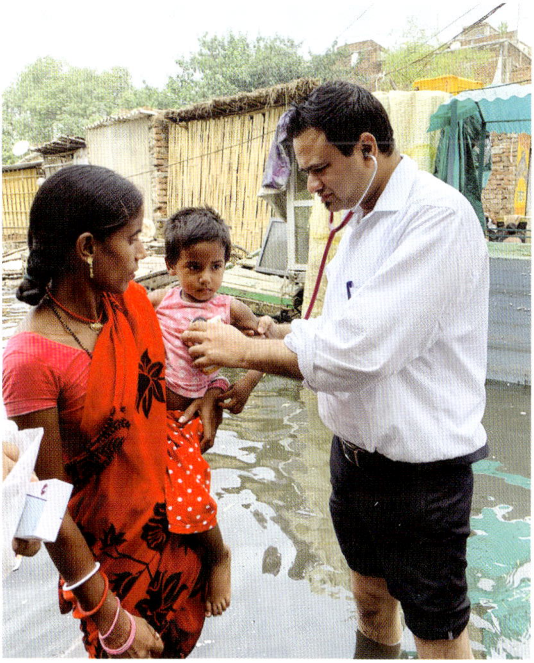

29

At a flood relief camp in Bihar in October 2019.

Below: With a young patient at a flood relief camp in Kerala in September 2018.

30

31 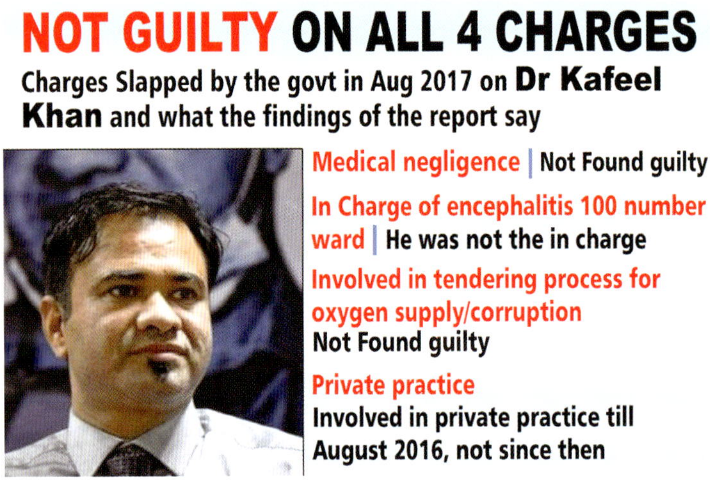

NOT GUILTY ON ALL 4 CHARGES

Charges Slapped by the govt in Aug 2017 on Dr Kafeel Khan and what the findings of the report say

Medical negligence | Not Found guilty

In Charge of encephalitis 100 number ward | He was not the in charge

Involved in tendering process for oxygen supply/corruption
Not Found guilty

Private practice
Involved in private practice till August 2016, not since then

A news piece about me in the *Times of India* that said I had been found 'not guilty on all 4 charges'.

32 

A protest held on 14 November 2021 at Jantar Mantar, Delhi, organized by members of the non-profit organization Medical Service Centre (MSC), against my termination from BRD Medical College.

he had mentioned earlier, the man was extremely rich. I did not speak to him, but he seemed like a young, down-to-earth guy. He had started in the business at a very early age, after his family had migrated from Delhi to Lucknow – in the wake of the 1984 anti-Sikh riots – where they had made great strides financially.

Mondays, which were parade days, were always very special for Shailesh. The superintendent, jailor, deputy jailor and medical officer used to visit each barrack and ask the inmates if they needed any help, or if anyone was bothering them. But they would spend five minutes in each barrack at most, and only the high-profile inmates were permitted to speak to them. This was also the day when Mantri-ji would come out and say hello to them and they, in turn, would treat him with respect.

Shailesh used to ensure there were fresh flowers on Mondays, the surfaces freshly painted, if necessary, and the whole barrack, toilets and garden were also cleaned. He felt proud when the officers declared his barrack to be the cleanest. He got personally involved in the cleaning so that by 10 a.m. on a Monday, the area looked spotless.

When the officers arrived on 18 September, they asked Shailesh how many of those arrested in the BRD case lived in this barrack. 'Seven,' he replied.

'They can't be here together. Transfer all of them, except Manish Bhandari, to the inside barracks,' one of them commanded.

Soon, Dr Satish Kumar was sent to the Nehru barrack. Uday, Sanjay, Sudhir and Gajanand were all shifted to different barracks. I was transferred to barrack number 13, the Kamaan barrack, which housed all the bhandara workers – those who worked in the kitchen. Half the barrack remained vacant during the day, but at night it was bursting at the seams.

I carried all my belongings in a bucket and a small bag and headed over to barrack number 13. The inner area of the prison complex was huge, containing many barracks and a field. It even included a hospital in a separate building. The inmates identified the barracks by the caste or class of the group dominant in each – there was a Thakur barrack, a Yadav barrack, a VIP barrack and so on. The gate leading to the inner part of the prison was called the devil's checkpost or *shaitan ki chowki* as it was here that the prison cops frisked the inmates after they had received visitors and relieved them of any food and money.

The buildings in the interior of Gorakhpur Jail are very old – most of them built before Independence – with cracked and broken flooring, dust and mud covering everything and roofs leaking after rains. All of this may not have mattered if it had not been for my being subjected, once again, to the same old questions.

'Oh, you are doctor sahab? The one we saw on TV. Why are you here? Who are the real culprits? What happened on that day?'

Of course, this was in addition to all the other things inmates say by way of introduction. Here is a sampler:

'I have committed six murders.'

'I raped two girls.'

'I am the bahubali (don) of Deoria district. I have seventy cases against me. I have been here for the past twelve years. If you need anything, you tell me – and I mean anything.'

'You are a doctor, you must have a lot of money, isn't it? He he he.'

'Want to smoke marijuana? What do you mean you don't? Then shall we bring milk for you? He he he.'

'Who all live in your house? How many cars does your family own?'

'Let's meet outside. Do you want to call your home from here? We can help you ...'

It was as if I was being ragged again in some deadly new hostel, but there was no appealing to any authorities against these men.

The same questions continued till the night, and I discovered that the place where I had been assigned to sleep was near the toilet – the long-term residents had fixed spots. If a spot became vacant because someone had got bail, only those who had paid a hefty amount could claim it. Without a permanent space to sit, keep my possessions and sleep, I had to carry my belongings with me at all times, lest someone else start using my toothpaste, bucket, soap, towel, blanket or bed sheet.

Smoking ganja and the consumption of prescription medicines continued all through the day and night. Even after the barrack closed, everyone smoked in front of the prison cops. They paid for their right to smoke. They also claimed that the cops were the ones who got them the stuff, so why would anyone stop them? It is a business, and the money goes into everyone's pockets. All the drugs – clonazepam, alprazolam, tramadol and amitriptyline – come from the prison hospital and are sold to each barrack by the circle officer or the writer at a higher price.

It felt like I had stumbled into a scene from the film *Dum Maro Dum*.

But there were also those who sang bhajans every evening for two hours.

Being deeper inside the prison complex came with certain advantages. There was a huge central canteen where bread, butter and tea were available at any time, and sometimes samosas, too. A doctor, who used to run a nursing home and had been charged with rape, ran this canteen.

However, any advantage was voided by being in a new environment, where unknown people could come up and make a threat, use your belongings and borrow your money and never return it. For me, it was especially depressing because I was asked to explain the same story to many people. The toilets were filthy. The main residents of the barrack – the bhandara workers – had to make 10,000 rotis daily in a coal furnace. It was a stressful, laborious job, and sometimes they fainted from exhaustion.

My sister Farro and my younger sister's husband, Samar, came to see me as soon as she returned from hajj. Ammi, who was still staying at my sister's house in Lucknow, had been told that I was okay – undergoing police interrogation, but not in jail. They wanted to break the news to her gradually. My brother Kashif was in Mumbai. The whole family was concerned as to who would be the next target of malice and false accusations.

The meeting with my sister was much more emotional than the one with my brother. Farro came running and hugged me like a child. She asked through her tears, 'My brother, *mera bachcha*, how could this happen? How are you coping? I just can't imagine your pain.'

I cried, too. Even the people around us were affected by our meeting. My bond with Farro has always been the strongest since we were children. We were best friends who shared every secret. She is two years younger than me, and we have always meant the world to each other. Adeel bhai is the eldest and the three younger ones were a group of their own.

During her visit, Farro wasted no time on whys and wherefores. She just consoled me the best she could. '*Ya Allah, ye kya ho gaya, mere bhai? Bahut duayein sabne ki hai Medina mein. Puri duniya tumhe bekasoor manti hai.* (Allah, how has this happened to my brother? Everyone has prayed devoutly for you in Medina. The whole world knows that you are innocent.) Everyone was saying you deserve praise,' she kept telling me.

I tried to console her in return and told her I was fine.

'Anyone who came to know that I am your sister would say good things about you to us.' As usual, I could feel her love for me and could tell that she was speaking on behalf of Ammi and our other elders.

Samar bhai then asked me not to worry about Shabista, Zab and Ammi. 'We are here to take care of everyone,' he said. I learnt from him that they had been repeatedly questioned and harassed by the STF and were struggling to keep the news from the kids. My niece Rid's classmates had said to her, 'Your mamu is a thief!' She had cried a lot, and Samar and Zeenat had to meet the girl's parents and explain the situation.

I told them that I had been moved to a new barrack and asked if Adeel bhai could have me restored to either Millennium or Nehru barrack.

'Are the police still coming to the house?' I asked Samar bhai next.

'Yes, but the frequency has decreased. It seems like the visits are related to the news in the media. They come on the day something has appeared in the papers or has played out on primetime TV. Then they ask strange questions, harass us for a few hours and leave. We are just praying that you can get out soon. We will make sure Ammi is protected from the whole thing,' he said.

Farro had brought me letters from Shabista, my nieces Zara and Rid, and Ahmar bhai. I wrote a note for Farro to take back to Shabista, asking my wife to go home to her parents in Pipiganj, another area of the city, for some time. Farro seemed extremely distressed about my situation, so I did not share too much with her. Even though I had never kept a secret from her my whole life, I wanted to spare her my troubles. As she was leaving, she gave me some money and made me promise that when she came back to India next, I would be in Delhi to receive her at the airport. She was due to fly out again on 25 September.

After their visit ended, I had to give the usual amount to the prison cops and discovered that now there were three checkpoints, and I needed to pay ₹50 at each point. One officer asked me for ₹100 instead, and I refused to pay, so he let me go after cussing at me and making a threat.

Around three o'clock, when I stepped out of the barrack to have some tea, the same prison cop came and started beating me with his stick. 'You are not allowed to leave the barrack!' he shouted. 'The rest can go, but BRD inmates are not allowed to roam free.' The man was simply releasing his frustration because I had not paid him the ₹100. People began staring at me. My hand was throbbing where I had been hit on the wrist while trying to save myself from being slammed on the back.

That incident pushed me into the worst depression I had ever experienced after entering the prison. My life had never seemed as dark as it did that afternoon. I sat in a corner, not saying anything to a few inmates who tried to console me. I entered the barrack for *asr* namaz, and then sat outside again till 6 p.m., cursing myself. When they called for the counting, I joined the queue.

Inside the barrack, I spread a bed sheet on the floor near the toilet, lay down, covered my face with the blanket and cried for hours.

I got up only for *fajr* namaz and for my *sajda*. I could not help but offer up a long and agonized prayer to Allah. 'Please show some mercy, please!' I begged. 'I just went to save those dying kids, so why this punishment?'

Completely despondent, I realized that day just how much I hated the new barrack. People smoked up and uttered the vilest abuses. Even the writer was part of these activities. He was obsessed with money and kept tabs on who was going for meetings and what they were getting from home. He did a lot of drugs himself and was thus hardly in the position to stop anyone else.

That afternoon, Shailesh came to see me and brought me a paratha. That was the first meal I had eaten in two days. I hugged him and he promised to move me back.

The next morning, I began my day by cleaning the toilets. This was my job twice a day, once in the morning and then in the evening. Although two other inmates were also assigned toilet-cleaning duties, they used to do it just as a formality – throw some water around, smoke, chat and leave.

The writer had said that he would let me have another spot vacated by anyone who received bail. So I spent the day waiting to see if I would get a better place or if someone would come to visit with some good news. That is the way one's days pass in prison. You spend them in anticipation – of a meeting with your visitors, of good news, of the day when you will be released, of being proved right, so that the world knows you have not done anything wrong and your family can welcome you back home.

Anticipation is what keeps one going in prison. You eat to survive, you tolerate abuse and torture to survive. But it is anticipation that gives you the will to do so.

When Adeel bhai came to visit on Friday, 22 September, I hugged him and cried ceaselessly. 'Please bhai, help me return to Nehru or Millennium barrack!'

He said that he had spoken to the doctors and asked me whether I was willing to be moved to the hospital, to which I said, 'No, why should we do something illegal? Can't we just get my barrack changed?'

He was clearly irritated and berated me, '*Ye koi hotel nahi hai jo tumhe option milega. Bahar hum log kaise survive kar rahe hain, tum nahin samjhoge* (This is not a hotel where you can ask for options. You have no idea how we are surviving outside).' I kept quiet. I understood how he felt. But who else could I talk to about my distress? I needed to tell somebody, share my pain with at least one other human.

When he was leaving, he said he would try to do something about the barrack change, but it would take another two months for me to get bail, since all the advocates were advising us against moving for bail at this time.

'Two more months?' I was stunned.

'Yes, because the DM and other higher officials are also involved; there is a lot of pressure on the district judge not to grant bail. Once the media noise dies down, or someone else gets bail, things will move.'

Internally, my mind was screaming: *How would I survive? What had I done wrong? When I had not done anything wrong, why should we be scared? Let the judge reject my bail application; we would plead my case before higher authorities ...*

But I did not utter a word.

I was gradually learning the most important lesson of all while in prison: Your advocate would first say it would take only two weeks for you to get out, as there is no case against you. But after fifteen days, he would say another fifteen days, and fifteen more days after that, and so it would go on and on, sometimes taking months and even years for the prisoner to get out of the cage. No wonder that whenever a new prisoner came in and repeated these words of their advocate – that he would get bail in two weeks – older prisoners would just laugh out loud. I now understood why.

It was surreal how things were unfolding. On the first day, I did not want to enter the premises at all, and hated the Nehru barrack, but now, all I wanted for my survival was to be back there as soon as possible.

In just a couple of weeks I had learnt a lot about human nature. It is possible to survive in the most basic conditions. God has given human beings so much patience that even when faced with the worst of punishments, the will to live does not get extinguished. A convict sentenced to death will try to move their application before the Supreme Court or submit their mercy appeal before the president.

In prison, I had developed a thick skin for the sake of my own survival. In the past, I could never tolerate a rude form of address such as '*tu*' or '*abey*'. But now, when a guard addressed me as 'motherfucker' or 'sisterfucker', I endured it. In the past, I would not have tolerated a slap, or even a push or a shove, but now I was unaffected even when beaten with a stick.

Earlier, I would never eat until the plates were washed and dried properly, and I now ate, sitting on the floor, on a plate that I had to wash with mud and water. I would never have eaten the unhygienic food I was given in prison, which I now stood hours in a queue for, waiting eagerly for lunch and dinnertime. I would first check the quality of the washroom before checking in at good hotels, but now I was cleaning toilets. I even slept near the toilets.

After Adeel bhai's visit, I realized, in a flash of insight, that this meant I was not dying; rather, I was surviving.

I do not know whether it was because of Adeel bhai's efforts, or Shailesh's. But the next afternoon, for whatever reason, the head prison cop Surya Pandey came and asked me, 'Where is your card?' Once I handed it to him, he told me to pack my bag.

What was there to pack? I put all my belongings in the bucket again. Pandey-ji took one hour to return, and in that hour, I had made several assumptions – that I was going to the hospital, or the Nehru barrack, or some other, unknown, place ...

When he came back and asked me to walk with him, he returned my card, which now said 'Millennium Barrack'.

Sweet relief! I felt a rush of elation coursing through my body.

Just like the first time, the person I met first was D. Ram, who welcomed me with open arms. Dr Satish and

Manish were staying in the same barrack, which meant what I had heard on the prison grapevine was correct. I did not ask Dr Satish how he had managed to come back. Shailesh gave me a place near him, and we talked for hours. Shailesh told me that he had made a request to the jailor who had agreed.

It took a mere few minutes for me to get back into the skin of a practising doctor. Mubarak Ali and his group, who had been caught cheating in the high court judiciary exam, had been tortured in police custody. One of them, Shyam Bihari from Siwan, had developed an abscess on his upper arm. I recommended a ceftriaxone injection and Amikacin for the next seven days, and a dressing on alternate days. Once again, the inmates began to treat me with respect and loyalty.

And thus life went on, one day at a time.

PART THREE

Discovery

15

Threads Unravel

My long journey – from a relatively happy-go-lucky doctor to an unjustly imprisoned professional dispensing medicine to fellow prisoners – had brought with it several realizations.

In the weeks that I had spent in Gorakhpur Jail, I had discussed every detail of the BRD oxygen tragedy with my co-accused as well as several other inmates – this allowed me to identify several important threads. These helped me understand how the tragic events had unfolded and also how they could have been prevented.

Before 2013, the BRD Medical College received its oxygen supply from Modi Gas Ltd, a company favoured by the local member of parliament. After the installation of the liquid oxygen supply, the company was still supplying 300 to 500 cylinders per month to BRD. But when the new principal, Dr Rajiv Mishra, joined, he gave the contract to IGL in April 2017, an Allahabad-based company. Some said this was because of the company's connection to a cabinet minister from Allahabad. The proprietor of Modi Gas was obviously angry. The decision to award the contract to a company so far away was a blunder, especially because oxygen is an emergency drug that should be supplied within hours of demand, preferably from within the city itself.

The BRD Medical College's liquid oxygen supply was maintained by a three-way contract drawn up in 2013. This contract was between Inox (dealer), Pushpa Sales (middleman) and the BRD Medical College (buyer). The role of Pushpa Sales was confined to installing and maintaining the equipment, sending invoices to the hospital for payments, collecting payments and forwarding them to Inox after deducting a commission.

Questions were now being raised about why a middleman was even necessary.

This opened up a very important line of enquiry. When the liquid oxygen tender was floated, it was meant only for ward 100, a newly installed ward for treating encephalitis cases. So why had the ex-principal extended the supply to wards 12, 14, 8, 6 and the trauma centre? Who had given permission for this increase in the total consumption of liquid oxygen from 20,000 litres to 1.5 lakh litres? Had this consequently increased the liquid oxygen bill every month?

On 3 August 2017, a preparation meeting about the upcoming chief minister's visit had taken place. It was conducted as a videoconference between the principal secretary of medical education, the DGME from Lucknow, the DM and the BRD college's principal at the Gorakhpur District Court complex. The principal mentioned a legal notice that had arrived from Pushpa Sales on 30 July 2017. The notice stated that if the payment of his dues was not completed within fifteen days, he would stop the supply of liquid oxygen. According to the contract, BRD was supposed to pay his dues every fifteen days, and the overdue amount was never meant to be more than fifteen lakh. The DM and the principal requested the two officials from the Department of Medical Education to release the amount before the chief minister's visit on 9 August 2017.

Finally, after having discovered so much about the web of intrigue that surrounded the supply of life-giving oxygen at BRD, I was back to my original problem – how could I, a junior professor still on probation, with only a year of service and no knowledge of the central supply system, be held responsible for a failure that was well beyond my grasp?

But I knew the answer to that was clear.

I could ask the ultimate ruler this question a dozen times a day as to why I was being punished. However, the rulers on the ground had their own reasons, and these could not be questioned.

I was in prison for drawing too much attention and praise for a mere humanitarian duty during a crisis.

When the entire state machinery singled me out, two things happened. One, the majoritarian media, eager for the approval of the government, began to make much of my being a Muslim, and how this meant that I was a potential terrorist and wrongdoer. Second, people with secular values began expressing outrage at how I was being victimized only because I was a Muslim.

Both these stands served to distract from the tragedy that had occurred on 10–11 August 2017.

I believed, and I have stated this at multiple forums, that I would have been treated in the same way whether I was Kapil John, Kapil Singh or Kapil Pandey. That is, whether I had been a Christian, Sikh or a Hindu doctor, I would have incurred the wrath of the authorities for actions which were thought to draw too much attention to the tragic events at the BRD Medical College.

The outrage over my religion being the reason for my persecution managed to distract from the negligence and corruption that were coming to light. Targeting me thus made complete sense. While those who followed the news on TV and the nation's leading intellectuals were caught up in either attacking or defending my honour, the lives of the parents who had lost their children remained the same – devastated. Nobody even knew the names of those little ones who had died, what sacrifices their families had made for them, and how they had brought laughter and cheer to the hearts of their loved ones, before being snatched away by a man-made tragedy.

This was my most important realization in jail – a period that allowed plenty of time for reflection.

By the end of September, I had begun to follow my own well-established routine in jail. After completing my *fajr*, I joined the 6 a.m. queue for the counting. Next, I stood in the queue for the toilet, cleaned and used it, brushed my teeth, cleaned and swept the barrack and then sat down to have my tea. My breakfast was usually just fruits, following which I read the newspaper for an hour. If it was a meeting day, a Tuesday, Thursday or a Sunday, I would get ready and wait for Dadhi Kaka. Otherwise, I just walked around the barrack and talked to Dr Satish or Manish. I had a bath, washed my clothes, ate my lunch, offered *zohar* and went in before the barrack closed at 3 p.m. Then I cleaned and swept the barrack again, walking around and pondering over the same question: Why? I offered *asr* and stood in the 6 p.m. queue for the counting, after which the barrack closed for the night. I watched some television with the inmates – serials like *Gangaa* or *Bhabi ji Ghar Par Hai!*, before offering *maghrib*. Then I read novels until it was time to offer *isha*, which was when I read the Hadith. Then, I continued poring over books for hours, at times going to sleep by 2 or 3 a.m.

The heat and humidity made me restless. Even though I drank lots of water and splashed my face and head with it many times a day, I was constantly reminded of the contrast between my life now and how I used to live before arriving in jail. During the summer, I would use the AC everywhere – my home, car, hospital, classroom. Now, the intense crowding in the prison also added to the heat and made it unbearable. There were people around me at all times.

Soon, a spell began during which I spent all the festivals and special days in jail.

That year, Dussehra fell on a Friday, on 30 September. Meetings were not permitted because it was a gazetted holiday. There was a small celebration at the prison hospital and inner barracks, and a few people performed pooja in our barrack, but overall it was quite subdued. The next day was Muharram. The day after that, 2 October, was Gandhi Jayanti, another holiday. This meant there were four consecutive days when we did not know what was happening in the outside world.

But the inmates were all gearing up for the biggest festival of all, Diwali, which was round the corner. By 18 October, I saw that ours was the only barrack getting a complete whitewash for the festival. Since Shailesh had become the writer for this barrack, he had ensured that the whole barrack was painted once every year. He arranged the white lime for painting in a canvas bag, and everyone else participated. A few inmates led by Rohu painted the whole barrack and the outside wall in a single day, working non-stop from morning till evening. Mantri-ji provided money for his barrack to be painted as well.

We kept our belongings outside and spent the whole day in the sun. I read *The Pillars of the Earth* by Ken Follett the whole time. People were playing cards. It was a relaxing day, and there were no meetings. Most of the officials were on leave, there were fewer cops and no new inmates.

The next day was Diwali, which kept Shailesh busy

all morning, as he was collecting money for the evening's celebration.

We decorated the premises with diyas and candles. The evening pooja was led by Mantri-ji. Laddoos were distributed, and there was *halwa-puri* and a *paneer sabji* for dinner. I served dinner to everyone – all seated outside – feeling gladness in my heart after a long time. It was quite a feast.

Everyone hugged and wished one another a happy Diwali. The prison cops, having collected their *baksheesh* earlier, were now all drunk, and were shouting and dancing. In that moment, I could find it in my heart to forgive even them.

Unbeknownst to me, my own Diwali celebration would actually take place a few weeks later, when I was to be taken to court on 25 November to be served with my chargesheet. That morning, I got ready and wore the jeans and T-shirt I usually wore when they took me out to the district court. I was to accompany Principal Rajiv Mishra.

I steeled myself for the same horrible experience of going to the court handcuffed while onlookers stared at me but was surprised when the judge announced that many of the charges against me had been dropped. Apparently, no material and substantive evidence could be found by the investigating officers to prove that I had been involved in any corruption, indulged in private practice or violated any provisions of the IT Act.

'The charges under the Prevention of Corruption Act (Sections 7 and 13), forgery under IPC 420, private practice under IMC Act (Section 15) and IT Act (Section 66A) cannot be proved against you, so they are dropped,' the judge said.

I pleaded: 'Why not all the charges, my lord? I have been in prison for three months now.'

He sighed and told me, 'It is better if you do not waste any more time here.'

The disappointment hit me hard. I felt like I was sinking. When I read the 800-page chargesheet, I was shocked to see the parents' statements recorded by the investigating officer. All the statements were written in the same handwriting and were completely identical. 'No, the death was not due to a lack of oxygen. The deterioration in their health caused their death while they were being treated.' The only relief was that they had accepted I had arranged for many cylinders that night. I also realized while going through the chargesheet that Pushpa Sales agents had stated to the investigating officers that the authorities were asking for 10 per cent commission to clear the dues.

I came back to the filthy waiting room for the prisoners and had to stay there until 5:30 p.m. I was hungry and my stomach was hurting. When I got into the cramped prison van for the return trip, my mind went into a whirl again as I wondered how much more I would have to endure before seeing a glimmer of justice.

16

Notes that Mattered

I had never understood the power of letters before my incarceration in Gorakhpur Jail. A prisoner who used to work as a mechanic told me he had not written anything in such a long time that his fingers struggled to sign his own name. Then he remembered his wife's expression when she had come to visit him ten days ago. She looked so defeated that he immediately realized that writing to her was important, however tough it might prove to be.

As someone who had grown accustomed to writing short text messages on the phone and the instant communication possible on social media, it was surreal for me to realize just how much a letter could convey, how it could be treasured and savoured again and again. Most of all, receiving letters from my family was a reminder of how much they meant to me, how precious those relationships were in my life.

30 November 2017

Dear Mamu,

How are you? Hope this letter find you in good health. I am writing this letter to ask about your health. My mother told me that you are not well. Please look after your health. I prayed to God for your early recovery, and I am very excited to meet you. I am having lot of plans for when we meet.

Your loving niece,
Zara

On 3 December, my brother-in-law Ahmar bhai and Kashif came to meet me. It was the first time Kashif, my youngest sibling, would meet me in prison. We embraced and he told me, as if donning the role of an elder brother, to keep calm. When I began usual complaints and laments, he said, 'You should be thankful that nothing has happened to your brothers, your wife and kids.'

These words hit deep and gave me a reason to console myself every time I began sliding into depression and cursing myself.

Now, whenever I would start to feel upset, I would silently remind myself: 'Be happy that at least your family is okay.'

Farro's letter reached me next:

> Asssalamwalaikum
>
> I won't ask your well-being. I understand how difficult it is for you to pass each day, each hour. Except for the time when I am asleep, I am praying for you each moment. I cry as though some part of my body is aching. Ahmar bhai is giving me all support. He is also in pain. I firmly believe in you, know that you have not done anything wrong, and soon you will be out, and all the charges would be dropped, just as these corruption charges had to be dropped. Everyone has got some relief and thanked Allah. People know you are innocent, but *afsos*, still many are trying to give it a religious colour. I have explained to Zara and Jasir what noble work has been done by their Mamujani.
>
> *Bahut baichani rehti hai, bhai* (I am terribly restless, brother). I don't feel like doing anything. Sometimes I keep things to cook on the stove and forget. The kids complain about my aloofness. My friends here are very cooperative, they are helping to take care of the kids. I fear I will go mad, thinking such thoughts. Sometimes, I feel like screaming loudly and crying. But losing all hope is *kufr*. One should try to be cheerful.

> I have booked my ticket to India for 9 January 2018. I hope you are able to come to receive me. Insha'Allah.
>
> I can't come to see you inside the prison again. It breaks my heart.

I replied to them, saying that I was well and would soon be reunited with everyone.

I wrote to my niece Rid, who had been taunted by a classmate about her uncle being a thief. The vicious campaign unleashed in the media after the August tragedy had affected the minds of God knows how many children.

> Dear Rid,
>
> Asssalamwalaikum
>
> How are you? I hope you are doing fine. How is your school? I heard you fought for me, for your Mamujani. Don't fight with anyone again. *Allah sab dekhta hai* (Allah sees everything). Your Mamujani has not done anything wrong, so there is nothing to be ashamed of.
>
> Just pray. I promise you, when you come home for the Christmas holidays, I'll be there to receive you, and we will go to the water park every day.
>
> Love you and take care of your Ammi, Abbu, Dadi and lil star Rahil.
>
> Allah Hafiz

The next day, on 7 December 2017, Samar bhai and Shabista came to meet me. Zab was looking dull, and I immediately asked them what had happened to her, even though Shabista tried to hide it from me. Samar told me that Zab had been having high-grade fever for the past three days and had experienced difficulty in breathing. Shabista started crying. 'I got scared, Kafeel!'

It was a deeply painful moment. I, a paediatrician, could not treat my own daughter. My wife had to take her to other doctors. What punishment was this?

I told Shabista to start Zab on the inhaler, as I suspected a hyperactive airway disease, since she had experienced similar recurrent episodes and there was a strong history of atopy on her maternal side. Her weight was also stagnant at eight kilograms. I hugged my daughter close. The prison walls had never felt so thick and high as they did at that moment.

Christmas in 2017 arrived on a Monday. I was unable to keep my promise to Rid that I would be home for the holidays.

I missed celebrating Christmas as I had done for several years. I used to organize a health camp at an orphanage on 25 December and spend the day with the kids there. I would dress up as Santa Claus and distribute gifts, mainly books and stationery, and savour lots of cake with them.

Before we knew it, the last day of 2017 had arrived. It was a Sunday, and the spirit of celebration was all around. One of the big mafia inmates had sponsored food for the whole prison. There was paneer, puri and sweets – the common items for all the festivals in jail, be it Eid or Holi. At night, we were permitted to watch TV till 1 a.m. Inside the barrack, Azad and Vishwa danced. Shailesh was in a good mood. I, too, enjoyed the dancing and the night's bonhomie.

Privately, I was praying with ardour. 'This terrible year is now over,' I thought to myself. 'The new year will be better. In 2018, I will go home.'

The year 2018 arrived and soon it was Republic Day. On 26 January, a Friday, there was a flag hoisting at the central area of the prison, Girdha – which is what the meeting area was called – but we were not allowed to attend. Instead, we took it upon ourselves to sing the national anthem and distribute sweets.

It had become so cold that I had to wear a jacket and keep it on even while sleeping at night. The large windows let the cold air drift in, making me shiver all night long and crave for hot cups of tea. Now the crowd of people in the barrack did not seem as suffocating. It was so cold that washing my hands and feet for *vazu* before the prayer had become a challenging task.

On 14 February, some people celebrated Mahashivratri. The prisoners who were fasting were given a banana and 250 millilitres of milk, for which they had to sign up beforehand. During the day, they got a boiled potato. The whole prison was in a religious spirit in the run-up to Mahashivratri. Most of the inmates used to pray for one hour in the morning and an hour in the evening. Even the jailor and other officials were fasting.

In the neighbourhood where I grew up, I used to play Holi with a group of people outside my home. This year, Holi was on 2 March. We were not allowed to play with colours inside the prison, only *gulaal* was allowed, but everyone mixed the coloured powder with water to throw on each other. My bag, clothes and books – everything got wet. I ran and locked myself in the toilet, but the half door could not protect me, and I got thoroughly soaked with colour. Mantri-ji had organized *gujias* for everyone. At dinner, we were again treated to halwa-puri and paneer sabji. We hugged one another and exchanged Holi wishes before retiring for the night.

In the midst of all the festivities, I received some letters from my family.

On 20 March, I got a surprise visit – one that I had often thought about, but with a sense of dread.

My sister Zeenat had come to see me, but she had not come alone. My mother and my elderly aunt had accompanied her.

When I saw the three women walking towards me, I could not believe my eyes. My old Phuphijan was in a wheelchair, but my Ammijan walked up to me with a sense of pride mixed with grief. This was the first time I was meeting her since my arrest. All the months I had been in jail, I worried about how the news and our altered lives were affecting her.

We hugged for a long time, both of us too overwhelmed with emotion to speak. When she finally spoke, it brought me a lot of strength. 'I am proud of you, my son,' she said. 'You have proved that what was taught by Abbujan and me in your childhood was the right thing. I told the chief minister that my son is innocent and that he has been framed.'

I was shocked to hear that she had met the CM. 'When did you find out that I was in jail?' I asked her.

'When I was on hajj,' she said. So, all the while my whole family were trying to hide the news from her, she had already known? She told me that she had gone to Gorakhnath temple and met the CM at his *janta darbar*. I could feel my heart swelling with pride and love – she was such a brave woman.

Phuphijan, too, leaned forward on her wheelchair and hugged me.

'Shave your beard! It has grown too long,' she said, making us all laugh. It felt so good to be sharing a laugh with my family after such a long time.

With my mother having come to see me, and sensing her joy on meeting me, I began to feel much happier.

But as they say, happiness is often short-lived.

One morning soon after my mother's visit, I experienced some abdominal pain. I needed to go to the toilet urgently and requested the others to let me jump the morning queue. The moment the barrack gates opened that day, I ran towards the toilet. But, as soon as I entered, a swarm of bees from a beehive nearby stung me on my face. I came out screaming, to everyone's amusement. The fresh pain from the bee stings made me forget my stomach pain.

As quickly as he could, Shailesh put toothpaste over the stings. It was a good thing I had a beard, or my swollen face would have looked even scarier than it already did. The worst part was that I had to then wait my turn to go to the toilet – at a time I had been in a great hurry.

The next day, when Shabista came to meet me, she was horrified. She thought I had been beaten up, even though I told her about the bee stings. I tried assuring her that this was not the case, as I held on to Zab, who was trying to play with my beard, which made my swollen face hurt all the more.

Soon after, when I was happily getting ready for another meeting day, I suddenly slipped while cleaning the toilet. My head hit the floor with a loud bang. Everyone came to witness the embarrassing scene, but they quickly helped me up and laid me down on the filthy toilet floor. Once I could get up, I forgot the pain, wrapped a towel around myself and bathed for fifteen–twenty minutes, thoroughly cleaning myself with soap. Even the next day, when I thought about what had happened, I felt like retching. Both my legs were hurting, and I limped around for two or three days after my fall. It was inevitable that this would cause my mood to plunge, triggering the 'Why me?' question in my mind repeatedly.

Around this time, my next pesi date came up and, for the first time, it was to be held in court. I had heard that it was a horrible, painful experience, but some of the other inmates described it as an outing and a chance to eat food cooked in one's home.

The previous evening, the pesi writer had come and announced everyone's names. So, that whole night was spent listening to stories and advice from others about what to do and what not to do. 'Keep a newspaper with you, and a water bottle. Wear jeans, as you have to sit on a dirty floor.' I did not sleep all night. Even though there were so many people to advise me, no one I knew would be accompanying me to the court. I was worried about how the hardcore criminals would tease me and laugh at me on the way to the court. The only positive thought was that I was going to be on the other side of these huge walls and that I may be able to see someone from my family.

The morning slip came around 7 a.m. By 9 a.m., I had to get ready and wait in Girdha. I had two apples for breakfast, and Shailesh took me to Girdha at 10 a.m. 'Why go early when you will just have to wait there?' was his reasoning.

Nearly 200 inmates from different barracks were already waiting there, including ten or twelve women.

I requested the deputy jailor to tell one of the prison cops who were taking us to court to protect me from the others. He looked at me as if I had said something exceptionally stupid.

The pesi writer called everyone by name. First, all the women and thirty or so inmates left. My number was called out for the third vehicle, a small prison van for fifteen or twenty people, which had more than fifty people stuffed inside, and the door was locked. The small window was not shut, but thank Allah, it was netted. Still, it was so jam-packed that the twenty-minute journey felt like an hour and that happy feeling of going out disappeared the moment I entered the van.

The other inmates did not seem to be affected in the same way. Some of them were laughing and screaming at the people on the streets, who in turn looked back at us with hatred and disgust. Children were clapping and making fun of us: '*Dekho, dekho, chor gadi* (Look, look, a van of thieves).'

We reached the court shortly after. This was the *kachaheri*, or Gorakhpur's district court. Even though I belong to this city, I had never had any reason to visit the court in my life.

The van stopped in front of an old, one-storey building. Nearly seventy of us were asked to remain on the ground floor, while the rest had to go to the first floor. The ground floor had two halls – there was a room on the side for the women.

I had been told that the advantages of the first floor were that you could smoke, drink, play cards, look outside, and shout out to your family members standing by the building. But I preferred the ground floor.

It was so dirty, the whole area looked like it had not been cleaned even once in seventy years. The toilet door and flush were broken, the walls were covered in paan stains and tobacco spit. The big waiting room smelled of urine.

A police constable was announcing the names, and once your number came up, two cops would take you to the respective magistrate's courtroom. After the attendance and upon being given the next hearing date, you came back, escorted by the two cops. Only hardcore criminals or former fugitives were handcuffed and escorted by three or four cops. It usually took an hour, but could sometimes take three or four.

At some point, if you knew your escorting cops well, you might be allowed to eat some food your family would have brought for you, drink whiskey or vodka out of a plastic bottle. All these tips had been given to me the previous night. But the whole time, I stood near the window mesh to simply breathe. My number was called only past 2 p.m., after one van had already gone back to the prison.

Four cops accompanied me, two of them holding my hands. My face was covered with a handkerchief, but I still had the feeling that everyone was looking at me. Adeel bhai was waiting outside the magistrate's chamber. We looked at each other but could not talk. Then they took me inside. It took just a minute to sign in a register.

On the way, my brother tried to give me some home-cooked food, but one of the cops took it and put it in a dustbin. My brother told me it was paratha and bhindi sabji, my favourite.

Now, as we were made to wait in the stinking room again, all I wanted to do was return to my barrack as soon as possible.

I could see that Adeel bhai was walking around outside. He wanted to talk to me while we waited but the cops refused to let him. Other inmates were talking to their family members by shouting through the window meshes.

At around 5 p.m. they said we would go back. They did a head count and stuffed more than fifty of us into the small van. Throughout the journey, the standing inmates bumped against one another, smelling of sweat, chewing tobacco, farting. I felt nauseous. *They were right*, I thought to myself. It was a horrible, painful experience.

When I reached the barrack, D. Ram told me to first take a bath. I agreed, running to get my bucket and towel. I sat under the tap until 6 p.m., when they called us for the counting.

Inside the barrack, everyone came up to me and asked about my experience of the outside world.

But for some reason, I began thinking again of those hours on the night of 10–11 August, and the events began flashing before my eyes. The faces of the parents, the helpless children turning blue one after another, me having to rush from one bed to the next, the truck we used to bring oxygen cylinders. The only thing I felt sure of: if I had to do it again, even if it meant I could save only a single child, I would. I did not regret it then and I do not regret it now.

17

A Crack of Light and Hope

The first person to file their bail application was Dr Poornima Shukla, the wife of Dr Rajiv Mishra. She did this against the advice of the people who had asked her to stay out of the limelight. Already there had been a lot of noise about how she was the real power centre of the medical college. We had to file our bail applications in the lower court, where Judge Shivanand Singh had been appointed to hear the cases related to the BRD tragedy.

In court, Dr Shukla's advocate argued that she was neither a professor at BRD, nor was she working in any capacity that could have allowed her to be involved in the college's administration. They maintained that the public's perception had no value in the eyes of the court. Unfortunately, her bail was rejected on 3 October 2017, on the grounds that the investigation into the tragedy was ongoing and there was a possibility that if she was given bail, she could threaten witnesses or tamper with the evidence.

Manish Bhandari was the next person to apply for bail. He had been charged with bailable offences under sections 406 and 120B of the IPC. His chances of getting bail were supposed to be greater, and everyone felt that he would soon be out. He was also quite confident.

But a mere two days before his hearing, the district judge transferred our file from Judge Shivanand Singh to another judge, Justice Rakesh Dubey, for some inexplicable reason.

In his arguments, Manish had mentioned that the UP government had submitted an affidavit to the high court saying that no deaths had occurred due to a shortage of oxygen. But his bail too was rejected on 12 October 2017, once again on the grounds that the investigation was still ongoing. Justice Dubey rejected Sudhir's bail plea the day after, writing the same order.

On 7 November 2017, he gave the same explanation in his order rejecting the bail plea of Principal Mishra.

My bail application had been filed last. This was because we had listened to the advice being dished out by all and sundry that since I had faced a media trial already, I should wait for things to settle down. Even though I had told my brother, 'Let them reject it, we will go to the high court and, if necessary, the Supreme Court ...' no one listened to me. Everyone cited the same argument: the advocate has advised against it. It was extremely frustrating.

My whole family was living in fear. During the visits to the jail, they would tell me, 'You don't know how the world is treating us. We have become social pariahs. Our business is ruined. No one wants to even talk to us. No one picks up when we call, everyone is running away. So just keep your mouth shut and wait.'

Meanwhile, Manish Bhandari filed his bail application in the high court the moment it was rejected in the lower court. Without wasting any time, he hired a very senior advocate, whose fee was ₹5 lakh in the high court per appearance, and a few advocates from Lucknow and Delhi. He prepared a whole team to defend himself, even though the charges against him were mild, unlike ours, which were corruption and an attempt to murder. He clearly did not want to take any chances. He said to me, 'I would earn many times what I am spending in fees in a single week. So why shouldn't I arrange the best legal representation?'

He was right, of course. But it left me thinking: *How am I supposed to gather lakhs of rupees for lawyers and court fees?*

My bail application got rejected on 17 January 2018 by the ADJ of corruption prevention. The only relief I got from the lower court was that under Section 409 (criminal breach of trust by a public servant), according to the judge, the evidence produced by the investigating officer was insufficient. He also mentioned that bail was being rejected solely due to the graveness of the matter.

Even though I had been denied bail, it made me wonder why we had waited so long to file it, and why it had taken so long for it to get rejected. I was still under the impression that the moment we would file an application in the high court, we would be granted bail. I had never considered that the wait was going to be so long and hard.

Life in prison had gradually begun to take on a different shape. I started spending my days waiting for my next hearing date, or those of my co-accused, with a great deal of anticipation.

Rather than holding a hearing, the judge had set the next date of 3 March. This meant I would have to wait eighteen more days.

The way our criminal justice system works can be exhausting. Having never experienced it first hand, I had only seen or heard about the excruciating process in the movies or in newspapers. But the reality was as disappointing, all the more so because it was happening to me.

During the days, weeks and months of waiting, I developed a strong reading habit and devoured any books I could lay my hands on – these ranged from novels by Ken Follett, Robin Sharma, Mario Puzo, Dan Brown, among others. Reading helped pass the hours and it provided a glimpse of the world that still existed beyond the prison complex.

With matters still 'under investigation', we read in the newspapers of five separate instances of fires that had broken out at BRD Medical College since August 2017. One of the fires had broken out in the principal's office and the adjacent record room, in which many documents from the past years were supposedly destroyed. Inside the jail, we discussed these incidents and wondered who could be responsible for them. How did so many fires start, particularly *after* the tragedy? Each time, we also heard of a committee being set up to enquire into the causes of the fire. But none of the reports of any of those committees ever came out into the public domain.

By April 2018, Manish had filed his bail application in the Supreme Court after his bail got rejected by the Allahabad High Court. He had engaged Mukul Rohatgi as his lawyer, a senior advocate who had served as the attorney general under the Narendra Modi-led NDA government.

Rarely in the Supreme Court's history has a person charged under Section 406 (criminal breach of trust) applied to the apex court for bail. Usually, an individual charged under this section receives bail at the police station itself, as per the Supreme Court's ruling which stated that 'bail is a rule, jail is an exception'. It also says that all those charged with offences that result in less than seven years' imprisonment should be granted bail at the magistrate level and need not be sent to prison.

Getting one's application accepted in the Supreme Court is difficult, because it is first scrutinized by the registry that decides whether it is fit to be put before the court, after which the Master of the Roster, that is the Chief Justice of India, allots it to a particular judge or bench for hearing. In practical terms, an application is usually accepted by the registrar if one has a senior-enough lawyer to represent them in court.

At Manish's first hearing, Mukul Rohatgi pressed hard, arguing that it was a bailable warrant, and his client should not have had to come to the Supreme Court for bail. This set a wrong precedent, he said. Chief Justice Dipak Misra agreed to hear the plea, issuing a notice to the UP government, and fixed the next hearing for 9 April 2018.

All our bail applications were pending at the high court level. We were simply given the next date of hearing every time our case came up, thereby extending our custody from fourteen days to twenty-eight days each time. This stagnation was most disheartening.

As I chafed under this delay, all the questions I wanted to ask the high court judges kept resounding in my mind.

Unable to ask these questions of the judiciary, I channelled my energies into writing letters instead. I wrote to the Indian Medical Association at the beginning of April, asking for their help and intervention in my case.

To: The President, IMA, Gorakhpur

From: Dr Kafeel Khan lifetime member IMA, Suspended lecturer, BRD Medical college.

Respected Sir/Madam,

I hope everything at your side is going well.

I am languishing in Gorakhpur jail for the last eight months, for a crime I have not committed. One thing is loud and clear, that I was in no way involved with the liquid oxygen/ jumbo cylinders purchase, order, procurement, supply, payment in BRD medical college. When I was not involved in any of these duties, how could I be held responsible for the mishap that occurred?

The moment I got information, I ran to do all I could, as a human, and as a doctor, to save children's lives. I have not done anything wrong. I did my best. I request you to kindly look into this matter humanely and help us to come out of these wrong accusations.

Hoping to get a positive response from your side,

Thanks, and regards

On 4 April, my third wedding anniversary, I was missing my wife terribly, recollecting every moment we had spent together and longing to be with her again. She gave me the strength to live. I poured out my feelings in a long letter to her.

My sister Farro sent me a letter around this time.

Asssalamwalaikum Kaife,

Today, I will ask how you are despite knowing your answer. I know you are very strong and patient, and perseverance is in your nature. We always thought that you won't be able to tolerate this hardship and would break, but you have proved everyone wrong. Your determination that you would continue to serve kids and showing no regret about going to the hospital that night shows that you have not done anything wrong.

Outside, on social media, there are so many people who have started writing about you, and most importantly 90 per cent of them are non-Muslim. They are all asking for your immediate release. You won't believe it, but once you are out, you would be surprised to see the love and affection that so many people have for you. My prayers that Insha'Allah, you get more success and achievement in your life, my brother. It will be a new life. I think then you will get that question answered that you have asked me so many times – why Allah has punished you, despite your good deed?

Ammi was telling us you have lost weight and are looking weak. Bhai you have to take care of yourself. Believe me, sometimes I too lose my patience and scream. Sometimes

I get such a severe headache it feels that my head could burst anytime.

How Shabista is coping is really commendable. Poor girl has to take care of Zab and run to the court, DM, SSP. She even went to meet the CM! I hope you both would be together soon.

Take care my love.

Allah Hafiz

I wrote a letter in reply to hers, thinking I would hand it to Shabista when she came to the jail for our next meeting.

Asssalamwalaikum

I hope you are okay. Convey my salaam to everyone.

You are right about my being an emotional person, and even I don't know how I spent these eight months. But I am not the 'Himmatwala (courageous one)'. All my himmat comes from my family who have stood like a rock, and together we have faced these eight months. It's true every hour, every minute, is really hard to pass but when I think of Adeel bhai, Kashif, Shabista and Samar bhai running from pillar to post and doing all they could possibly do, I think you guys are suffering more than I am. But I am getting news about you that you are not eating properly, praying all night and reading the Quran, that your eyes have sunken deep in your face, that you have lost a lot of weight and are having suicidal thoughts.

Please, please, for my sake take care of yourself. If anything should happen to you, I won't be there to help you out. Promise me you will eat properly, sleep well, my love.

I am okay.

Adeel bhai is a brave person and, as we say, he is like our father. He has been acting like my father only, talking to everyone, and explaining again and again that 'my brother is innocent'. His business has been ruined and he shows no regret about that. But he, too, has to look after himself.

He has gained so much weight. Already, our family has a strong history of diabetes and heart disease. Another thing, tell him to control his anger. Kashif and Samar bhai were telling me that even on the phone he talks loudly these days and gets irritated very easily. Once he gets angry, he loses control over what he is saying. He himself used to say to me, '*Sarkar se nahin lad sakte* (we can't fight with the government)'. Now he himself is saying so many things. Please tell him to be careful. I am worried – if cops do something against him or any other family member, I'll break into pieces.

Kashif, poor fellow, he is looking older than me. He has lost so much hair. When he should have been spending time with his wife, he had to run around for this.

Samar bhai's idea has infused so much enthusiasm and energy in me. I don't know whether our decision to go full blown before the public and take the fight to the street, to tell the world what had happened that night, is a good one. But it is appealing, for sure. I have always held the view that when I have not done anything wrong, why should we keep quiet? Only the thought that my family could get harassed has made me shut up. But what did we get? It has been 8 months. The whole family is suffering, anyway. Financially we have broken completely. Look at Shabista, Zab, Ab, Bhabhi, Ammi. They have gone mad. They are also suffering. Everyone is suffering ... We have no other option left ...

The water has crossed above our necks. Everyone is struggling to breathe. Everyone is suffocating, everyone is dying, dying every day.

Shabista has to give an interview. They are saying they may have to go to Delhi, sit on dharna at Jantar Mantar. She is a shy girl, has never given any interview in her life. And Zab so small, she won't leave her mother for a second. Please talk to her regularly, boost her confidence and guide her. Money is another hurdle, tell Ahmar bhai to help.

> Anyway, we have decided now that we are going to the public and telling the world the truth, the real truth behind the man-made massacre.
>
> Love you, take care of Ahmar bhai and the kids, and most importantly yourself.
>
> Allah hafiz

On 9 April 2018, a bench of Chief Justice Dipak Misra, Justice A. M. Khanwilkar and Justice D. Y. Chandrachud granted bail to Manish Bhandari, after it was pointed out that Manish had already spent seven months in jail.

The press reported how Manish had been unable to secure bail until the apex court intervened in a matter that should have been settled by the lower court without delay.

This news made me more determined to break my silence, as I, despite having arranged oxygen cylinders during the crisis, was still rotting in prison.

PART FOUR

Determination

18

A Question in Court

Soon after that momentous breakthrough for Manish, the Indian Medical Association took action after eight months of silence. All those people in the IMA who had not responded to several of my letters decided to hold a press conference in support of doctors. Dr Satish and Dr Mishra's families were supposed to attend the conference, but they did not make it.

My wife and Ammijaan were the only family members in attendance that day. A report in *Outlook* magazine dated 10 April 2018 captured the press conference well.

> **IMA Comes Out in Defense of Dr Kafeel Khan Arrested in Gorakhpur Hospital Tragedy Case, Calls it Conspiracy**
>
> Dr Kafeel Khan, who has been in the jail for the past seven months in the Gorakhpur hospital tragedy case, is a victim of conspiracy, said Indian Medical Association.
>
> IMA Secretary, Dr R P Shukla, said the situation of lack of oxygen arose due to administrative slack, unaccountability and corruption. For this, officials from Gorakhpur to Lucknow are to be blamed and not doctors. Whereas, state had all the amenities to prevent the situation from happening, but it couldn't, on the contrary they arrested the doctor who with limited amenities tried to prevent the situation.

Dr Shukla said that doctors were not even allowed on bail and neither was any thorough investigation done in the case after the incident. He demanded a high-level probe in the matter.

On *The Citizen*, a digital news platform, the report read:

'They terrorized us for days on end, a large number of policemen would break into our house in the late hours of the night, make us all get up and sit around, would threaten to take us into custody, my one year old baby would be howling, they would roam through our house, I cannot even begin to tell you what we have gone through,' said Shabista, the young courageous wife of Dr Kafeel Khan, who has now broken her silence to speak out for justice and her husband who has been in jail for seven months without bail.

Initially, when the family learnt that Dr Khan had fainted in jail their only focus was to 'save his life' and have him shifted into better lodgings in jail. They met every single official concerned but nothing was done. In desperation the family went to meet Chief Minister Yogi Adityanath who merely repeated the oft heard platitude, justice will be done. And to the family's plea to move him out of the general cell, asked, 'Do you think people go to jail for rest?'

Not a single rule was followed with male police men [*sic*] entering Khan's house in Gorakhpur at will. The harassment continued for days. They lost count. They were threatened, with the cops not even listening to the mother's pleas to leave as their little girl would howl in terror. Instead, they would move around the house at will ...

Asked why they had remained silent, the family members said that if they spoke, or anything about them got into the media, it would have a direct bearing on Khan in jail. He would face the music as it were, and hence the family bore the harassment silently, trying instead to get justice from the administration and the government. But in vain.

> Dr Khan's bail application has not been heard for months, with the Allahabad High Court continuously postponing it as either the government lawyer has not turned up, or the reply by the government needs more details. In what local lawyers admit is totally unprecedented, the High Court at one point showed two dates for the hearing as 'pending.' At the moment a new date for the hearing has still not been given with Khan's lawyers having written to the judge for a date.
>
> There is some optimism now following the Supreme Court's bail to Manish Bhandari, the oxygen supplier to the Gorakhpur hospital. It was alleged that a shortage of supply of oxygen killed the children, even as Dr Khan worked around the clock to arrange for the same from other sources on the fatal days.
>
> The difficulty for Khan is that he cannot even move the Supreme Court for bail, as his High Court hearing has not even come up. As the local lawyers said, these doctors are all in for first time offences, are not criminals, and yet they are being harassed and victimized by the Yogi government beyond all comprehension.

Two days after Manish had got bail, I received a visit from Nadeem Khan and Masihuzzama Ansari, both social activists who lived in Delhi. I told them how hard it had been for the whole family and how hard we had been hit financially – my brother's business had been destroyed, my wife's hospital was sealed, and I was in prison with no income. Nadeem Khan was of the view that we should move the Supreme Court and said that he would approach well-known lawyer and legal luminary Indira Jaising to take up my case pro bono. She had served as the Additional Solicitor General (ASG) of India and was reputed for being a champion of human rights. I felt as if a lifeline was being offered to me.

I told Nadeem to go ahead and contact Indira Jaising. He also advised me to write an open letter so I could refute some of the misinformation floating around and make the public truly aware of the terrible events of 10–11 August 2017, and how I had been treated since then.

Ahmar bhai, who knew of our financial condition, was sceptical of my decision to go public with my narrative. Around the same time, in April 2018, the trial in connection to a horrific rape case in Jammu's Kathua district had begun; the shocking incident in which a little girl had been gangraped had rattled the people of Kashmir and across the country and the world.

At such a time, Ahmar bhai held out little hope that my plight would draw the extent of public sympathy needed to counter the official pressure that was influencing the case. He wrote to me:

> People do have sympathy for you and appreciate your role in the BRD crisis but are also preoccupied by burning issues such as [the rape and murder of] Asifa. Do bear in mind that Adeel and Kashif are also having to deal with financial matters, and for any such agitation they need to have a free mind so that they can focus and continue the agitation. As regards your question of doing something, I am not sure how far it can help We need to calculate or estimate the impact of such a decision. In case all of the concerned persons feel it is ok we can revisit our decision. As of now, I cannot be physically present for such support.

I could see that he was probably right, but now that we had decided to move ahead, I did not want to turn back. 'Why should I be scared when I had not done anything wrong?' I would always tell myself in these situations. And, more importantly, what had I achieved for myself and my family by being silent for eight months?

'*Hasbunallahu Wa Ni'mal Wakeel* (Allah alone is sufficient for me, and the best disposer of my affairs),' I said to myself repeatedly as I prepared to write my letter to the public. On 18 April 2018, my wife came to inform me that she was going to Delhi with my brothers to talk to the Supreme Court lawyers, as the Allahabad High Court was postponing hearings and there seemed to be no other recourse.

I requested the office writer to give me a few pages and a pen. I wrote a ten-page letter, describing every single event that had happened in those fifty-four hours at the BRD Medical College, when our team of doctors was trying hard to save the lives of our patients. As I poured it all out in those pages: the eight months in prison without bail, the encounter with the CM, my family's harassment by the police officers, the torturous conditions in jail and how slowly the wheels of justice were moving, or that it often seemed like they were not moving at all.

Who could be the possible culprits? As my hand moved across the pages, I felt furious. I decided that enough was enough – we needed to speak up. Whatever the consequences, we had to tell the world the truth. My wife and my brother agreed.

This is what I wrote:

> 8 Months, In Jail Without Bail!
>
> Am I Really Guilty?
>
> I [remember] each moment. Every scene is still alive like it's happening right now in front of my eyes, even after 8 months of unbearable torture, humiliation behind the bars. Sometimes, I ask myself, am I really guilty? And the answer pops out from the core of my heart – no no, a Big No.
>
> The moment I got that WhatsApp message on that fateful night of 10th August 17, I did everything a doctor, a father, a responsible citizen of India would/should do.

I tried to save each and every life who was in danger due to sudden stoppage of liquid oxygen. I did my level best to save those innocent kids who were dying because of lack of oxygen.

I frantically called everyone. I begged, I ran, I drove, I ordered, I yelled, I screamed, I consoled, I counselled, I spent, I borrowed, I cried. I did all that is humanly possible.

I called my head of the department, my colleagues, principal BRD, acting principal BRD, DM GKP, AD health GKP, CMS/SIC GKP, CMS/SIC BRDMC informed them about the grave situation arising due to sudden stoppage of liquid oxygen and how kids' life are in danger due to lack of oxygen supply. (I have all call records)

I begged gas suppliers Modi Gas, Bala ji, Imperial Gas, Mayur Gas[es] Agency, all the hospital around BRD Medical College after arranging their contact number for jumbo cylinders to save hundreds of life of innocent kids.

I paid them in cash and assured them will pay rest on delivery. (We arranged 250 cylinders/day until liquid oxygen tank arrived. One jumbo cylinder cost Rs 216/-).

I ran from one cubicle to another, from Ward 100 to Ward 12, to the Emergency Ward, from point of oxygen supply to the point of delivery to make sure uninterrupted oxygen delivery.

I drove to get cylinders from nearby hospitals in my car, when I realized that was not sufficient. I drove to SSB met its DIG and explained him the unprecedented situation, their response was very quick and supportive. They arranged a big truck and group of soldiers to carry empty cylinder from BRD to gas agency, filled it, brought to BRD and ran again to refill.

They worked for continuous 48 hours. Their spirits boost ours. I salute SSB and very thankful for their help. Jai Hind.

I spoke to my junior/senior doctors, I ordered my staff. Don't get panic, don't be disheartened, don't get angry with agitated parents, don't take break, we had to work as a team to treat efficiently to save every life.

I consoled grieving parents who have lost their kids. I counseled those agitated parents who were getting angry after losing their kids. There was so much chaos, I explained them – liquid O2 (oxygen) is finished but we are trying to make it with jumbo oxygen cylinders.

I yelled/screamed to everyone to focus on saving life. I cried, actually everyone in the team cried to see the havoc created by the administrative failure to pay the dues to liquid oxygen suppliers, resulting in such a grave situation.

We did not stop trying until liquid oxygen tank arrived, around 1.30 am on 13.8.17.

But my life turned upside down when CM Yogiji Maharaj arrived next morning on 13.8.17. He asked – "so you are Dr. Kafeel, you arranged cylinders? I was like – yes sir. He got angry – so you think by arranging cylinders, you became hero ... I will see it."

Yogiji was angry because of how this incident came into media. I swear to my Allah I did not inform any media person that night. They were already there that night itself.

Then police started coming to our home, howling, threatening, torturing my family. People warned they would kill me in an encounter. My family, my mother, my wife and my kids were so scared that I do not have words. I surrendered to save my family from the humiliation, misery thinking when I have not done anything wrong, I should get justice.

But numbers of days passed, weeks, months passed – from August, 17 to April, 18. Holi came, Dussehra came, Christmas gone, New Year came, Diwali came – every date – *Tareekh Par Tareekh* hoping will get bail ... (Even they acknowledged the same)

Sleeping on floor with more than 150 prisoners in a cramped barrack with millions of mosquitoes in night and thousands of flies at day. Trying to swallow food to live, bath half naked in the field and shit in a toilet with broken door, waiting for Sunday, Tuesday, Thursday to meet my family.

Life is hell, miserable not only for me but for my whole family. They had to run from one pillar to another – from police station to court, from Gorakhpur to Allahabad – in hope of justice. But all in vain.

My daughter whose first birthday I could not celebrate is now 1 year and 7 months old. As a pediatrician it is very painful disheartening not to see his child grow. As a pediatrician I used to taught parents importance of milestones and myself don't know when my daughter started walking, speaking and running.

So now again that question haunts me – am I really guilty? No no – NO.

I was on leave on 10th August 2017 (its sanctioned by my HOD). I still rushed to do my duties – is that wrong?

They made me head of the department, vice chancellor of BRD, 100 ward prabhari. As I am junior most doctor and joined only on 8.8.16 as a permanent employee. I was working as nodal officer with NHRM and lecturer pediatrics. My whole work is to teach students and treat kids.

I was nowhere involved with purchase/tender/order/maintenance/supply/payment of liquid oxygen/jumbo cylinders.

If Pushpa Sales stopped liquid oxygen supply, how am I responsible for that. Even nonmedico could tell doctors' work is to treat not to buy oxygen.

The guilty are DM GKP, DGME, principal secretary health education for not taking any action against 14 reminders sent by Pushpa Sales for his 68 lacs dues.

It was total administrative failure at higher levels. They did not realize the gravity, just to save themselves, they made us scapegoats and put us behind the bars.

When Manish Bhandari got bail, we saw some light that may be now we would also get justice and come out to live with my family and serve again.

But No – we are still waiting.

Supreme Court says, bail is the right, prison is the exception. Then this is a classic example of miscarriage of justice.

I hope time would come I will be free with my family with my daughter.

Truth would come [out], justice would be served.

A helpless broken-hearted father/husband/brother/son/ friend

Dr. Kafeel Khan

On 19 April 2018, this handwritten letter was translated into many languages, and both audio and visual versions of it were shared and read by millions.

I woke up to a surprise on the morning of 19 April. Little did I know that on this day my life was going to change again. I was taken to the district hospital in the morning for a medical examination. When I reached, the local media tried to speak to me and, as I was attempting to answer their questions, I was roughed up by the cops. A video of this went viral on social media.

In the afternoon, my wife held a press conference where she released my letter and pleaded my innocence.

That evening, until late at night, she appeared on many prominent news channels, as part of their prime-time news coverage, and narrated the whole story – how our entire family was being harassed while the real culprits continued to roam free. This news coverage came as a surprise for many. Many people had been under the impression that I was imprisoned for a few days and later released.

It shocked the whole country – and people internationally expressed outrage as well – that a doctor who had tried to save children by arranging for oxygen was still behind bars after eight months, and his whole family had suffered a great deal during that time. They became aware of my daughter crying for her father, my mother pleading with the chief minister for my release, my wife running from police station to lower court to high court and now to the Supreme Court. Finally, after months of silence, there was an uproar. From media commentators to politicians, Bollywood stars, social activists to NGO workers and sports personalities – everyone tweeted and issued statements on video in my favour and demanded my immediate release. On 20 April, when my case came up for hearing in the Allahabad High Court, for the first time, the honourable justice read my file and asked, 'Is Dr Kafeel a doctor?'

For the first time in eight months, advocates from both sides argued on the matter – my advocate, Nazrul Jafri sahab, and the advocate general of Uttar Pradesh.

For the first time, the court fixed the next date of hearing, for 25 April, issuing a notice to the UP government based on my plea.

For the first time, the honourable judge read my file and expressed surprise. 'Being a junior doctor, when he tried to save innocent lives, why is he behind bars?' he asked aloud.

'Well, that is what I have been asking myself for the longest time!' I wanted to exclaim. It had taken so many adjournments – 16 February 2018, 13 March, 30 March, 6 April, then 9 April and finally 20 April – for his lordship to raise the one question to which I was still desperately seeking an answer.

19

The Turning Tide

Although I had more or less disappeared from public memory after a concerted media campaign was unleashed against me soon after the oxygen tragedy, many months later I was rediscovered and lauded by the public. Now there was no looking back. As a massive uproar on social media about my ongoing detention even after eight months gained ground, we needed to highlight our family's continuing ordeal.

On 21 April, my wife, Adeel bhai and Zab appeared at a press conference at the Press Club of India in Delhi, attended by reporters from numerous prominent electronic and print media houses. Ravi Nair, the director of the South Asia Human Rights Documentation Centre (SAHRDC), and Dr Harjit Singh Bhatti, the president of the Resident Doctors' Association at AIIMS, Delhi, were also in attendance.

In a poignant moment during the press meet, when Adeel bhai asked Zab, 'Where is your father?', she went running to the entrance to the room, as if to check if I was outside.

Shabista explained that she was in Delhi to explore legal options for my release. She emphasized, 'My husband has done no crime. If he wanted, he could have stayed home that night in August. On many occasions, he has himself paid for supplies such as masks, gloves and sanitizers. The deaths were a result of administrative failure ...'

The next three days in jail were spent with everyone discussing what had happened at the press conference and if it had improved my chances of being granted bail. Dr Mishra and Sudhir were confident that I would get bail on the 25th. Even I felt hopeful, since my lawyers had not got the opportunity to present any arguments prior to the latest hearing, and there was usually a large time gap between them. But this time, they were able to argue my case, and the next hearing was set four days away.

Across the country, a campaign asking for my release had been gaining momentum. Ordinary citizens from all sections of society, including lawyers, began reaching out to my family with offers to help. Within the jail, however, veteran inmates like Mantri-ji and the prisons authorities told me that due to the release of my open letter and my wife's press conference, I would not be let out. Mantri-ji said, 'I told you the day you came here: If you keep quiet you have a chance of being released, or else you will rot in prison.'

'Yes, I followed your advice for eight months,' I reminded him. 'But when I have not done anything wrong, why should I stay quiet, and why should my family and I suffer like this? I don't care anymore. I will no longer keep quiet. I will fight this fight.'

In Delhi, my brother and my wife were being sought after by news channels. Every day, there was some news about my letter, and the video of me getting roughed up at the hospital was played on television. Several eminent lawyers, former judges and human-rights activists raised questions about my prolonged detention when in fact the chargesheet had been filed and another co-accused had got bail.

Kashif came to see me on the 23rd. Looking more at ease this time, he told me how the world was reacting in disbelief that I was still in prison and at how I was being mistreated by the police in front of reporters. He also apprised me that many organizations had called for a Bharat *bandh* if I was not granted bail on the 25th.

The night before 25 April 2018, I remained awake and restless. The following morning, I was still agitated, feeling palpitations in my heart, wondering if I would finally get bail or a date for yet another hearing. I sat quietly, having skipped breakfast, alone with my thoughts, the prison activities around me carrying on as usual.

The writer attached to the office came to inform me that I would have to go to the district hospital for a medical checkup. This time they were careful to keep it so secret that no reporter or any member of my family could reach the hospital. Even Shailesh did not have a clue. I began rehearsing in my mind what I would say if anyone from the media was present to ask me questions.

They took me to the district hospital in a jeep packed with six policemen. My face was covered. The vehicle was parked outside the hospital while a police officer went to find out if the doctor was available. He took an hour to return, and in all that time, they did not even allow me to look outside. I tried to peek out and search for any health reporters I could recognize, but could see none.

Once inside, the cardiologist – who was very friendly towards me – examined me and advised a complete blood checkup. I tried hard to find someone who could convey a message to my family, but this time the cops were more vigilant than ever. The moment my test was over, around 2 p.m., they whisked me back to prison.

But what about my hearing? Had my bail application been rejected or granted? I feared it was the former, or the prison grapevine would have picked up on the good news instantly. I tried asking the deputy jailor what had happened, on the way back to the barrack, but he replied that he did not have a clue.

Feeling sad and stumped, I went into the toilet and locked myself there for an hour, just wanting to be alone. At any other time, it would not have been possible to stay inside the toilet for so long, but if anyone knocked on the door then, I screamed at them and told them that I had diarrhoea.

We sat and discussed all the possibilities. We concluded that I must have been given another date. Someone would come to visit me on the meeting day, which was the following day, so I would just have to wait until tomorrow. Shailesh put on the TV to check the news, but there was nothing related to me, and the other inmates were clamouring to watch the entertainment channels. 'Do you want to give one of the prison officers ₹100 and make a call?' asked Shailesh. I refused. I did not want to try anything that could invite further trouble.

Like the previous night, this one, too, I spent sleeplessly. At least earlier I had some hope and had felt more optimistic. But now, I was clueless about what had happened in court and had no choice but to await the next day's meeting to get some news.

On the morning of 26 April 2018, the moment the counting was over, I requested Shailesh to get the newspaper. We normally had to wait till 10 a.m. for it. He came running back with it, and there it was on the front page.

'Infants' death case: Gorakhpur BRD hospital doctor Kafeel Khan gets bail'. Shailesh was laughing out loud in delight. We embraced each other tightly, my heart feeling lighter than it had in ages.

Dr Satish and Sudhir had heard as well and came running. We screamed, we laughed, we cried. I had lost track of how many times I had cried in those eight months, but this was the first time the tears were of relief. Everyone in the barrack, except the newcomers, came over to congratulate me. Mantri-ji was so happy he congratulated me and ordered sweets as well.

All the police officers started approaching me for baksheesh. Manish had given anywhere between ₹200 to ₹2,000 to each of them, and they were expecting the same from me. 'Arre bhai, I am not that rich,' I explained with a laugh, and asked them to wait until my family visited.

It's hard to describe what I was feeling in that moment. I began remembering the other times when I had felt this happy. When Zab had come into this world ... when I got selected for the MBBS programme ... the days Adeel bhai and Kashif got married ... when Fazeel cleared the medical entrance ... when I first took tiny Zara in my hands ... when Shabista said yes ... when Rid's surgery was successful – all moments of pure delight. This moment was just as sweet, but uniquely so.

I was all of a sudden consumed by a deep longing for my family. I wanted to hug Ammijan, lay my head in her lap and cry. I wanted to see Farro, and give Adeel bhai and Kashif tight hugs. I wanted Shabista to kiss me, I wanted to make love to her ...

The feelings bubbled over until I wanted to scream, laugh, run, dance, cry and bang my head against a wall.

Overwhelmed with emotions, I ran to offer the *shukrana* namaz.

Dadhi Kaka came in, carrying *imartis*. 'Your brother is waiting outside,' he said.

The release process was arduous. Between 10:30 a.m. to 11:30 a.m., I went to the main gate many times to ask for a meeting slip. As soon as I got it, I asked Shailesh to take me to Girdha. 'What's the use? They are not there yet,' he reasoned.

But he eventually relented, laughing, and told the prison officer, 'I am taking Kafeel; send the rest of them with the junior writer.'

I reached the spot and stood there, looking at the entrance.

The deputy jailor called out to me, offered his congratulations and asked me to sit, pushing a chair forward. 'Tea?' he asked. I was stunned. For eight whole months these officials had behaved with me rudely and made me feel like a pariah. But, in that moment, all these gestures seemed welcome, and I just could not feel bad about the stark contrast in their behaviour.

'Your medical advice for my daughter was very useful. She has started eating better and gained some weight. Please give me your number – I will bring her to you for consultation,' said the deputy jailor.

I thought to myself: *How fast people change*.

Anyone passing us, office workers, inmates going for meetings – all came and congratulated me. Uday and Gajanand also came running and hugged me. During the mulakat period, the principal and his wife came forward to congratulate me. The eight months we had spent inside had dissipated everyone's bitterness and attempts to blame each other. All they wanted was to get out of this hell.

People from other barracks started coming over to talk to me, and soon it seemed as if everyone around me was talking about my bail.

I finally spotted Kashif and his friend Pintu Gupta at the entrance. Both carried bags full of newspaper clippings and printouts of social media posts. I ran towards Kashif and embraced him. He is younger than me and did not cry, but I wept like a child. Pintu joined us in a group hug.

'Kafeel bhai, you got it!' exclaimed Kashif. 'The "chor" and "murderer" tags are now gone from your name. The world sees you as a hero. Since your letter became public, you have been the top trend on the news. And now, the news of your release has led to a mass celebration. Our home is full of relatives and well-wishers. People are telling Ammijaan how her son has made them all proud. In so many debates on TV, even any of the authorities are not saying anything against you. Everyone is only talking about how you have been kept captive and punished for so long. You are the top search on Google, people are writing about you on social media, and we are all so happy that we want to take you home today itself ...'

My heart skipped a few beats. 'I won't be going home today?' I asked.

Kashif saw my expression and reassured me, 'No, nothing to worry about. There is just some paperwork left. Today Adeel bhai will get a certified copy of the order, tomorrow he will submit it to the local court and furnish the required bail bond. You will be home by tomorrow evening.'

'Understood, bhai. I just want to see everyone as soon as possible,' I told him.

Kashif's face turned serious. 'There is just one thing. Adeel bhai has asked me to tell you that you should maintain a strict silence as far as the media is concerned. There will be a lot of reporters waiting. Everyone in the family, even Nadeem bhai and our advocates, all feel that you must control your words and emotions at that time. Look at Manish – he didn't speak a word, and left immediately.'

'Come on, it's time to go,' the prison cops reminded us, and we pleaded for five more minutes. They relented, with a reminder to Kashif, 'Don't forget to give him some money so he can pay us our baksheesh before leaving.'

Kashif hugged me again before turning around. Watching him and Pintu disappear into the distance, I did not feel sad that day. I wanted to go into the barrack, talk to my fellow inmates, and read all the clippings Kashif had given me.

As I reached the barrack, everyone gathered around. I began telling them what had happened. Prison cops kept coming every ten or fifteen minutes from different barracks, asking for *vidai* (farewell) money. Now they were all giving me respect, even the jailor, who was always unpleasant to me. But I did not dwell on this shift in their attitude. Nothing mattered in my euphoric state except a single, dominant, thought: I would be home soon.

Other inmates started coming to exchange contact details with me. Some were hoping I would find them legal help, because they had no contacts or resources of their own in Gorakhpur. Time was flying now, and soon it was 6 p.m. The same barrack that used to seem hellish and plagued me no end, no longer evoked feelings of depression.

I chatted late into the night with my fellow inmates, sharing biscuits, namkeen and fruits around my blanket. The atmosphere in the whole barrack was charged. Shailesh was very happy for me. I promised to do my best to get him bail and told him that I would never forget him. Everyone was in a good mood and seemed to have chosen to ignore their sadness for the time being.

I thought about D. Ram, the Mubarak gang, Rohu, Azad and so many who had left during my time in jail. We would remember them sometimes – usually whoever left never returned. Some came back for a visit in the initial months, but no more after that. So, maybe the promises we were making to one another were mere words. But in that moment, I truly felt that I would never forget my friends and their camaraderie that had helped me though the most hellish periods in incarceration.

After everyone had said goodnight, I finally had a chance to read the newspaper clippings Kashif had brought for me – they were like a balm to my pain. An online news website called *The Citizen* said that I had been 'jailed for over eight months in an ordinary criminal cell for a "crime" manufactured by Uttar Pradesh Chief Minister Yogi Adityanath's government'. An article in the *Quint* quoted the Allahabad High Court as saying, 'No Evidence Against Dr Kafeel, No Inquiry Was Done'. Several had quoted from the order of Justice Yashwant Verma to establish that the Gorakhpur police had already dropped the charges of corruption and private practice against me, that there was no need for custody since the chargesheet had already been filed in the case, and most importantly, as the bail order stated, '… there is no material on record, which may establish medical negligence against the applicant individually.' The reports further stated that the judge had 'observed that Dr Kafeel was not stated to be part of the tendering process that resulted in the enlistment of the entity, which was charged with the supply of medical oxygen.'

It fully dawned on me then. Tomorrow I would be free. A survivor. After months of tossing and turning on my otta, at last I slept in peace.

20
Homecoming

'Truth prevails. The truth can never be defeated.'

Several inmates from other barracks came to see me and said these powerful words.

When I was given my visitors' slips for the day, I found Shabista, Adeel bhai and Samar bhai's names on them. At 10 a.m., Dr Satish and I were asked to meet the prison doctors Dr Goyal and Dr Verma. We were served tea and hot pakoras, and told, 'We knew you guys were innocent. Now you owe us a party outside!'

I remembered the days when I used to beg them to convey one message to my family, or to give me my medicine for hypertension. They used to make some weak excuse or react rudely. But now, I decided to let go of all such thoughts, sitting there with a smile on my face, thinking of what I would say to each member of my family.

I came back to the barrack and had a long chat with Shailesh. He was the one person I knew was sincere in his actions and feelings towards me. My whole family had got to know him.

Then it was time for my meeting. Zab came running to me first. How time had flown! When I was arrested, she could hardly walk, and now she was running with abandon. Before I could ask, Adeel bhai said to me, 'Today we will take you home.'

The same euphoria that had taken hold of me when I learnt of my bail returned in an instant. I felt like I was walking on air. From Adeel bhai I heard about the tense atmosphere in the courtroom, which had been packed with reporters. Justice Yashwant Verma had asked, 'Why do you still need him? Is the investigation not over? What have you found in eight months against him? Nothing. So just tell me some good reason not to grant him bail.' The government advocate could not give a reply and stayed mum.

'Bail granted.'

The verdict had been pronounced, and the entire courtroom erupted in joy.

Shabista found a moment to whisper to me, 'Now promise me you won't leave me and Zab again.'

'Promise,' I said. Her eyes were shining with tears of joy. 'There's a surprise waiting for you,' she said. I smiled.

Adeel bhai and Samar told me how reporters were camped outside the prison waiting to interview me. 'It is like a *mela*,' said Adeel bhai. 'But you have to stay calm. No need to talk to anyone today. Just sit in the car and we will go home.'

I could see Samar bhai did not agree with this approach. I, too, was feeling rebellious. Why should I stay silent when I was finally getting to share my side of the story?

After the visit, I came back to the barrack and started giving away my possessions. First my blanket and some of my clothes: jacket, jeans, T-shirt. Next I gave away my shoes, sweater, bedsheet, bucket, mug, toothpaste, soap, shampoo, towel and my bag for fruits, biscuits and namkeen. Finally my boxes, Ludo set, chess set … had I really accumulated so much stuff?

I collected my books in a bag and put on a T-shirt and shorts.

Jail custom dictates that you should not leave anything behind when you leave, otherwise you might have to come back. But the superstition did not bother me. I left everything behind, except my books and what I was wearing. Everyone gave me their blessings as I waited for the clock to strike 5:30, when the writer who announced the *rehai*, or bail, would arrive. The rehai list is brought along with the inmates returning from court.

Once the man arrived and began reading out the names, I eagerly asked for my name to be called out. But he said, 'Your name is not on the list.'

What? But Adeel bhai had clearly said that I would be released today ...

A part of my brain told me to stay calm. Manish had received bail on the 9th, but he could leave only by the 13th. But another part was fast filling up with troubling thoughts. Several inmates had told me, 'Until you go out of that gate, nothing is certain.'

I had not eaten dinner, thinking that I would have dinner at home. Now, after the counting, I had to get in the queue again. The people who had got my blanket and bedsheet gave it back; I did not ask for anything else, nor was anything returned. I stayed quiet but people around me were talking. Shailesh consoled me, saying, 'You will definitely go tomorrow.' I laughed uneasily.

The next day, on 28 April, I had a half-bath since I had no clothes to change into anyway. I told myself that there must be some paperwork holding things up. The day went by quickly; many people came and talked to me, we exchanged numbers, hugged and promising to meet on the other side. I tried to see every inmate in the barrack. The torture and humiliation I had suffered there was coming to me only in flashes, but the pain of the last several months was gone.

In my head, I started making plans. A long holiday, a trip with the family, eating non-vegetarian food two times a day for some time, sleeping, exercising, laughing and watching movies. I wanted to spend time with my family more than anything else. In the eight months I had spent in prison, I had become eight years older. My face had started showing some wrinkles, I had lost hair, some of my hair had turned grey, my arms and legs had become thinner, and my stomach had grown bigger.

At 5 p.m., the writer from the office came to ask me for *vidai* money. 'Tell me, when is my vidai actually going to happen?' I asked him.

'First you must pay,' he replied. I put some money into his hand.

'You are leaving today. Your papers are here. Your family is waiting outside,' he revealed.

Indescribable relief coursed through my body, as everyone started surrounding me. I shared some last hugs with many of my fellow inmates.

Outside the barrack, I gave a short speech:

> Life has been very tough for me and my family, but truth has prevailed. I have learnt a lot living with all of you in prison. Have faith in yourself, and don't get disheartened by bad news. Give your family importance, because they suffer more than you. God is there to take care of you and your family if you are true. Hate the crime, not the criminal and remember that books are our best friends. Respect everyone. Life is a school and people around are there to test us and teach us lessons. When we learn those lessons, we move to a higher class. As for me, I have no regrets about going to the medical college that night, nor will I stop serving poor people. If such a calamity strikes again, then regardless of the consequences, I will be there again, even if it means facing action; and remember one thing – one day everyone will go beyond these walls.

I was taken to Girdha where about twenty other inmates who had got bail were also waiting to be released.

The superintendent, jailor, all three deputy jailors as well as the whole office staff were in attendance there, which was most unusual, as a single deputy usually handled the rehai.

The prison officers told me that more people and reporters were thronging the prison gates than they had ever seen before. The jail superintendent, Dhani sir, called me over and congratulated me. 'Please forget any bad treatment you got here and start a new life. Leave the city for a few days, keep away from the media and spend time with your family,' he advised. Then he suddenly noticed my clothes. 'Why are you wearing shorts? Please wear jeans. There are hundreds of people outside.'

'I gave all my clothes to the other inmates,' I replied.

'What's in your bag?' he asked.

'Books,' I said. He shook his head incredulously.

The jailor and deputies also came forward and apologized for their behaviour. Then the whole process I had undergone when I came was repeated (except for having to strip off my clothes). Name, father's name, wife's name, two identification marks were confirmed, a signature and thumb imprint given.

I had a round stamp on my arm, that said WASTE REHAI, meaning release, and carried the date and the deputy jailor's signature. I was told that this stamp allowed you to travel for free if you showed it on public transport.

With so many farewells and promises of parties, I had to wait another hour as the same process was repeated for the other inmates. 'Please, let me go as my family is waiting!' I told the deputy, but he said, 'No, the rules are for all to be released together.' Shailesh told me the delay was deliberate, as they were waiting for the local cops to disperse the crowds gathered outside.

At last, at around 8 p.m. they called my name, I signed and gave my thumb imprint, and the jailor also signed on my palm with a red pen. After all the inmates had their palms signed, we stood in a queue to leave those huge walls behind and walk out of that massive gate.

I hugged Shailesh and Dadhi Kaka, thanked everyone again, shook hands and promised to come and meet them all. Then I went through the first gate.

Between the two huge gates, they checked my belongings. There, I was asked to sign in one more register, my stamp was checked, I was congratulated, asked for baksheesh, and was counted one last time. They told me to squat on the floor and wait, but I refused, and remained standing.

Minutes later, I finally stepped out and could breathe in the open air. I thanked Allah, looked back at those walls and the prison gate, reliving the moments when I had been brought here. The memories and wounds were still fresh and painful.

I had not shaved my beard or trimmed my hair in jail for fear of contracting hepatitis B or HIV.

Kashif came towards me, along with my friends Aftab and Mahtab. They tried to form a protective ring around me as a crowd of reporters rushed forward and were pushed back by the local cops. 'Kafeel sir! Kafeel bhaiya!' people were shouting.

I had decided to talk. Kashif kept looking at me, signalling that I should keep silent.

People started pushing against me, even as the police constables were herding us up, saying '*Baahar, baahar* (Go outside).' The reporters were pleading, 'Doctor sahab, please speak up!' There was a huge commotion around us.

In this chaos, I screamed, 'Let me speak – just give me two minutes!'

Everyone went quiet.

'I am really tired, please try to understand, mentally tired, physically weak, and emotionally drained. I will speak, but after two or three days. I won't forget these months of unjust incarceration. But right now, I just want to go home, hug my mother and sleep. I really miss my family. Thank you to the countless people who supported me through social media or in any other way. Thank you, thank you, all.'

'How tough was it for you to get bail after such a long wait?' a journalist shouted.

'It was absolutely horrible. I can't forget the cramped and depressing conditions. The people who should have been prosecuted are the ones who filed the FIR, headed the enquiry. We have been victimized, and I don't know why. I did no wrong, only did what a father, a doctor, a Hindustani would have done. And for God's sake, stop calling me an "*Oxygen kand ka aaropi* (accused in the oxygen scam)". Please know that the honourable court has categorically said that the UP government could not produce even a single piece of evidence against me.'

'Doctor sahab, if you are not guilty, who do you think are the real culprits?' somebody else shouted.

'I have already written a letter. You have read it. I don't need to state it again and again.'

Now the cops began pushing us and threatening to file an FIR if we did not leave immediately. My family, relatives and my friends pushed me outside as well.

The moment the gate opened, my younger sister Zeenat came up to me. I held her tightly. Suddenly, numerous other people ran to me and tried to shake my hand or give me a hug. I saw my nephew Rahil being crushed by the crowd and took him in my arms. Then I looked up.

There were thousands of people holding up posters and banners.

'Our hero is back! Dr Kafeel is back!' I cannot express the happiness that overcame me when I saw that scene. My friends, relatives, neighbours, colleagues from the BRD Medical College, people from my city, people whose faces seemed familiar and many I did not know at all – they were all there.

Parents of children I had treated had come, too. Even

those parents who had lost their children were holding up placards that said 'Welcome back, sir'.

As I tried to shake their hands and thank them for coming, I felt surprised and wondered why many people I knew well had not come to meet me for eight months. Were they being kept away?

Suddenly, I spotted Shabista and handed Rahil to Zeenat, took Zab in my arms and kissed her all over her face. I hugged Shabista for a brief moment, before people started pushing us again, trying to take a selfie with me or simply to congratulate me. It was a near-stampede. Adeel bhai and Samar made a circle around me with a few close friends and guided me to the car. I waved, and several people in the front of the crowd patted me on my arm. I smiled at them, screaming, 'Thank you, everyone, thank you!' Kashif pushed me and shut the door, and the driver started the car.

Inside the car I was reunited with my bhabhi, Rid and Ab. I had missed them so much! Rid immediately started filling me in about her last few months. When Farro called, we could hardly talk – both of us just sobbed on the phone. I could feel her happiness and relief. Out of nowhere, I felt as if I was choking, and a bout of coughing took hold of me. I could not breathe. The car had to be stopped and I went to the side of the road and vomited. A nearby shopkeeper offered me water so I could rinse my mouth and wash my face.

Shabista was looking at me, extremely worried. 'I am fine,' I told her. 'It's nothing, I just think my body had got accustomed to the cramped atmosphere of the jail.'

'What's the surprise?' I asked, and she smiled and said, 'I'll tell you later.' Then she held out her hands. They had applied mehndi on her hands and legs, just like on the day of our wedding. She was looking so beautiful. I wanted to kiss her right then, but the kids were there, and Bhabhi was smiling ...

I opened the window of the car and the air felt so fresh. The roads looked familiar, the route looked beautiful. I had been brought the same way in a police jeep. Now I was going home, a free man, the murderer tag removed from my name. It was a heady feeling.

The narrow lane outside my house was packed with people.

Home, sweet home. Never had that phrase meant more to me. I closed my eyes for a second. The car stopped. The moment I opened the door, people showered me with flowers, hugs and smiles. Then, hearing 'Kaife, Kaife!', I ran to my Ammijaan who was waiting at the gate with my badi phuphi and chhoti phuphi (elder and younger paternal aunts). She held me, gazing at me with a mother's love. I melted into loud sobs.

'*Mera beta, mera beta* (my son, my son),' she kept repeating, while I kept saying, '*Ammi, hum wapas aa gaye, Ammi hum zinda hai* (Ammi, I am back, I am alive).'

Even after we had gone inside, she kept crying. I had never seen my mother crying in my life, even when her husband, my father, had died. She had kept her tears in check then. When she married off her daughters, she was calm and composed. She used to say, 'I have to take care of six kids – I want them to be strong, stronger than me.' But today she was crying inconsolably. She kept saying '*Aa mere bete, mai tujhe kaleje mein chhupa loon* (Let me keep you hidden in my heart, my son).' She was holding me tight as if she feared that I would be lost again and unable to come back from prison. She said she used to worry that she would never see me again, that her son would be killed.

My aunts comforted her and gave us both water.

I had a similar reunion with Adeel bhai, who had made it his responsibility ever since my father died to look after us all, even though he is only two years older than me. So many people had come to greet me that it took more than an hour just for handshakes and hugs.

Tarique Anwar from NewsClick, Aishwarya Paliwal from Mirror Now, and Kamal Khan from NDTV talked to me. Adeel bhai appreciated the research they had done on the oxygen tragedy. When we were thus busy, Bhabhi handed me a bowl of the first thing I would eat after I coming home. Heavenly kheer!

This incredible reception charged me up and made me feel energetic, enthusiastic and happy.

By 1:30 a.m., most people had left. Only my close relatives and friends were still with me.

I finally sat down to have dinner with all of them. Mutton do pyaza, roast chicken, pulao and shirmal – every morsel tasted delicious. I took my time to enjoy every bite. My mother herself had cooked some of the dishes. As we ate, my family was talked about the reaction in the city, in UP, and in India. They marvelled at how everyone – across the political spectrum, across religions and castes – had expressed their happiness at my release. They noted how the same people who were earlier scared to be seen with them were now offering their unconditional support. I cherished most the details they shared about how the whole family had stood together like a rock and fought the propaganda, political games, administrative pressure, police interrogations and legal troubles. Each member of the family had played their part.

My wife was looking at me. She got up, with Zab in her arms, and said, 'I must put her to sleep. I am going up.' This made the rest of us begin clearing up, as we shared some laughs about the jokes people had cracked on social media about rumours of my plans after being released. I sat with my mother for some time. At 4 a.m., when I got up to go to bed, she said, 'Please have a bath before entering your room.'

I entered the bathroom that I had known since my childhood, but it seemed to have changed. It looked bigger, with its bathtub and shower. I took a long time to bathe, using soap, shampoo, conditioner, scrubbing my body hard in my attempt to wash off the smells of the barrack.

Then I put on a light kurta-pajama, offered shukrana namaz and went to my room.

It felt very strange to enter my room after all this time–a place so familiar, but it was as if I was seeing it after decades.

I could smell her perfume, but where was she?

I discovered the big surprise she had teased about. I was not expecting it at all. Our room had been decorated like it had been on the first day of our marriage and Shabista was wearing red bridal clothes and looking really beautiful.

It felt as if life had come full circle, but this time, for us to move ahead with much better prospects. In that moment, I realized how much I loved my life and my precious family.

21

A Shooting and Return to Jail

Even though I had such a warm homecoming, in some ways, it took me a while to truly return.

On the night after my release, I could not sleep in the comfort of my room. My bed felt unfamiliar. I went up to the rooftop and spent some time alone, breathing in the clear, fresh air, looking up at the sky and trying to come to my senses – that this was no prison. Then I came down and finally got some sleep.

I was woken up by a loud scream. It was Zab, frightened on finding herself next to a stranger sleeping in her bed. Shabista tried to console her, while I felt sheer agony at her not being able to recognize me, her own father, who now had long hair and a shaggy beard. It suddenly struck me – those months spent apart from her would never come back.

But soon after, when I had come down and had tea with my mother and Samar bhai, Adeel bhai called the barber and I was relieved of my nine-month-old beard and hair. Zab looked at me and said, '*Papa aa gaye* (Papa is back)!' and held out her little arms.

We got ready and went to my father's grave to offer *fatiha*. I thought of how much I missed my father, and how he had always wanted me and my brother to become doctors. 'I am glad you did not have to see me in prison, Abbu,' I said quietly. 'But I am sure you would have been proud of me.'

The next few days, my happy, smiling family gathered around me, doing their best to bring me back fully into their loving midst.

In those initial days after being back from prison, I used to get up at 5:30 every morning, a habit developed in Gorakhpur Jail. Even at night I would get up many times, imagining that a prison cop was calling me, or that someone was screaming or had put their arm or leg on my face. I would throw off the arm, realizing only a moment later that it was actually Zab. Sometimes I got off my bed and slept on the floor. I used to shiver when the AC was on, hearing people talking, coughing, making loud sounds right next to me, only to wake up and realize there was no one around.

All kinds of weird dreams haunted my nights. The judge had rejected my bail and I was going back to prison ... Shailesh was calling me for the counting ... Satish sir was saying, 'Don't go!' I would get up screaming and sweating bullets because I thought some prisoner was trying to kill me. Shabista would try to rescue me from these nightmares by talking softly to me and patting my head and shoulders. I would go to sleep holding her with one arm and Zab with the other. Then I would hear Dadhi Kaka's call, '*Mulakat, sun lo*!'

As soon as my eyes opened, unknowingly, unintentionally, I would walk out of my room like a zombie, and then realize that it is not the barrack, but my home, and go back again to bed. I left my slippers outside my room. When I needed to use the bathroom, a voice in my head would say, 'Join the queue!' At other times I would just run to the toilet and forget to latch the door. The luxury of having a bath for as long as I wanted felt very good, but I would begin washing my clothes immediately after, just like I did in prison. I had also begun to wash my plate after lunch and dinner.

I felt terribly hungry at 11 a.m. and 5 p.m., the lunch and dinner times in prison, and very sleepy and lethargic between noon and 3 p.m. In the evening, I sometimes heard prison cops calling my or some other inmate's name, saying '*Kal tumhari pesi hai* (Your attendance appearance is tomorrow)' or '*Rehai sun lo* (listen up, those who have got bail).'

My mother made all my favourite dishes – mutton, chicken, *bhindi, nenua*, roti, basmati rice, kheer. I ate a lot and laughed even more. Every day well-wishers visited. Slowly, after receiving a lot of love, I began regaining some normalcy.

I was considering all the things I would do. My first priority was to spend time with my family, then go back to working at the Nehru Hospital once I could return to the BRD Medical College. Then it hit me: What if the government did not reinstate me?

In fact, as events unfolded, not only was I not reinstated, but my family continued to be persecuted in many different ways.

By May 2018, the police had begun circling around us, once again, because I had been vocal, and people had shown me love and admiration in person as well as on social media. I would be asked to take selfies and shake hands with people when I went to the movies with my family, or even at department stores. The news channels and papers continued to discuss my unfair imprisonment, asking the underlying question as to who really was responsible for the Gorakhpur hospital tragedy.

With the cops asking my family questions once again, in the first week of May, we had to decide what to do. Our long ordeal had taught us that feeling scared and staying silent brought no rewards. So, we decided to go on the offence and hold a press conference in both Lucknow and Delhi, to apprise people of the current situation. At the conference, we asked for a CBI enquiry, or for an independent enquiry to be conducted into the circumstances of the children's deaths. I also revealed what I would do if the government did not reinstate me at the college. I hoped to set up a 500-bed charity hospital in Gorakhpur to battle the disease that is still a big threat to the lives of children in the poverty-stricken regions of eastern Uttar Pradesh and Bihar.

On 9 May 2018, at a conference moderated by Seema Mustafa, editor of *The Citizen*, I addressed the media at the Press Club of India. My declaration that 'I will not leave Gorakhpur. I will not leave India. This is my home, my soul resides here, in this soil,' drew huge applause.

I went to BRD Medical College on 19 May 2018 and met the new principal, Dr Ganesh Kumar. There I handed over a letter requesting the authorities to reinstate me and reminding them that the high court had cleared me of the charges of medical negligence and corruption. Then I went to Lucknow to meet the enquiry officer Himanshu Kumar, who was also the principal secretary of food protection and drug administration. He promised me a fair enquiry and said that he would finish it within a month.

The month of May brought news of the Nipah virus wreaking havoc in some parts of Kerala. I volunteered to go to Kerala to help the health administration, a decision that triggered opposition from the UP government who pointed out that I could not offer my services as a doctor anywhere else as long as I was an employee of this state government. I received a notice from the DGME asking for an explanation about my offer of help to Kerala.

But I was determined. I wanted to apply my knowledge and skills wherever they were needed most. The government was already not letting me return to BRD or releasing my salary arrears. What was I supposed to do?

In June, we got a frightening reminder of the kind of measures that could be unleashed on my family if I did not fall in line.

Early in the month, I had gone to an iftar party thrown by Ankit Saxena's father at his home in Delhi. Ankit was a young man who had been shot dead by the family members of the Muslim woman he loved, because they were opposed to an inter-religious match. His father's gesture of having an iftar function at his home was a clear indication that he did not want his son's death to be the cause of further hatred.

Soon after, I was invited to various universities, and by other organizations across India, and warmly welcomed and celebrated. With a few days remaining until Eid, I received my most precious gift – my sister Farro arrived home, and this completed my homecoming. Since I had come out of jail, my happiness had seemed hollow, as if something was missing. I had tried to identify the missing link but simply could not find it. The moment I saw her, I realized what it had been ... it was her that I had been missing so much. I hugged her immediately. She broke down, and so did I. Farro, my sister, my best friend, was finally home. Our family was finally doing all the things we were supposed to do in normal conditions – talking, laughing, going shopping for Eid together.

On 10 June 2018, I attended a conference on 'Encephalitis Control – Challenges and Solutions' organized by Dr Surheeta Karim of the All India Professional Congress (Gorakhpur Chapter), at Star Hospital. In the evening, Adeel bhai and I had gone to Kushinagar, for an iftar event hosted by an acquaintance Irfan Shaikh, where we were treated by all with great respect. We completed the *tarabi* namaz at Kushinagar's biggest mosque and got home by 10 p.m. I had gone to take a bath when I heard Adeel bhai scream, 'Kafeel, come out quickly!' I rushed out as fast as I could.

My brother Kashif had been shot, just 500 metres away from the Gorakhnath temple, a high secure area where the chief minister was staying.

The next few minutes passed in a blur. Utterly stunned, I drove with Adeel bhai to Star Hospital, where some people had taken Kashif. My hands trembled at the wheel. I sped down the streets, praying, '*Allah rehem*. Please let him live.' When we reached, Kashif was in the emergency ward and the medical officer at the hospital was recording it as a medico-legal case.

He was alive but screaming in pain.

There were two bullet holes in his neck, one on his right elbow and three on his chest – a bullet had pierced through one side of his chest to the other. The doctor on duty cleaned the wounds and put on a dressing. After that, I put in an IV line and started the fluids. An inspector from the Kotwali police station arrived and began taking notes. Dr Wajahat Kareem, the hospital's owner, had also arrived and, based on his advice, we got an urgent CT scan done, which showed one bullet stuck near Kashif's left carotid artery. My brother would have to undergo surgery on his neck so that it could be removed. The surgery was to be performed by the neurosurgeon Dr Ranvijay Dubey – he was around the same age as me and an acquaintance.

This is when things began to go further awry. The inspector from Kotwali had gone back and now returned with circle officer. This was the same man to whom the special task force had handed me over in the guest house at Shahjanwa, where he had mistreated me. A month later, around 28 July, a picture of him in uniform touching the chief minister Yogi Adityanath's feet would go viral.

'We have to take your brother to the district hospital, as this is a very high-profile medico-legal case,' he said.

'But let us remove the bullet from his neck. They were just going to operate,' I requested.

'No, he got shot near the Gorakhnath temple. As the CM is at the temple tonight, this is a major security breach. We have to follow all protocols.'

He was adamant, even though both Dr Ranvijay and I tried to explain the dangers in delaying the surgery.

We reached the district hospital at around 12:45 a.m., where Dr Ashwini Gupta, the doctor on duty, told us, 'It's an emergency – the bullet has to be removed immediately from the neck. We don't have any neurosurgeon available; you have to take him to the medical college.'

'I know there is no neurosurgeon there!' I said. 'And why should we go another twelve kilometres, when we have a neurosurgeon right here?' Yet the circle officer insisted that we take Kashif to BRD. The circle officer's phone rang continuously, and he talked in cryptic terms, 'Yes, sir, yes, sir, you don't worry.'

My brother was bleeding profusely. His vitals were dipping. I knew, as a doctor, that he could die anytime. I told the circle officer, 'I am not going to the medical college. I am taking my brother to Star Hospital.' He tried to stop us, and we had a heated argument. Some people had gathered by now and there was a mild scuffle between the cops and my well-wishers. I took the referral letter from the doctor on duty, put my brother in the ambulance and told the driver to drive as fast as possible to Star Hospital. We were zooming through the city streets with the cops chasing behind. They made it seem like we, and not Kashif's perpetrators, were the assailants.

We reached Star Hospital, where about twenty-five policemen from different police stations were waiting for us – the superintendent of police was also present. He said that my brother could be treated only in a government hospital. I resisted, after which they took Dr Wajahat Kareem into a closed-door meeting. When they came out, Dr Kareem told us to go to the medical college, as the police were insisting. Dr Ranvijay Dubey said he would come with me, but I refused. 'Why should we go there when we know there is no neurosurgeon, the road is bad, and it is over twelve kilometres away?'

They did not listen to me and put my brother back in the ambulance. I jumped inside. My mind was racing. I gave Kashif fluids and noticed that his pulse was becoming feeble. He had stopped crying in pain and was now slipping into a coma as he had lost a great deal of blood. Feeling incredibly worried, I screamed at the cops to stop, but they were in no mood to listen. The ambulance was being escorted by four or five police jeeps carrying the station house officer, circle officer, superintendent of police and some twenty-five cops.

I called Adeel bhai and told him about the situation. He asked me to send pictures that he could forward to people in Delhi.

Within minutes, it had become national news and was flashing on TV. 'The brother of Dr Kafeel, accused in the BRD oxygen tragedy, has been shot where the CM was staying.'

It was a rollercoaster ride to BRD Medical College as the road was in a bad state. The only good thing was that there wasn't much traffic, and the speeding cops got us to BRD at around 2 a.m. The police superintendent explained to the medical officer on duty that there were orders from above for Kashif to be treated only at this hospital.

'Sir, but we don't have a neurosurgeon,' said the medical officer, 'and the surgeon will only be available in the morning. Right now, we can't do anything. There was no need for a second medico-legal examination, as the necessary formalities had already been carried out.'

To this, the superintendent replied, 'Then refer him to Lucknow.'

'No, sir, if we do that, we will lose the patient. He is not in a position to go to Lucknow at this hour with a bullet stuck in his neck,' the medical officer confirmed.

When I heard him repeating what I already knew and had told the police, somehow I mustered the courage to start shouting and arguing with the cops. 'If you won't allow us to go, I am going to start a *dharna*!' I told them. The circle officer came running to the superintendent, saying, 'Sir, you have a call.' He took the handset and said to the person on the other side, 'Yes, sir, yes, sir, okay, sir.'

Suddenly, his attitude changed. 'Okay, you can take your brother wherever you want,' the superintendent said. I felt furious but controlled my anger. I just took my brother and left immediately. Reporters began following us trying to get a sound bite. I did not speak to any of them. On the way, I gave Kashif painkillers and kept up the fluids. I started him on inotropes dopamine dobutamine, kept a resuscitation kit ready, and began giving him oxygen. I was also monitoring his condition. He received at least four litres of normal saline and Ringer lactate fluids. I called Dr Kareem and requested him to prepare the operation theatre.

By the time we reached, Kashif's wife Khalida had come with my bhabhi. She was crying inconsolably. I assured her that nothing would happen, even though I was quaking on the inside. Dr Ranvijay was feeling confident. 'Give me ten minutes, just ten minutes,' he said. But he was fast – he removed the bullet in just six. It was like magic.

This urgent surgery which should have been done by 10:30 p.m. could only be performed at 2:30 a.m. Four golden hours had been lost, and we had no answer as to why the police had delayed us so much, only to agree to let us go to a private hospital in the end. Despite the numerous unnecessary obstacles, my brother Kashif survived the attack.

Ammijan woke up around 3:30 a.m. Every day, she used to get up at the same time and call everyone for *sehri*.

On that particular morning, she was surprised to find everyone missing. *Are they still sleeping?* she thought. She went up to find my nephew Ab sleeping and Bhabhi and Adeel bhai missing. She went to Kashif's room, and both Kashif and Khalida were missing as well. She knocked on Shabista's door and asked 'Where is Kafeel?' Shabista was wide awake, watching TV. In tears, she said, 'Ammijan, everyone is at Star Hospital.' Then she told my mother everything.

My mom was stunned, but she is a strong woman. She promptly put on her burqa and left the house. After walking alone in the night for a couple of kilometres, she found a rickshaw and reached Star Hospital just after 4 a.m. There, she did not ask anyone anything, but went straight to the ICU. She put a few drops of water on Kashif's lips and sat there. She prayed, got up, offered fajr, and gave an interview to all the major news channels whose reporters had been waiting outside. 'Enough is enough,' she said to the media. 'Stop haunting my family. Give us security. My whole family may be in danger, but we are not cowards.'

The same thought echoing in my mind, I heard an inner voice say clearly, 'I won't bend.'

An FIR was filed against 'unknown assailants' who had shot at my brother from a scooter and fled. On 29 June, after Kashif had been discharged from hospital, Adeel bhai met the CM in the janta darbar at Gorakhpur and complained about police laxity. This became big news, after which he spoke to a few reporters.

A few days later, we learnt that an FIR had been filed the very next day after Adeel bhai's meeting with the CM at the janta darbar. This FIR, registered at the Kotwali police station, was based on an allegation that he had opened a bank account in 2009 using fake documents.

Meanwhile, I started conducting free medical camps for poor and marginalized children – something that gives me the greatest joy.

On 10 August 2018, the first anniversary of the BRD oxygen tragedy, my call to light a candle by the Mahatma Gandhi statue in Gorakhpur, in memory of the children who had lost their lives, saw thousands of people gather. This threw the local administration in a panic, and I was stopped by the police on the way to the venue.

The following day, I observed the BRD oxygen tragedy anniversary in my own way through a free health camp at Piprauli in Gorakhpur district, where 182 poor children were examined and treated.

Three days later, on 14 August 2018, a Right to Information enquiry revealed how the government had tried to cover up serious lapses. A news article about it on *The Logical Indian* read:

> The response to an RTI filed by an activist regarding the infamous Gorakhpur hospital tragedy of 2017 has revealed that there was indeed a shortage of oxygen cylinders on the fateful night of August 11, 2017, due to which 63 children died in BRD Medical College Hospital.
>
> This report indicates that a cover-up of the case had taken place and that Dr Kafeel Khan, who had tried to arrange for the cylinders on his own and managed to save a few lives, was wrongly implicated ...
>
> The response to the RTI filed by a Lucknow activist, Sanjay Sharma, dated April 19, 2018, has cleared up the debate surrounding the legitimacy of Dr Kafeel's claims. The response clearly shows that the hospital had acquired six oxygen cylinders from Anandlok Nursing Home in Gorakhpur, and Dr Kafeel had arranged cylinders on August 11, 2017. The contradiction between the claims by the UP government and their reply to the RTI implies that the several investigative probes conducted by the state government into the matter were complete failures.

The CM responded to the news on 26 August, saying, the issue of deaths at BRD hospital had been 'blown out of proportion due to internal politics at the hospital' and 'there was no shortage of oxygen'. The next day, I called his statement 'incorrect'. If the entire episode had been about 'internal politics' and 'there was no shortage of oxygen', why did we languish in prison for close to a year?

By now, I was regularly getting invited to events across the country where I spoke to students at schools and colleges – these activities had been noted by the authorities. But I continued to conduct free medical camps all over India. This had become the means for me to find inner peace. When I spend time with children, when I treat them, meet their parents and give them advice about their children's health, when I teach them good practices, make health bulletin videos, successfully treat a child suffering from a severe disease, I feel satisfied and am able to sleep well at night. The health camps in Kushinagar, Khalilabad and Maharajganj brought me back into the midst of some of the children and families who had been in the wards on that fateful night in August 2017. I had not forgotten them, even though the authorities had not reinstated me at BRD.

In between camps, I had to go to court and appear before the enquiry committee. Before Himanshu Kumar, I asked that the ex-principal Dr Rajiv Mishra, Dr Bhupendra Sharma, Dr Mahima Mittal and the DGME be cross-examined. I pointed out the CM's statement that internal politics at BRD had fuelled the controversy. In fact, the CM had said that no deaths had been caused by a shortage of oxygen and that there had been no oxygen shortage at all at the hospital. I filed a counterclaim, enclosing the affidavit the government had filed with the Allahabad High Court, accepting there was a shortage. Parents who had lost their little children now started speaking to the media about those deadly fifty-four hours. Providing my own documents and testimony was like disturbing a hornets' nest. There were bound to be painful repercussions.

Soon, I began receiving death threats from anonymous sources on the phone.

'*Ab teri bari hai, bachega nahi ab tu* (It's your turn now. You cannot escape).'

Undeterred, I submitted an application to the SSP for an investigation before resuming treating underprivileged patients.

Alongside these attempts, from July to August 2018, I was beginning to see the worst effects of the persecution unleashed against me since the BRD tragedy on my family. The bad times just seemed to go on and on. That summer, we spent every day in fear, wondering if Adeel bhai would be arrested, or if someone would attack our family. The children had stopped laughing and playing. The house remained silent as if no one lived there. Ammijan fell sick, and once she took to her bed, she could not get up for the next few months.

People started avoiding us again. The business ground to a halt. Adeel bhai's suppliers stopped giving him any goods, and distributors stopped picking up products from him. Those who had already picked up goods from him stopped making payments. People began to look at us with pity. Meanwhile, we followed whatever advice we received from advocates and well-wishers.

As ordinary, educated, rule-abiding citizens, we were new to this kind of vicious politics. We didn't know the police could be so merciless, and people could carry so much hate on the basis of religion. Every day brought a new experience, most of them negative. So many people were trying to exploit us. One camp was provoking us to continue the fight, another was calling us mad, a third wanted money, and yet another just watched and laughed at us.

Our family's financial crisis deepened, and we started selling things we owned to survive. To pay our electricity bills, phone bills, school fees, grocers and general merchants, and the salaries of our staff. Adeel bhai sold all his pickup vans one by one. The Innova he had bought only two years ago was sold for just ₹5 lakh. He cut down his expenses.

Yet another realization for us was the importance of money. The battle we were fighting required huge amounts of it. Every professional who helped us in our fight had to be paid something. Every process in the courts came with a price tag – we paid for stamp papers, registration fees, lawyers' fees. Our home electricity supply was cut due to arrears on bills. Every day, the only discussions we had at home were about how to cut down further on our expenses. Our creditors were at our doorstep. Banks put up a notice to auction Parveen Plaza and the only other piece of land we had. A shopping complex with a hundred-odd shops, the plaza had been built by my father and named after my mother, Nuzhat Parveen. After his death in 2003, while all of us were studying, this had been the only source of income for the family besides the pension.

After the cars and pickups had been sold, it was the motorcycles' turn to be disposed of. Finally, we had to mortgage Ammijaan, Shabista, my bhabhi, Zeenat and even Farro's jewellery. It was humiliating, but we had no other option. Severely cash-strapped, we were flailing about when Bilal Zaidi of Our Democracy came to our aid with a crowd-funding campaign on Ketto. The target was ₹20 lakh over sixty days, but ₹22 lakh came pouring in within three days.

On the one hand, I was immensely grateful so many people believed in our struggle and were opposed to the treatment we had received. On the other, I began getting criticism from many people too, that those who once travelled in Fortuners and Innovas were now reduced to taking money from others. Some of the resentment against us was also due to the fact that organizations and NGOs had approached us to join their cause, and we had turned them down.

While my whole family believed that Allah had given us this opportunity to be known and loved so that we could better serve humanity, we wanted to do just that, instead of becoming brand ambassadors for any one cause or group.

Now, the cops started harassing the whole family. They took us to the police station, and kept us there till the evening, raided Adeel bhai's office and our home, and took away his papers, computers, laptops and mobiles.

Whether it was the oxygen tragedy, or the attack on Kashif, the message seemed to be: Keep quiet and don't question anything, or your hardships will continue.

September 2018 saw disastrous floods wreak havoc in Kerala. I travelled to the state and worked at health camps in the Thrissur, Wayanad and Kozhikode districts for a week. The conditions I saw in the Dalit basti I visited, with a high prevalence of tuberculosis and alcoholism among adults, and rampant malnutrition in the children, affected me terribly. Why should people have to live in such abject conditions seventy years after Independence? I made a request to the government to pay special attention to the adivasis living in abject poverty and suffering from poor health. I expressed my worries about the third of the state's population – people who were struggling to return to their lives after the floods because they are socially and economically many leagues behind their fellow citizens.

I returned home to find that more than seventy children had died within one month at the district hospital in Bahraich in Uttar Pradesh. The government was calling the cause of the deaths a 'mystery illness'. The opposition parties and local citizens were outraged. I suspected encephalitis to be the cause behind the deaths. I decided to put together a fact-finding team of doctors and head to Bahraich. I called a few doctors I knew, and several agreed.

A local doctor put me in touch with the chief medical officer at Bahraich, Dr Pandey, who agreed to our visit. On 21 September 2018, I announced on social media that I would be going there with a few other doctors.

We left in the morning. Even before we reached, while we were still on the way, we got the news that Dr Pandey had been transferred, and another doctor, Dr Singh, had replaced him. I immediately called Dr Pandey to verify this. He said, 'Don't worry, he will be in charge only from Monday.' I called the doctor who had introduced me to Dr Pandey, and he, too, told me that he had spoken to the CMO and we should go ahead. But something seemed suspicious.

Next, the circle officer for Bahraich called, and asked me where I was. I told him we would reach by the afternoon but did not give him my exact location. We got a call from a local politician warning us not to come. Finally, someone from Gorakhpur police station called to warn us to not go any further as the superintendent of police was apparently planning to arrest my brother and me.

We reached Bahraich in the afternoon. Some local doctors were waiting for us. We first visited the OPD and asked the doctor on duty to give us permission to meet the patients' parents. On talking to the parents, I found that all those who had arrived with a history of fever and seizures, and in an unconscious state, were symptomatic of Acute Encephalitis Syndrome.

The hospital staff told me, 'The parents are poor, sir. When we refer them far away to Lucknow, they don't go. And as we don't have ventilators or a good ICU facility, these kids are dying.'

The picture was becoming clear to me ...

We were preparing our report and were going to address a press conference, when suddenly a few cops arrived and took me into custody. Apparently, the doctor in charge of the paediatrics ward had lodged a complaint that I had created a ruckus in the PICU and had attempted to forcibly treat patients, even though I had not entered the PICU at all and he was not at the hospital when we reached.

Due to this incident, a second suspension order was passed against me on 31 July 2019 on charges of 'forcibly treating patients and criticizing government policies'. After two years of endless enquiries, the honourable Allahabad High Court stayed that suspension on 9 September 2021.

That day, from the hospital, I was taken by the police to a guest house on the outskirts of Bahraich. There, a magistrate came to record my statement and served me a challan under Section 151 of the IPC. But they did not release me. They said they were waiting for the release order. When the sub-divisional magistrate (SDM) issued my released order, they still seemed hesitant to release me so the SDM got angry and left.

The local policemen then took me to another town, in another car with some plainclothesmen inside. From there to another car, and so on, for the next sixteen hours. They shifted me from place to place after taking my phone and not allowing me to contact my family.

I couldn't shake off the feeling that I might die in a fake encounter in the darkness of the night. I was told that I would be freed at around 4 p.m., after the CM had left the city. Then I was finally brought back to Gorakhpur and handed over to the Gorakhpur police. I argued many times, 'Why are you not letting me go when the SDM has ordered my release?' I was held in a room at the Bichia police station on the outskirts of Gorakhpur.

Once the CM had left Gorakhpur, I was taken to Cantonment police station and told to sign a few papers, which I refused to do. When they took me away for a medical examination, I was shocked to see Adeel bhai in the room. 'What are you doing here?' I asked him incredulously.

Adeel bhai was nervous and scared. He said that he had been arrested in the same forgery case for which an FIR had been filed in June. 'But why has my name been added?' I asked. Adeel bhai said, 'That is because they had to suddenly change their plans after the Bahraich SDM gave you bail.'

I was aghast at the kind of absurd allegations that had been brought up. But as I have heard the police say themselves, it was up to the accused to go to court and prove the allegations wrong. Until such time, they would have to stay in jail. This awful absurdity is the reality, whether you like it or not.

While coming back after our medical examination, we were surrounded by reporters.

Adeel bhai shouted, 'This is true anarchy! They are framing us using false, baseless charges.'

'This is the punishment for speaking the truth – we are living under an undeclared Emergency,' I said.

After that we were taken to court. The magistrate was in his chamber. The inspector of the Cantonment police station went inside the chamber and returned after ten minutes. I told him angrily, 'Sir, please allow us an advocate or at least listen to our arguments.' But all we got was fourteen days' judicial custody.

I was back at the same gate out of which I had emerged just five months ago. This time I was enraged, not sad, and more determined than ever to keep fighting.

22

On the Road to Health for All

My second stint in jail reunited me with Shailesh and some other friends. It also resulted in Mantri-ji repeating one of his favourite lines, '*Suraj par thookoge to girega tumhare hi upar, patthar se takraoge to phootega sir tumhara hi* (If you spit at the sun, the spit will ultimately drop on your face, if you dash against a rock, it is your head that will break).' I took it all in my stride. This time it was my brother Adeel who was feeling as tormented and anguished as I had the last time. I was comparatively much calmer. Thankfully, Adeel bhai was granted bail after about a month. I underwent a longer imprisonment and returned home in time for Diwali on 3 November 2018. Even though the local administration submitted an affidavit stating that a grave law-and-order situation could be created if I were to be released before Diwali, the judge declared, 'You are wasting the court's time with these baseless cases.'

While walking out of prison a second time, I made a few promises to myself:

'*Darna ata nahi,*
Chahe jitna bhi dara lein,
Uthenge har bar ek nayee takat se,
Chahe jitna jhuka lein.'

(I don't know how to feel scared,
However much they may try to scare me,
I will rise every time with a new strength,
However much they try to make me bend and kneel.)

My son was born in February 2019, and my brother Kashif also became a father to a son in March 2019. There was good news for us on the family front, although our financial troubles continued. This entire period was yet another emotional rollercoaster. My mind was racing a mile a minute, and my heart was pacing to its limits, but an inner voice kept reminding me, 'You are on the right path,' even though it was a very tough time, with my family under attack and no significant support from any quarter.

I decided to move court, asking for a speedy conclusion to the enquiry being conducted into the allegations against me at BRD.

On 7 March 2019, the Allahabad High Court ordered the Uttar Pradesh government to conclude my departmental enquiry within ninety days on my writ to revoke my suspension. It was not a good order, as it had already been eighteen months since the enquiry had begun. According to the rules, any departmental enquiry should not last longer than ninety days. And this is why I decided to move the Supreme Court.

On 10 May 2019, a division bench comprising Justice Sanjay Kishan Kaul and Justice Indira Banerjee ordered the timely conclusion of the enquiry regarding my suspension and directed that my dues be cleared – finally providing a huge relief to us financially. After this, I started receiving half of my salary from the government. I was also paid half of my salary that had accrued over the past twenty-four months.

The apex court had upheld the order of the high court. The latter also asked me to approach the apex court again, should the state government not follow the order of the high court in letter and in spirit. I was represented pro bono by the senior advocate Meenakshi Arora while the advocate-on-record (AOR) was Fuzail Ahmad Ayyubi. Advocate Ibad Mustaq helped me with drafting and filing the writ.

By now I had completely devoted myself to the mission of bringing health and hope to the poorest amongst us. With this motivation and the assistance of Samar bhai and some friends, I launched Health for All on 7 February 2019 in Hyderabad. Through my work in health camps in Assam, Muzaffarpur, the areas around Gorakhpur and even in Kerala, it became clear to me that those who are in the greatest need of healthcare have the least access to it. Health for All was going to be my attempt to fix a broken healthcare system, into which the Gorakhpur oxygen tragedy provided only a brief albeit brutal peek.

Even while I was travelling to different places for free medical camps, I finished writing the second edition of the *Manipal Manual of Clinical Paediatrics* and submitted it to the publisher. My days were becoming hectic, but I was running again with full zeal and enthusiasm. In between, I had to visit the Gorakhpur district court or the Bahraich district court every fourteen days, for my pesi, just to sign documents. Every other week, I had to shuttle between Allahabad and Lucknow to meet advocates or appear before the court.

In June 2019, there was an outbreak of AES in Muzaffarpur and the adjoining districts in Bihar, which resulted in the death of more than 300 children. Immediately people from many NGOs started calling me.

As a doctor, I knew the symptoms well, Whether it is UP's 'Japani bukhar' and 'nawki bimari', Kerala's 'Nipah virus encephalitis', Bihar's 'chamki bimari' or Assam and Bengal's 'moshtishko jor', that is, brain fever, they all indicate AES.

I went to Muzaffarpur with a team of four doctors, eight nursing staff, two pharmacists and some volunteers. We left Gorakhpur with a few cartons of medicines in mid-June. Upon reaching, I was horrified to see the conditions in the hospital. It was the same as BRD Medical College. The Shri Krishna Medical College and Hospital, the only medical college in the area, caters to the whole of northern Bihar.

The paediatric ward was a small hall containing more than 100 children and 200 relatives. In June, the hottest month of the year, with the temperature soaring to forty-five degrees, and no fans or windows, the packed hall was so stuffy that it felt like I could not breathe. There were only two junior doctors and four nurses. Two to three children were lying in each bed, with IV fluid bottles strung by a rope. Some children were lying on the floor. It was total chaos. It struck me that *even the Gorakhpur Jail hall was in a better state.* The so-called eight-bed ICU was not fit to be called an ICU.

Most of the parents had brought their kids from distant villages, often travelling for hours and, by the time they reached the emergency ward of the hospital, half of them would be declared 'brought dead'. Private hospitals were too few and too costly. The primary health centres, which allows the first contact between doctors and these villagers, were in complete disarray. They were like white elephants, working only on paper. So-called doctors without any formal training were taking care of 78 per cent of the population's health.

The whole area is behind by decades in terms of everything – health, education, industry, transport; even electricity is a privilege. Numerous people in the state, as in many Indian states, struggle to get two meals a day.

I found more than half of the children to be malnourished, stunted, and every other female was anaemic. The lack of facilities for safe drinking water, the poor hygiene, the hot and humid climate, lack of awareness, poor vaccination coverage and open-field defecation made it very easy for the spread of the deadly AES virus.

The general elections held in May 2019 had contributed to a spurt in cases. While all of India was busy with elections, Bihar's vaccination and awareness programme got derailed. Local people blamed it on lychee toxins. This theory gained currency as Bihar is the largest producer of lychees. The children of parents working in the fields often eat unripe lychees, which contain toxins like methylene cyclopropyl ascetic acid and hypoglycin A. These cause hypoglycemia, and hypoglycaemia, in turn, induces seizures and brain swelling. But it seemed that the same seven 'P's as in the Gorakhpur AES cases were playing a role here.

The promise of a virology centre and a 100-bed encephalitis treatment centre by the then union health minister, Dr Harsh Vardhan, during the last spurt of AES in 2015, had never materialized. He repeated this promise again in 2019, during his visit to the same hospital.

I spent the next two months in Muzaffarpur and its adjoining areas. With the help of local people, especially Zafer Alam, the vice president of Insaf Manch, I treated more than 10,000 children. More than 'chamki bukhar', common diseases were affecting children. There were numerous cases of diarrhoea, pneumonia, skin diseases and ear and eye diseases. Girls were affected more than boys. I even found that hernia and vitiligo were considered normal.

I saw severe cases of scabies that had disfigured the face of the child, as well as children losing their hearing because of frequent ear discharge and subsequent negligence. I realized many patients were told that treatable diseases like nephrotic syndrome, bronchial asthma, cardiac valve defects, infective endocarditis and juvenile rheumatoid arthritis were incurable. I found every second child to have rampant dental caries, extensive pyoderma, dermatitis and fungal lesions.

Many mothers complained that their child was getting a typhoid fever every ten to fifteen days. I asked them how they measured the child's temperature. 'We know when their head is warm, or their palm or soles feeler warmer than usual,' was the common reply. I told them that due to high basal metabolic rate (BMR), their body temperature is higher than ours. So, temperature was best measured by a thermometer. Soon we started distributing thermometers to each household.

The parents would complain that their child's liver was weak. When asked how they knew, they would say, 'S/he passes stool after each feed.' I explained that this is the gastrocolic reflex, particularly in babies and infants. A child's digestive system is such that whenever s/he eats, a signal goes down to empty the already digested food.

Hypothyroidism results in short stature. We could see it in the children there – some of them were the textbook definition of a coarse face, a history of constipation, weight gain and stunting. Medicines for these issues cost just a few rupees. By just giving a child thyroxin tablets daily, you can change their life. But there is no doctor to diagnose the condition, and no one to treat it. I once asked a local practitioner, '*Bachchon mein bhi thyroid hota hai?* (Do children also get thyroid?)' to which he laughed. In the same way, the people of the village asked me, '*Bachchon mein bhi BP hota hai?* (Do children also have BP issues?)' when I was checking the blood pressure of a six-year-old child. I had to tell them that children could also be hypertensive and diabetic.

There were so many cases of mental illness – the

common belief was that '*Atma aa gayee hai* (a spirit has entered the body).'

Many teenage and adolescent girls came with complaints of abdominal pain, headaches, backaches, fainting episodes and increased breathing. The most common cause I found was the huge number of restrictions put on them by parents, relatives and neighbours. There were so many cases of seizures – not all caused by 'chamki bukhar' but because the dosage of medicines had not been given according to the child's weight and age. Once the child had seizures, they would face social stigma.

Developmental delays were common, as were cases of cerebral palsy due to complications during labour. The worst was their acceptance of diseases preventable by vaccines. Mumps, measles, chicken pox, hepatitis A and pertussis were considered routine – they would not even approach a doctor for any of these problems – many preferred local '*jhaad phoonk*' or occult practices as a remedy. Going to a doctor was thought to be a costly affair. The local doctors had never even used vaccines which were now available against pneumococcal bacteria, typhoid, human papillomavirus and rotavirus diarrhoea. I had to deworm every child, as the most common complaint was worms in the stool. Menstruating girls were considered impure and disallowed from entering the kitchen, taking baths, touching pickles or going to school, and had to use pieces of dirty old clothes as menstrual napkins. I counselled them day and night to help them shed these old customs.

My daily routine was to get ready by 6 a.m., go to a village and spread awareness among the people. Our awareness programme covered AES – what was chamki bukhar, what were its signs and symptoms, how they could measure fever, what to do if the child was having seizures, and vaccination and diet advice. By 10 a.m., we would start a medical camp in another village – in a school or at the village centre. Lunch was at 4 p.m. By 7 p.m., we would go to yet another village, attend their *chaupal* (public space) and raise more awareness. By the time we reached our rooms at 10–11 p.m., we were so tired that we slept the moment we hit our beds. It was so hectic, but just as satisfying.

We donated blood when required, we skipped lunch if needed, we slept on a *charpai* when nothing else was available, we travelled by auto, bus or truck when we had to, and we walked miles in the scorching sun when there was no public transport. I do not know how Allah gave me so much energy that I wanted to work round the clock to allay the suffering of these innocent children. Gradually, more medical activists joined us, and when I appealed on social media for medicines, I had never imagined the response we received. People sent medicines from Bangalore, Calcutta, Ahmedabad and Delhi. One well-to-do lady was so moved by my video that she asked her manager to fly over to us with several boxes of medicines.

In August 2019, Assam saw devastating floods – usually an annual occurrence. After the water subsided, it left in its wake all types of infectious diseases like cholera, malaria, skin issues, hepatitis, eye diseases, ear infection, and many other ailments. I went with an organization's medical services team to Assam by train. In this state, many people live on islands in the Brahmaputra that lack basic facilities. There is no safe water supply, no electricity, and boats are the only means of transport. We found that, due to the floods, the primary health centres were shut, schools had been destroyed and communities hit hard.

We conducted several medical camps. We went from village to village by boat and stayed on various different islands. We took baths in the open, defecated in fields, washed our clothes by the lake or riverside, and ate fish and rice. It was sultry, with no electricity, but it was satisfying. I enjoyed the natural surroundings, drinking tea in the rain and walking for miles with the local people. We were accepted warmly by the locals. In the evenings we sang and danced, though I felt a pang on missing Zab's birthday, on 24 August, for the third consecutive year.

The next month, in September 2019, I continued hosting free medical camps in different parts of India. We went wherever there was a calamity – floods, cyclones, disease outbreaks.

But what about the case against me? While I was glad to be of service to these people, I wondered if I would ever be reinstated as a doctor at the BRD Medical College. While I had no answer to this conundrum, the contrast between me and my fellow accused in the oxygen tragedy was self-explanatory. They spent a longer duration in jail and got bail months after my bail order. At the time of writing, all the doctors, accountants and the pharmacists got their jobs back at the hospital, although the enquiry into their purported involvement would continue. Dr Rajiv Mishra, Dr Poornima Shukla and Gajanand Jaiswal retired after serving for a few months. Dr Satish Kumar went on to become the HOD of the Department of Anaesthesia and the accountants got their respective posts back as well. Since 2018, Inox Air Products has started directly supplying liquid oxygen to the BRD Medical College.

I am the only one of the nine accused who was terminated from their position, despite being cleared by not one but several enquiry committees:

- District magistrate, Gorakhpur, Uttar Pradesh, submitted a report on 12 August 2017.
- Central Government Health Ministry enquiry, headed by Professor (Dr) Harish Chellani and head of Vardhman Mahavir Medical College, Safdarjung Hospital, submitted a report on 14 August 2017.

- Commissioner, Gorakhpur zone, Uttar Pradesh, submitted a report on 16 August 2017.
- The SG-PGIMS, Lucknow team, headed by Professor (Dr) Hem Chandra, medical superintendent and head hospital administration, SG-PGIMS, Lucknow, submitted a report on 18 August 2017.
- High court-initiated enquiry submitted in September 2017.
- Bal Ayog enquiry report on 9 November 2017.

Although I was promised the departmental enquiry would be concluded early, it kept getting delayed.

On 20 December 2018 and then 17 April 2021, I wrote to the chief minister of Uttar Pradesh, asking him to reinstate me.

Meanwhile, through the RTI reports and the chargesheet submitted by the investigation officer, we collected vital important information that I submitted during the enquiry.

- Dr Bhupendra Sharma, associate professor of the paediatrics department, had been the officer-in-charge of AES from 11 May 2016. We also submitted a copy of the RTI reply along with the principal's order dated 11 May 2016.
- There was a shortage of liquid oxygen for fifty-four hours at the BRD Medical College from 10–12 August 2017, and I had indeed arranged jumbo oxygen cylinders to save many children from dying.
- Twenty-three children and eighteen adults died on 10 August 2017.
- I was on leave on 10 August – a copy of my leave letter and attendance register were submitted as proof.
- I was appointed on 8 August 2016 as a lecturer on probation for two years. I had no financial and

administrative responsibilities. [Towards the end of 2016, I was appointed as a nodal officer with the NRHM, but even that didn't entail any such responsibilities.]

- Pushpa Sales had written fourteen letters to the authorities demanding a payment of their dues of ₹68 lakh, including letters to the CM and the health minister of UP.
- The honourable Allahabad High Court, in a judgement dated 30 April 2018, observed that there was a shortage of liquid oxygen due to the abrupt disruption of liquid oxygen supply, which took place due to non-payment of dues to the supplier.
- An affidavit filed by the UP government in Allahabad in March 2018 had accepted that there was a shortage of oxygen supply.
- I was in no way involved in the tender/supply/payment/order/maintenance of either liquid oxygen or jumbo oxygen cylinders.
- The SSB accepted that I did come on 11 August 2017 asking for help, and they had provided their vehicle and their soldiers, who worked for two days ferrying oxygen cylinders to BRD Medical College.
- My call records from 10–11 August revealed that I had called twenty-six people, including the HOD, principal, acting principal, Balwant, junior , the SIC, the CMS, the DM, the CMO, the AD health, gas suppliers and other hospitals.
- The purchase receipts of the jumbo cylinders I had paid for.
- The honourable Allahabad High Court, in its order dated 25 April 2018, made certain important observations and stated that there was no material on record which could establish medical negligence against me individually. Further, the high court

also concurred that I was not said to be part of the tender process that result in the enlistment of the entity which was charged with the supply of medical oxygen. Additionally, the high court also observed that the charges under Section 7/13 of the Prevention of Corruption Act, 1988, against me had been dropped in the course of the investigation.

- The Allahabad High Court, in an order dated 7 March 2019 in the matter of WRIT-A No-3511, directed the disciplinary authority to endeavour to conclude the enquiry with expedition and preferably within a period of three months.
- The Supreme Court said the same thing in their order dated 10 May 2019.

Finally, after the high court and Supreme Court orders, enquiry officer and principal secretary Himanshu Kumar concluded his enquiry on 15 April 2019, which stated that the following:

- I was the junior-most doctor in the paediatrics department. I had joined BRD Medical College Gorakhpur on 8 August 2016 as a lecturer under probation.
- Despite being on leave on 10 August 2017, I had rushed to the Nehru Hospital on that fateful night and tried to save every innocent life possible. I and my team managed to arrange 500 cylinders in those fifty-four hours.
- I called twenty-six people that night, including all the officials of BRD Medical College and the district magistrate of Gorakhpur.
- There is no evidence to suggest my involvement in corruption.
- I was not responsible for the payment/order/tender/ maintenance of the oxygen supply.

- I was not the head of the encephalitis ward.
- There is no evidence that I was engaged in private practice after 8 August 2016.
- The charges of medical negligence levelled against me had been found to be baseless and without any substance.

Even though the enquiry committee submitted its report in April 2019, in my opinion, it was not released due to fear of backlash in the Lok Sabha elections held in May 2019. In September 2019, Himanshu Kumar's enquiry report was made public.

It is barely possible to describe how my family and I felt after the two long years of blame, harassment and persecution that had gravely tarnished our reputation.

I was of course elated beyond belief. It was the good news that my whole family had prayed and waited for throughout the course of this long ordeal. As the announcement of the report's findings began to come out, there was an eruption of joyous celebration within my family. My brave and strong mother, who had never let her sons down, was visibly proud, and said with great dignity, 'I never lost hope that your innocence will be proved. When my son has done no wrong, why is there even a question of punishment?' I fell to my knees, and she hugged me close. It was the biggest blessing I had received – that my mother never once lost faith in her son's integrity.

In my excitement I hugged Shabista so hard that she screamed, and Zab and Zain, my son, started crying due to all the noise. Bhabhi and Khalida stuffed sweets into my mouth. Zeenat cried, Samar bhai sang. Farro and Ahmar bhai celebrated in Oman. Adeel bhai hugged me, his eyes wet with tears. 'Kafeel, we won. We won!' he said.

Kashif, who had paid a bloody price after our family was targeted, ran and brought home sweets and crackers.

Soon our house was full of visitors, relatives and, yes, even reporters. It was a magnificent celebration, the spirit of which spread across India and beyond, with people distributing sweets, bursting crackers, dancing and hugging one another. The media broke the news under large headlines: 'Dr Kafeel Khan Jailed Over UP Child Deaths Cleared.'

Many prominent journalists apologized to me, after the enquiry report became public, for their earlier stories in August 2017 showing me in a negative light.

Actor and former BJP MP Paresh Rawal, who had tweeted about me on 14 August 2017, saying 'Yes, a hero but in the eyes of the termite clan,' again took to Twitter to express his apology. This time he said: 'There is no shame in apologizing when one is wrong…I apologise to @drkafeelkhan.'

Apart from my personal satisfaction at having my name cleared by the UP government's enquiry led by Himanshu Kumar, I was still concerned about the fact that the loose ends of the oxygen tragedy had not been properly tied up. Therefore, after my acquittal, I demanded that the following:

- The UP government should revoke my suspension at the earliest and give my job back with due respect and arrears.
- The BRD oxygen tragedy should be investigated by the CBI to rule out any complicity of state officials in these incidents.
- The UP government should publicly apologize to the grieving parents who lost their children and compensate them for their losses.

Immediately after the report became public, Himanshu Kumar went on a study leave only to return on 15 November 2021, after two years.

As for me, they suggested that out of four charges, two which alleged that I was practising medicine privately had been proved even though the enquiry report clearly mentioned that it was before I had joined BRD Medical College on 8 August 2016. Nonetheless, when that too failed, the government opened another enquiry. They suspended me again, stating that I was speaking against the government while still being a government employee. They also started an enquiry into the Bahraich incident.

I wondered how they could suspend me again when my previous suspension was still in place at the time.

In April 2021, a tsunami of deaths struck various parts of India in the form of the deadly second wave of the Covid-19 pandemic which exposed our country's already collapsed healthcare system. As I watched the people of my country grappling with a severe shortage of oxygen, I was haunted by a feeling of acute déjà vu ...

During this time, it occurred to Dr Harjit Singh Bhatti, me, and other similarly minded doctors and health activists that rural India must be in terrible shape if the big metros of Delhi, Bombay and Bangalore were reeling from the effects of the outbreak.

This is how Doctors on Road was initiated, after a visit to Valmiki Nagar, a suburban locality in Delhi, on 14 April 2021. We distributed masks, thermometers, oximeters and basic medicines, taught the people there Covid-appropriate behaviour and how to treat common diseases.

On 21 July 2021, Doctors on Road completed a hundred days of operations covering the states of Delhi, Haryana, Rajasthan, Punjab, Uttar Pradesh, Bihar, Jharkhand, West Bengal, Assam and Telangana.

When it comes to choosing the right path, I always listen to my heart. I take risks and push myself to the limit. Once I believe I have chosen the appropriate path, I leave things to Allah. If there is something that keeps me motivated, energized and determined to keep doing my best to ensure good health for the people of my country, and especially its children, it is the enduring love I have received from so many in my hour of need, a love that has only strengthened my resolve to continue serving as a doctor and a citizen, against all odds.

EPILOGUE

A Doctor and a Citizen

My transformation from being a relatively privileged, nonchalant person to one who is intensely concerned about the welfare of my fellow humans has been described in some detail in this book. It has been four long years since the events of that night in August 2017 that triggered my ordeal and resulted in my growth – as a doctor, a citizen and a human being.

The most important thing I have learnt from this journey is that the way forward for me will be filled with obstacles. It continues to trouble me that the real culprits in the BRD hospital tragedy continue to roam free, while my torment goes on, and the parents who lost their children still await justice.

On 29 January 2020, I was arrested a third time under the National Security Act (NSA) based on the allegation that I had given an inflammatory speech at Aligarh Muslim University against the draconian and discriminatory Citizenship Amendment Act, passed by the central government in December 2019. This time I remained behind bars for seven months. On 1 September 2021, the charges were quashed by the Allahabad High Court as well as the Supreme Court of India, which called the whole process illegal. The order by an Allahabad High Court division bench of Chief Justice Govind Mathur and Justice Saumitra Dayal Singh observed: 'A complete reading of the speech prima facie does not disclose any effort to promote hatred or violence ... The address gives a call for national integrity and unity among the citizens.'

But my family continues to suffer to this day, while I struggle to make a living.

I filed a writ petition on 3 July 2021 at the Allahabad High Court against my first suspension. At the first hearing, on 29 July, Justice Yashwant Verma asked the UP government to 'justify the continuance of the order of suspension which has continued for more than four years'.

In response, on 6 August 2021, the state's additional advocate general informed the court of its decision to withdraw the order of 24 February 2020 – the second departmental enquiry, which was initiated after the Himanshu Kumar-led probe gave me a clean chit. The court noted that while the FIR had initially been registered against nine individuals, seven of them had since been reinstated at the hospital. It also ordered the government of UP to justify my continuing suspension. On 10 August 2021, at the next hearing, the counsel of the state told the court that various incidents had transpired since my first suspension, leading to independent disciplinary proceedings being initiated wherein orders of suspension were passed separately against me. At this, the court ordered the UP government to produce facts about the other disciplinary proceedings and the suspension within two weeks.

In the meantime, I filed a new writ petition challenging my second suspension. On 9 September, this was stayed by the high court.

A total of fifteen hearings took place regarding my four-year-long suspension. I received eight court dates between 10 August and 10 November 2021, with no verdict about the first order.

On the morning of 10 November 2021, I woke up hoping against hope that in the coming days I would be granted some relief by the judiciary. Later the same morning, my family, especially my mother and my wife, expressed their ardent wish that I be reinstated by the UP government so that there could finally be some semblance of normalcy in our lives. We waited the whole day in anticipation of some good news while I texted Adeel bhai, who was in Allahabad for the hearing, every ten to fifteen minutes.

But this wasn't to be. Instead, in the afternoon, he informed us that the next court date had been set for 7 December 2021. Yet another tareekh. Little did I know at the time that the evening would bring a much more staggering jolt.

Around 6 p.m., I started receiving calls from journalists asking for my response to the UP government's decision to terminate me from my position as a lecturer at the BRD Medical College. *Terminated? What on earth were they talking about?* Bracing myself for the worst and with a sinking feeling in my chest, I sought to find out. And this is what I learnt: Instead of informing me personally or submitting to the court the report that had apparently found me 'guilty of laxity' in the Gorakhpur hospital tragedy case, the principal secretary of medical education, Alok Kumar, had told reporters that I had been sacked from my job at the hospital. The next day, *Jagran* reported that 'After the Uttar Pradesh Public Service Commission (UPPSC) approved the dismissal of Dr Kafeel, the Medical Education Department on Wednesday issued the order of dismissal.'

More than a week later, I received the order by the state government of my termination as a lecturer from the BRD Medical College. Of the four charges against me that the hospital was investigating, the letter mentioned that I had been found guilty of three. The allegations were as follows: First, I had undertaken private practice while being employed by the UP government; second, I ran a private nursing home without having the required registration with the UP Medical Council; third, even though I was present on the night of 10–11 August 2017, I did not inform any of the authorities about the crisis, had conspired with the principal and therefore been negligent and corrupt; and, finally, I had not supported the staff adequately during the oxygen shortage as the nodal officer of ward 100 – the encephalitis ward.

The letter stated that I had been found guilty of running a private practice in 2014, but I had not even been employed by the BRD Medical College until 8 August 2016. It also pronounced me guilty of running a private nursing home, despite the fact that any person registered with the Indian Medical Council can practise anywhere and there was no evidence to suggest I had engaged in such activity after joining the medical college. As for the third allegation, the letter accepted that I had indeed contacted all higher officials on the night of the tragedy and acknowledged the high court's observation that there was no material evidence suggesting medical negligence or corruption on my part. It further noted that although I was on leave on 10 August 2017, I had made every attempt possible to save patients. The fourth and final charge – that I was the nodal officer of encephalitis ward – had also been found to be true. But the letter failed to provide any evidence that I had ever been appointed to that post.

The bottom line was that I was no longer in the hospital's employ. This thirty-four-page letter from the government authorities had delivered the biggest professional setback of my life.

Nevertheless, me and my family have realized in the course of the past few years, since that grievous tragedy of 10 August 2017, that someone has to speak up for justice, for all those oppressed by the powers that be. The news of that evening was devastating but I also decided, almost instantaneously, that I would keep up my fight and challenge in court what to me was an utterly wrongful termination.

Strange as it may seem, the attempts to intimidate me into silence have made me all the more conscious of what I owe to society. If I had remained silent in order to keep my job, even as little children perished and their parents mourned, could I call myself a good citizen? If I had become resigned to my fate, using my time only to placate the authorities, could I have called myself an ethical doctor?

Instead, I have found that working for the most marginalized sections of society and continuing to raise my voice against injustice is the only way I can be at peace with myself. I have also realized that fear and selfishness keep us chained and enable our tormentors to wreak further cruelty and injustice upon us. We owe it to ourselves to stand up, make our voices heard, and extend a helping hand to those who are less fortunate than us. For too long, communities at the periphery of society have remained invisible to the educated and privileged classes.

Putting me behind bars and trying to suppress my voice through physical and mental torture is therefore not going to break my zeal, my enthusiasm or my commitment to my country and its secular, democratic values.

The difficulties which my family still faces only make me more determined to achieve my objectives.

My medical team, working under the banner of Dr Kafeel Khan Mission Smile Foundation, with the help of numerous citizens, has conducted more than 250 free medical camps, treating more than 1,00,000 children across the country. With a team of twenty-five health activists, we have started a Health for All campaign to demand the Right to Healthcare legislation, as the Indian healthcare system desperately needs an overhaul.

I finished writing the first draft of this book on the fourth anniversary of the deaths of innocent infants and children at the BRD Medical College. Even today, the conditions remain the same for millions of families on the lower end of the social stratum. Many have become even further marginalized. The parents grieving the deaths of their children that night have received neither sympathy nor any assurance that such events will not recur.

Four years after that disaster, in 2021, the Government of India declared that no deaths had occurred due to a shortage of oxygen during the second Covid-19 wave, even after countless patients died gasping for breath, and cremation grounds and cemeteries overflowed with dead bodies.

The anguish of numerous citizens of our country remains unacknowledged and unaddressed.

Although the phase of my life described in this book may be over, my determination to create more awareness about the state of Indian healthcare remains as strong as ever.

There is much more to be said, dear reader, about the lessons I learnt on the ground through my medical work across India and how I, a doctor, was declared a history-sheeter by the UP government but somehow became an activist.

That story is for another day. For now, I only want each of us to consider how best we can relieve the sufferings of those who need our help. In India, today, this is the need of the hour.

Author's Note and Acknowledgements

I would like to render my heartfelt thanks and gratitude to every person across the world, including several NGOs, social and healthcare activists, who have stood by my side in a time of crisis and prayed for my well-being. Numerous people have shared my joys and sorrows faithfully through my journey in the past four years. Their support boosted my confidence and fortified my resilience.

The families of prisoners are the forgotten victims. I am grateful to my mother for inculcating in me the qualities of being a good human first, before anything else.

My brothers, sisters and in-laws are my pillars of strength. They have supported me in the face of great adversity.

My wife and our two children are my lifelines. The hardest and the most painful part of this journey was that I missed being able to witness my own kids grow up.

Special thanks to Scharada Dubey, Kanishka Gupta, Teesta Guha Sarkar, Isha Banerji, Mimi Choudhury, Greeshma Gireesh, Debasish Roy Chowdhury and Mrudula Bhavani.

I wish to acknowledge that as a member of the noble medical profession and as a paediatrician, I owe a responsibility towards any child who might need a doctor's help, irrespective of how I am viewed by my detractors. This book is in the public's interest and will hopefully serve as a wake-up call so that no parent or child will have to needlessly lose a loved one.

As citizens of the world's largest democracy, this is also a time for us to introspect, not merely to point fingers but also in order to understand why and how we have failed as a nation, and find the right way forward.

I dream of an equal India, where people are not looked down upon because of their economic status, caste or religion but are able to enjoy equal freedoms, rights and facilities, not the least of which is healthcare.

Gorakhpur, Uttar Pradesh
10 August 2021

Abbreviations

ABG: Arterial Blood Gases
ADJ: Administration of Justice
AES: Acute Encephalitis Syndrome
AIIMS: All India Institute of Medical Sciences
AOR: Advocate-On-Record
ASG: Additional Solicitor General
BMR: Basal Metabolic Rate
BRD(MC): Baba Raghav Das Medical College
BVM: Bag Valve Mask
CPMT: Combined Pre-Medical Test
CPR: Cardiopulmonary Resuscitation
CrPC: Code of Criminal Procedure
CMO: Chief Medical Officer
CMS: Chief Medical Superintendent
DGME: Director General of Medical Education
DIG: Deputy Inspector General
HFNC: High Flow Nasal Cannula
ICU: Intensive Care Unit
IGL: Imperial Gas Limited
IMA: Indian Medical Association
MMWC: Millimetres of Water Column

NICU: Neonatal Intensive Care Unit
NNF: National Neonatology Forum
NHRC: National Human Rights Council
NRHM: National Rural Health Mission
NSA: National Security Act
OB-GYN: Obstetrics and Gynaecology
OPD: Outpatient Department
PICU: Paediatric Intensive Care Unit
POCSO: Protection of Children from Sexual Offences
SAHRDC: South Asia Human Rights Documentation Centre
SDM: Sub-divisional Magistrate
SG-PGIMS: Sanjay Gandhi Postgraduate Institute of Medical Sciences
SIC: Superintendent-in-charge
SSB: Sashastra Seema Bal
STF: Special Task Force
UPPSC: Uttar Pradesh Public Service Commission
VC: Videoconferencing

Photo and Illustration Credits

1. Courtesy Manoj Singh (www.gorakhpurnewsline.com).
2. Courtesy the author.
3. Courtesy the author.
4. Courtesy the author.
5. Courtesy the author.
6. Courtesy the author.
7. Courtesy the author.
8. Courtesy the author.
9. Also appears in Anoo Bhuyan, 'Gorakhpur Deaths: Adityanath Government Ignored SOS on Oxygen Payments for Months', *Wire*, 9 August 2018.
10. Courtesy the author.
11. Courtesy the author.
12. Pranshu Mishra, 'Is "Hero Doctor" Kafeel Khan a Scapegoat in the Gorakhpur Hospital Tragedy?' News18, 14 August 2017.
13. 'Gorakhpur Hadsa: Dum tod rahe masoom ko bachane ke lie joojhte rahe Dr Kafeel', *Hindustan*, 12 August 2017.
14. Courtesy the author.
15. Courtesy the author.
16. Courtesy the author.
17. 'BRD Medical College me FIR darj, principal sahit 9 par lage hai ye aarop', *Dainik Bhaskar*.
18. A copy of the letter also appears in Bhuyan, 'Gorakhpur Deaths: Adityanath Government Ignored SOS on

Oxygen Payments for Months', 9 August 2018. Accessed from the chief secretary's report.

19. Courtesy the author.
20. A copy of the letter also appears in 'Gorakhpur deaths: Company supplying oxygen says it sent nine reminders to hospital for payment', *Scroll.in*, 14 August 2017.
21. Courtesy the author.
22. 'Doctors made scapegoats to let off big fishes: IMA', *Hindustan Times*, 11 April 2018.
23. Courtesy Kashif Khan.
24. Courtesy Kashif Khan.
25. Courtesy Kashif Khan.
26. Courtesy Kashif Khan.
27. Rohan Dua, 'No proof of med negligence by BRD doctor Kafeel: HC', *Times of India*, 30 April 2018.
28. Courtesy the author.
29. Courtesy the author.
30. For references to the author being called the 'vice principal', see Arshi Aggarwal, 'Gorakhpur hospital tragedy Live: Dr Kafeel Khan, vice principal of BRD college removed from post over negligence'.
31. 'UP: Two years after BRD College tragedy, govt probe absolves Kafeel Khan', *Times of India*, 27 September 2019.
32. Courtesy the author.
33. Courtesy Mammootty Anjukunnu.
34. Courtesy the author.

Notes on Sources

Names of several characters who appear in this book have been changed to protect their privacy. Certain dialogues and events are reconstructed to the best of my abilities, with every effort undertaken to maintain consistency. Although the events recounted in this book are still fresh in my memory, I may have missed a few details. However, I hope I have been able to vividly present my account to my readers, so as to provide them a clear understanding of how the events since the night of 10 August 2017 truly unfolded.

24 **I managed to get four cylinders from one hospital:** Neha Shukla and Arjumand Bano, 'RTI query reveals there was oxygen shortage at BRD Hospital', *Times of India*, 14 August 2018. Available: https://timesofindia.indiatimes.com/city/lucknow/rti-query-reveals-there-was-oxygen-shortage-at-brd-hospital/articleshow/65395029.cms.

48 **Two clerks in the paediatrics department:** As stated in the letter from the CMS to the principal.

52 **In his address, the DM said clearly that there was no shortage of oxygen:** '*Jaanch committee gathit, Aaj degi report*', *Amar Ujala*, 12 August 2017.

52 **'BRD has witnessed a disturbance in the liquid oxygen supply since last night':** '30 Children deaths in Uttar Pradesh's Gorakhpur after oxygen supply in hospital disrupted', YouTube, 12 August 2017. Available: https://www.youtube.com/watch?v– 0Jzqp24FBA4.

53 **'there was a shortage of oxygen but was managed through oxygen cylinders from SSB and other resources':** '*Jaanch*

committee gathit, Aaj degi report', *Amar Ujala*, 12 August 2017.

58 **statement against the principal's wife would be spared from further harassment or enquiry:** As stated in an affidavit submitted to the minister of medical education.

58 **Sudhir took this offer up and wrote a written complaint:** As stated in his affidavit to the hospital.

63 **On an average, twenty deaths were reported a day at the paediatrics ward of the hospital:** 'Gorakhpur tragedy: Is August the cruellest month for BRD Medical College?', *New Indian Express*, 15 August 2017. Available: https://www.newindianexpress.com/nation/2017/aug/15/gorakhpur-tragedy-is-august-the-cruellest-month-for-brd-medical-college-1643274--1.html.

63 **Unsurprisingly, locals refer to the college as the 'graveyard of Purvanchal':** Shikari Shambhu, '1 Year Gone What about BRD?', Medium, 17 August 2018.

67 **'*August me har saal bachhe marte hai*':** '"हर महीने अगस्त में मरते हैं बच्चे' इस बात पर गुस्साए ट्विटर यूजर्स, मंत्री सिद्धार्थ नाथ सिंह पर निकाली जमकर भड़ास", *Jansatta*, 13 August 2017. Available: https://www.jansatta.com/trending-news/health-minister-of-up-siddharth-nath-singh-as-trooled-in-twitter/401471/.

70 **'[My daughter] was alive until the morning':** Abdul Jadid, 'Went to buy medicines, when I returned my 10-day-old son was dead': Families recount Gorakhpur tragedy', *Hindustan Times*, 12 August 2017. Available: https://www.hindustantimes.com/lucknow/went-to-buy-medicines-when-i-returned-my-10-day-old-son-was-dead-families-recount-gorakhpur-tragedy/story-TvQ0iM3LZPBwyhTFvwPYwK.html; Kripa Padhy, 'India's Gorakhpur hospital: The night the children died', BBC News, 1 April 2018. Available: https://www.bbc.com/news/world-asia-india-43482471.

70–71 **'A resident of Bihar's Gopalganj district':** PTI, 'Man whose daughter died in Gorakhpur hospital seeks action against ministers', *Outlook*, 16 August 2017. Available: https://www.outlookindia.com/newsscroll/man-whose-daughter-died-in-gorakhpur-hospital-seeks-action-against-ministers/1125288.

72 **'Deaths of 11 More Children':** ANI, 'Not a tragedy, it's a massacre: Kailash Satyarthi on Gorakhpur hospital

deaths', *Outlook*, 11 August 2017. Available: https://www.outlookindia.com/newsscroll/not-a-tragedy-its-a-massacre-kailash-satyarthi-on-gorakhpur-hospital-deaths/1122160.

72 ***'August me har saal bachhe marte hai'***: '"हर महीने अगस्त में मरते हैं बच्चे" इस बात पर गुस्साए ट्वटिर यूजर्स, मंत्री सदिधार्थ नाथ सहि पर नकिाली जमकर भड़ास', *Jansatta*, 13 August 2017.

73 **I was being called a 'hero'**: Srawan Shukla, 'Gorakhpur tragedy: Meet Dr Kafeel Khan, the hero who saved the lives of countless children', *DNA*, 13 August 2017. Available: https://www.dnaindia.com/india/report-gorakhpur-tragedy-meet-dr-kafeel-khan-the-hero-who-saved-the-lives-of-countless-children-2528035' 'सोशल मीडयिा पर डॉ. कफील का 'सच' वायरल, 'कातलि' या मसीहा?', *Amar Ujala*, 18 August 2017. Available: https://www.amarujala.com/national/crime/gorakhpur-tragedy-dr-kafeel-a-hero-or-a-criminal-viral-on-social-media.

73 **'While other doctors gave up hope'**: 'Gorakhpur Tragedy: Here's how 'hero' Dr Khan saved as many children as he could', News Nation, 13 August 2017. Available: https://english.newsnationtv.com/india/news/gorakhpur-tragedy-heres-how-hero-dr-khan-saved-as-many-children-as-he-could-179396.html.

73 **'At least 63 kids have died'**: 'At Least 63 Kids Have Died in Gorakhpur Hospital In 5 Days, Yogi Govt Admits Oxygen Shortage', India Times, 12 August 2017. Available: https://www.indiatimes.com/news/india/at-least-63-kids-have-died-in-gorakhpur-hospital-in-5-days-yogi-govt-admits-oxygen-shortage-327676.html.

73 **'[Khan] collected as many as 12 oxygen cylinders'**: 'Allahabad High Court Grants Bail to Dr. Kafeel Khan in Gorakhpur Tragedy Case', *Libertatem.in*, 27 April 2018. Available: https://libertatem.in/law/high-court/allahabad-high-court-grants-bail-to-dr-kafeel-khan-in-gorakhpur-tragedy-case/.

73 **Crises brings out the best in some people:** 'Gorakhpur tragedy: How a doctor stepped up in desperate times to save lives', *Hindustan Times*, 13 August 2017. Available: https://www.hindustantimes.com/india-news/gorakhpur-hospital-tragedy-a-good-samaritan-who-responded-to-the-call-of-duty-in-desperate-times/story-vRsfbGKPjnW260w7UAtySN.html.

73 **'Even as the death of 36 children in Uttar Pradesh's Gorakhpur hospital once again exposed government':** Srawan Sukla, 'Gorakhpur deaths', *DNA*.

75 **The moment he and J. P. Nadda got out of their SUV:** 'CM Yogi Adityanath, JP Nadda visit Gorakhpur's BRD medical college 2 days after death of 37 children', ZEE News, 13 August 2017. Available: https://zeenews.india.com/video/india/up-cm-yogi-adityanath-jp-nadda-visit-gorakhpurs-brd-medical-college-2-days-after-death-of-37-children-2032611.html.

76 **'For the past thirty years':** Rajesh Kumar Singh, 'UP CM Yogi Adityanath visits Gorakhpur hospital, says guilty won't be spared', *Hindustan Times*, 13 August 2017. Available: https://www.hindustantimes.com/india-news/yogi-adityanath-visits-gorakhpur-hospital-says-nobody-more-sensitive-to-children-than-him/story-BLKZwtUJQIFUcISFuaRLgM.html.

77 ***'Toh tu Dr Kafeel hai?'*****:** 'Yogi Maharaj ne jab kaha, tumhe lagta hai cylindero ki vyavastha kar dene se tum hero ban gaye, mai dekhta hu ise', Patrika.com, 24 April 2018. Available: https://www.patrika.com/gorakhpur-news/brd-oxygen-tragedy-accused-dr-kafeel-wrote-letter-from-jail-2698990/.

77 ***'Toh tu sochta hai cylinders la ke tu hero ban jayega?'*****:** Shone Satheesh, 'Gorakhpur doctor jailed for infant deaths claims many adults may have also died when oxygen ran out', *Scroll.in*, 29 June 2018. Available: https://scroll.in/pulse/883944/gorakhpur-doctor-jailed-for-infant-deaths-claims-many-adults-may-have-also-died-when-oxygen-ran-out; 'My life "turned upside down" after Adityanath's visit, Dr Kafeel writes from jail', 23 April 2018. Available: https://www.ummid.com/news/2018/April/23.04.2018/dr-kafeel-khan-writes-from-jail.html; Soutik Basu, 'Kafeel Khan: National threat or symbol of repression?', BBC News, 3 September 2020. Available: https://www.bbc.com/news/world-asia-india-53995027; 'Was made scapegoat by Yogi Adityanath govt: Dr Kafeel Khan terms Gorakhpur deaths man-made massacre', *India Today*, 30 September 2019. Available: https://www.indiatoday.in/india/story/

gorakhpur-tragedy-scapegoat-yogi-adityanath-govt-dr-kafeel-khan-1604935-2019-09-30.

79 **'Japanese encephalitis and insanitary conditions':** 'Kids died due to encephalitis, insanitary conditions: Yogi Adityanath', *Times of India*, 13 August 2017. Available: https://timesofindia.indiatimes.com/city/allahabad/kids-died-due-to-encephalitis-insanitary-conditions-yogi-adityanath/articleshow/60041544.cms.

79 ***'Itni kadhor karyawahi Pradesh sarkar karegi ki woh manak banegi logon ke anushashan mein rehke karya karne ke bare mein'*:** Maulshree Seth, 'Yogi claims kept in dark on hospital, vows truth: "Treatment, or massacre"', *Indian Express*, 13 August 2017. Available: https://indianexpress.com/article/india/gorakhpur-hospital-tragedy-deaths-up-cm-yogi-adityanath-claims-kept-in-dark-on-hospital-vows-truth-treatment-or-massacre-4795324/.

80 ***Gorakhpur me 'bachho ka kaatil' kaun'*:** 'Gorakhpur me bachho ka kaatil kaun?', ABP News Hindi, 30 August 2017. Available: https://www.youtube.com/watch?v=FeW-djG3uxY.

81 **and then labelled as the villain of the entire episode:** Shashank Bengali and Parth M.N., 'Global Development: When an Indian hospital was running out of oxygen, these doctors tried to help. So why were they sent to jail?', *LA Times*, 29 June 2018. Available: https://www.latimes.com/world/asia/la-fg-india-hospital-2018-story.html.

81 **The doctors called in their parents and asked them to quietly:** Rajesh K. Singh, Gaurav Saigal and Abdul Jadid, 'Gorakhpur tragedy: A saga of negligence, cover-ups, kickbacks', *Hindustan Times*, 17 August 2017. Available: https://www.hindustantimes.com/lucknow/gorakhpur-tragedy-a-saga-of-negligence-cover-ups-kickbacks/story-pXyCYuFX9Rg6i51FQtOSaP.html; 'Gorakhpur tragedy highlights: Yogi Adityanth calls deaths a "despicable incident"; Anupriya Patel to visit hospital', *Firstpost*, 12 August 2017. Available: https://www.firstpost.com/india/gorakhpur-hospital-tragedy-live-60-children-died-in-5-days-up-govt-faces-flak-from-opposition-3921401.html.

82 **The CM and HM should resign, they had said:** ANI, 'Gorakhpur hospital deaths: Congress demands resignation

of Chief Minister Yogi', *New Indian Express*, 12 August 2017. Available: https://www.newindianexpress.com/nation/2017/aug/12/gorakhpur-hospital-deaths-congress-demands-resignation-of-chief-minister-yogi-1642196.html.

82 **Dr Kafeel Khan was a murderer:** 'सोशल मीडिया पर डॉ. कफील का "सच" वायरल, "कातलि" या मसीहा?' *Amar Ujala*, 18 August 2017.

84 **'On 11 August, when I reached the 100-bed encephalitis ward':** Manoj Singh, 'A Single Photograph Was All it Took to Dramatically Alter Dr Kafeel Khan's Life', *Wire*, 3 September 2020. Available: https://thewire.in/rights/dr-kafeel-khan-release-gorakhpur-brd-medical-arrest.

85 **'The allegations that Dr Kafeel is a chor are blatant lies':** Biswajeet Banerjee, 'Dr Kafeel: a villain or a victim in a political conspiracy', *National Herald*, 14 August 2017. Available: https://www.nationalheraldindia.com/national/dr-kafeel-a-villain-or-a-victim-in-a-political-conspiracy.

85 **'gross neglect of public health':** 'Gorakhpur hospital deaths: Congress demands PM Modi's apology in his I-Day address', *Indian Express*, 14 August 2017. Available: https://indianexpress.com/article/india/gorakhpur-hospital-deaths-tragedy-baba-raghav-das-hospital-yogi-adityanath-encephalitis-4795907/.

85 **'With great pain, we have to say that':** PTI, 'Gorakhpur tragedy: Dr Kafeel Khan made scapegoat, says docs at AIIMS', *Outlook*, 14 August 2017. Available: https://www.outlookindia.com/newsscroll/gorakhpur-tragedy-dr-kafeel-khan-made-scapegoat-says-docs-at-aiims/1123487.

85 **my efforts and SSB's assistance helped in fighting the crisis:** 'Is 'Hero Doctor' Kafeel Khan a Scapegoat in the Gorakhpur Hospital Tragedy?', News18, 14 August 2017. Available: https://www.news18.com/news/india/is-hero-doctor-kafeel-khan-a-scapegoat-in-the-gorakhpur-hospital-tragedy-1491285.html.

86 **'It was an unprecedented crisis situation':** Ibid.

89 **the media had been told that my resignation as superintendent:** 'डॉक्टर कफील खान बीआरडी मेडकिल कॉलेज के NICU प्रमुख से हटाए गए', Available: https://www.abplive.com/news/india/doctor-kafeel-khan-sacked-as-brd-medical-colleges-nicu-chief-670506.

90 **a statement questioning what good I could have done with four cylinders when fifty were already in stock:** '*Jab 52 cylinder uss raat ko stock mein they toh 3 cylinder Dr Khan laakar ke koi bahut teer nahi maar lenge: KK Gupta on Dr Kafeel Khan*', ANI UP, 7:17 p.m., 13 August 2017. Available: https://twitter.com/ANINewsUP/status/896729984554811392.

90 **I had indeed gone to the SSB office on 11 August:** Pranshu Mishra, 'Is 'Hero Doctor' Kafeel Khan a Scapegoat in the Gorakhpur Hospital Tragedy?' News18, 14 August 2017.

91 **They had written letters directly:** 'Gorakhpur deaths: Company supplying oxygen says it sent nine reminders to hospital for payment', *Scroll.in*, 14 August 2017. Available: https://scroll.in/latest/847209/gorakhpur-deaths-company-supplying-oxygen-says-it-sent-nine-reminders-to-hospital-for-payment.

91 **even though the firm didn't have the licence to supply medical liquid oxygen:** Anoo Bhuyan, 'Gorakhpur Deaths: Adityanath Government Ignored SOS on Oxygen Payments for Months', *Wire*, 9 August 2018.

91 **'The government must find why there were just around fifty cylinders':** Omar Rashid and Damini Nath, 'Gorakhpur hospital oxygen supply not cut, says U.P. firm', *The Hindu*, 18 August 2017. Available: https://www.thehindu.com/news/national/other-states/gorakhpur-hospital-oxygen-supply-not-cut-says-up-firm/article19512475.ece; 'Gorakhpur tragedy: Oxygen supplier says it never stopped supply, suspects cylinder theft led to shortage', *Firstpost*, 15 August 2017. Available: https://www.firstpost.com/india/gorakhpur-tragedy-oxygen-supplier-says-it-never-stopped-supply-suspects-cylinder-theft-led-to-shortage-3932347.html.

91 **'We personally handed the dues letter to the health minister on August 9th':** Piyush Srivastava, 'Nothing, nothing, nothing', *The Telegraph*, 15 August 2017. Available: https://www.telegraphindia.com/india/nothing-nothing-nothing/cid/1502328.

92 **Siddharth Nath tells reporters in Allahabad that the oxygen supply was disrupted:** Srivastava, 'Nothing, nothing, nothing', *The Telegraph*, 15 August 2017.

92 ***'Itna bada desh, hadse toh hote hain'***: Harish Upadhya and Snigdha Basu, 'Gorakhpur Child Deaths 'A Tragedy, A Mistake,' Says Amit Shah: 10 Points', NDTV, 15 August 2017. Available: https://www.ndtv.com/india-news/gorakhpur-child-deaths-a-tragedy-a-mistake-says-amit-shah-10-points-1737551.

92 **'natural calamity'**: 'PM Modi Terms Gorakhpur Tragedy As Natural Calamity', NNIS News, 15 August 2017. Available: https://www.youtube.com/watch?v=AQNwIFUHL6A; 'For Modi, Gorakhpur hospital deaths a natural calamity?', *Business Standard*, 15 August 2017. Available: https://www.business-standard.com/article/current-affairs/for-modi-gorakhpur-hospital-deaths-a-natural-calamity-117081500137_1.html.

93 **giving more statements to several media channels:** 'Private practice me lipt doctor par hogi FIR', *Jagran*, 17 August 2017. Available: https://www.jagran.com/uttar-pradesh/lucknow-city-fir-will-be-on-doctors-involved-in-private-practice-16555041.html.

93 **'that he had written several letters to top officials ...'**: 'Gorakhpur deaths: Company supplying oxygen says it sent nine reminders to hospital for payment', *Scroll.in*, 14 August 2017. Available: https://scroll.in/latest/847209/gorakhpur-deaths-company-supplying-oxygen-says-it-sent-nine-reminders-to-hospital-for-payment; Maneka Rao, 'Gorakhpur hospital deaths: Doctor explains why oxygen payments were delayed', *Scroll.in*, 13 August 2017. Available: https://scroll.in/pulse/847105/adityanaths-visit-to-gorakhpur-proved-deadly-as-oxygen-payments-were-delayed-by-a-day-says-doctor.

93 **'The government appointed Dr Gupta'**: 'Wrote several letters for clearing dues: Ex-principal', *Times of India*, 14 August 2017. Available: http://timesofindia.indiatimes.com/articleshow/60052869.cms?utm_source=contentofinterest&utm_medium=text&utm_campaign=cppst.

93 **'The budgetary allocation for 14 such medical colleges'**: 'UP government slashed medical education budget by 50%', *Times of India*, 17 August 2017. Available: https://

timesofindia.indiatimes.com/city/lucknow/up-govt-slashed-medical-education-budget-by-50/articleshow/60094209.cms.

94 **refrained from blaming the UP government for the tragedy:** 'Gorakhpur probe report says children died due to oxygen crisis, blames principal and doctors', *Hindustan Times*, 17 August 2017. Available: https://www.hindustantimes.com/india-news/gorakhpur-admin-report-says-children-died-due-to-oxygen-crisis-indicts-principal-doctors-and-supplier/story-x9pjtTGRnKe3kApr0X8NVJ.html.

94 **accused the Principal Rajiv Mishra of failing to alert the DGME and health departments to the impending oxygen crisis:** Snigdha Basu, '2 Doctors Blamed For Oxygen Shortage In Gorakhpur Report: 10 Points', NDTV, 17 August 2017. Available: https://www.ndtv.com/india-news/cant-link-gorakhpur-deaths-to-lack-of-oxygen-says-centre-team-10-facts-1738262?pfrom=home-lateststories.

94 **Another accusation was against Dr Satish Kumar:** Ibid.

95 **'The alleged oxygen breakdown does not appear to be directly responsible for the deaths':** As stated in the SG-PGIMS report.

97–98 **deaths at the hospital were not related to the snapping of the oxygen supply:** Virendra Singh Rawat, 'Gorakhpur hospital tragedy: FIR against 9, including oxygen supplier', *Business Standard*, 25 August 2017. Available: https://www.business-standard.com/article/current-affairs/gorakhpur-hospital-tragedy-fir-against-9-including-oxygen-supplier-117082400495_1.html.

97 **It came to light that a committee led by the chief secretary, Rajiv Kumar, had submitted its report:** Namita Bajpai, 'Gorakhpur tragedy: Chief secretary submits report, action follows', *New Indian Express*, 22 August 2017. Available: https://www.newindianexpress.com/nation/2017/aug/22/gorakhpur-tragedy-chief-secretary-submits-report-action-follows-1646796.html.

97 **Anita Bhatnagar Jain was transferred:** 'गोरखपुर ट्रेजडी: IAS अनीता की छुट्टी, पूरव परसिपिल और डॉ कफील समेत 6 के खिलाफ FIR दरज', ABP Live, 23 August 2017. Available: https://www.abplive.com/news/states/gorakhpur-tragedy-cm-

yogi-adityanath-orders-firs-against-college-principal-and-5-others-676090; IANS, 'Gorakhpur Tragedy: Top Uttar Pradesh Bureaucrat Removed', NDTV, 23 August 2017. Available: https://www.ndtv.com/india-news/gorakhpur-tragedy-top-uttar-pradesh-bureaucrat-anita-bhatnagar-jain-removed-1740883.

98 **seven different sections of the IPC: 409, 420, 308, 120B, the Anti-Corruption Act 7/13, the Indian Medical Council Act (Section 15), as well as Section 66A of the IT Act:** 'Gorakhpur BRD Tragedy: Arrest Of Doctors Likely', *The Hawk*, 27 August 2017. Available: https://thehawk.in/states/uttar-pradesh/gorakhpur-brd-tragedy-arrest-of-doctors-likely-95372/cid3285991.htm; Maulshree Seth, 'Since BRD case 3 yrs ago, Kafeel Khan fighting charges, in and out of jail', *Indian Express*, 2 September 2020. Available: https://indianexpress.com/article/india/since-brd-case-3-yrs-ago-kafeel-khan-fighting-charges-in-and-out-of-jail-6579500/.

99 **people were very angry with the principal and his wife:** 'BRD Haadse ke peechhe ek aur "madam"', Amar Ujala, Gorakhpur Bureau; 'Harsh va Dr Poornima ka agent ki Bhoomika nibhane wala kaun?', Rashtriya Sahara, 21 August 2017.

101 **on the morning of 2 September:** 'UPSTF arrests Dr. Kafeel Khan from Gorakhpur', ZEE News, 2 September 2017. Available: https://www.youtube.com/watch?v=zW0R7_wrWfA.

103 **'was arrested just before [I] was allegedly trying to flee to Nepal, police said':** Amita Verma, 'Gorakhpur tragedy: Doctor Kafeel Khan held while trying to flee to Nepal', *Asian Age*, 3 September 2017. Available: https://www.asianage.com/india/all-india/030917/gorakhpur-doctor-kafeel-khan-held-while-trying-to-flee-to-nepal.html.

103 **They asked me to sign a paper stating that they had caught me at the bus stop in Shahjanwa:** Amita Verma, 'Gorakhpur tragedy: Doctor Kafeel Khan held while trying to flee to Nepal', *Asian Age*, 3 September 2017; 'Gorakhpur tragedy: UP STF arrests Dr Kafeel Khan, in-charge of encephalitis ward of BRD hospital', IndiaTV, 2 September 2017. Available: https://www.indiatvnews.com/news/

india-gorakhpur-tragedy-up-stf-arrests-dr-kafeel-khan-in-charge-of-encephalitis-ward-of-brd-hospital-399403; 'Gorakhpur hospital tragedy: STF arrests accused doctor Kafeel Khan', *Times of India*, 2 September 2017. Available: https://timesofindia.indiatimes.com/india/gorakhpur-hospital-tragedy-stf-arrests-accused-doctor-kafeel-khan/articleshow/60340094.cms.

118 **'The court is inclined to accept the submission'**: PTI, 'Gorakhpur deaths: UP HC rejects oxygen supplier's bail plea', *Outlook*, 14 February 2018. Available: https://www.outlookindia.com/newsscroll/gorakhpur-deaths-up-hc-rejects-oxygen-suppliers-bail-plea/1252830.

129 **You don't want to work? Pay the kachchi baithaki of ₹200 per day:** 'Gorakhpur Jail ka Haal Gazab; 822 bandiyo ki kshamta wale jail me 1950 kaidi, bhojan ke naam par dete hai paani wali daal; har suvidha ke lie vasooli ka alag system', News India Live, 24 June 2021. Available: https://www.bhaskar.com/local/uttar-pradesh/gorakhpur/news/separate-recovery-system-for-each-facility-from-prisoners-in-gorakhpur-jail-128631088.html.

137 **He was an MP from the BJP when a communal riot broke out and an outfit torched many buses and public property:** 'Gorakhpur on the boil, BJP MP arrested', *Times of India*, 30 January 2007. Available: http://timesofindia.indiatimes.com/articleshow/1525851.cms?utm_source=contentofinterest&utm_medium=text&utm_campaign=cppst.

137 **a rail compartment carrying handicapped students:** 'What is the Yogi Adityanath hate speech case of 2007?' *Indian Express*. Available: https://indianexpress.com/article/what-is/what-is-the-yogi-adityanath-hate-speech-case-of-2007/

154 **'Clerk Sanjay Tripathi has been arrested from Cantonment police station area'**: PTI, '6 arrests so far in Gorakhpur children deaths case, clerk held', *Asian Age*, 12 September 2017. Available:

154 **'Former chief pharmacist of the medical college'**: PTI, 'Another BRD medical college clerk held in child deaths case', *India Today*, 14 September 2017. Available: https://www.indiatoday.in/pti-feed/story/another-brd-medical-college-clerk-held-in-child-deaths-case-1044582-2017-09-14

166 **at night it was bursting at the seams:** Vivek Pandey and Kundan Upadhyay, Gorakhpur jail me kaidi do-do shift me so rahe, *Hindustan*, 4 October 2017.

178 **this increased the liquid oxygen bill every month:** As stated in an affidavit by Pushpa Sales.

183 **authorities were asking for 10 per cent commission to clear the dues:** As stated by the authorized agents of Pushpa Sales to the IO in a court affidavit, part of the high court charge sheet.

195 **even though the charges against him were mild:** Manish Sahu, 'Gorakhpur tragedy: 7 chargesheeted in BRD hospital deaths', *Indian Express*, 28 October 2017. Available: https://indianexpress.com/article/india/gorakhpur-tragedy-seven-chargesheeted-in-brd-hospital-deaths-4910043/.

199 **five separate instances of fires that had broken out at BRD Medical College since August 2017:** 'BRD Medical College me phir lagi aag', *Hindustan*, 9 January 2018.

199 **One of the fires had broken out in the principal's office and the adjacent record room:** Arjumand Bano, '"Mysterious BRD fire guts files linked to oxygen case"', *Times of India*, 9 January 2018. Available: https://timesofindia.indiatimes.com/city/lucknow/mysterious-brd-fire-guts-files-linked-to-oxygen-case/articleshow/62422132.cms.

199 **'bail is a rule, jail is an exception':** '"Bail is rule, jail is exception"', *Free Press Journal*, 22 November 2020. Available: https://www.freepressjournal.in/analysis/bail-is-rule-jail-is-an-exception.

204 **The press reported how Manish was unable to secure bail:** PTI, 'Gorakhpur hospital deaths: Supreme Court grants bail to oxygen supplier', *Indian Express*, 9 April 2018. Available: https://indianexpress.com/article/india/gorakhpur-hospital-deaths-supreme-court-grants-bail-to-oxygen-supplier-5130597/; 'A Living Hell for Dr Kafeel Khan's Family', *The Citizen*, 10 April 2018. Available: https://www.thecitizen.in/index.php/en/newsdetail/index/2/13497/when-adityanaths-cops-turned-life-into-a-living-hell-for-dr-kafeel-khans-family.

204 **until the apex court intervened:** PTI, 'Gorakhpur hospital deaths: Supreme Court grants bail to oxygen supplier', *Indian*

Express, 9 April 2018. Available: https://indianexpress.com/article/india/gorakhpur-hospital-deaths-supreme-court-grants-bail-to-oxygen-supplier-5130597/.

205 **IMA Comes Out in Defense of Dr Kafeel Khan:** 'IMA Comes out in Defence of Dr Kafeel Khan arrested in Gorakhpur Hospital Tragedy Case, Calls it Conspiracy', *Outlook*, 10 April 2018. Available: https://www.outlookindia.com/website/story/ima-comes-out-in-defence-of-dr-kafeel-khan-arrested-in-gorakhpur-hospital-traged/310831.

206 **'They terrorized us for days on end':** 'Seven months and no bail hearing for Dr Khan', *Citizen*, 10 April 2018. Available: https://www.thecitizen.in/index.php/en/newsdetail/index/2/13497/when-adityanaths-cops-turned-life-into-a-living-hell-for-dr-kafeel-khans-family.

208 **The trial of a horrific rape case in Jammu's Kathua district:** Debjani Chatterjee, 'Kathua Gang-rape And Murder: Civil Society Outraged, Demands Justice', NDTV, 12 April 2018. Available: https://www.ndtv.com/india-news/kathua-gang-rape-and-murder-civil-society-outraged-demands-justice-1836652.

209 **'8 Months, In Jail Without Bail!':** '8 Months No Bail, Am I Really Guilty: Read Dr Kafeel Khan's Letter', *Quint*, 23 April 2018. Available: https://www.thequint.com/news/india/gorakhpur-infant-deaths-dr-kafeel-khan-full-letter#read-more.

213 **as I was attempting to answer their questions, I was roughed up by the cops:** 'Dr. Kafeel: A Scapegoat of Administrative Failure', NewsClickin, 19 April 2018. Available: https://www.youtube.com/watch?v=HJLZGurU3nQ.

218 **'Infants' death case: Gorakhpur BRD hospital doctor Kafeel Khan gets bail':** Omar Rashid, 'Infants' death case: Gorakhpur BRD hospital doctor Kafeel Khan gets bail', *The Hindu*, 25 April 2018. Available: https://www.thehindu.com/news/national/other-states/gorakhpur-brd-hospital-doctor-kafeel-khan-granted-bail/article23669929.ece.

223 **'jailed for over eight months in an ordinary criminal cell':** 'Dr Kafeel Khan Gets Bail!', The Citizen, 25 April 2018. Available: https://www.thecitizen.in/index.php/en/newsdetail/index/2/13635/dr-kafeel-khan-gets-bail; Pooja

Chaudhuri, 'The Punishment He Did Not Deserve: Last Eight Months of Dr Kafeel Khan's Life', Logical Indian, 3 May 2018. Available: https://thelogicalindian.com/exclusive/dr-kafeel-khan-life-after-bail/; 'After More Than 7 Months in Jail, Dr Kafeel Khan Gets Bail from Allahabad High Court', Kractivism. Available: https://www.kractivist.org/after-more-than-7-months-in-jail-dr-kafeel-khan-gets-bail-from-allahabad-high-court/.

223 **'No Evidence Against Dr Kafeel, No Inquiry Was Done':** 'No Evidence Against Dr Kafeel, No Inquiry Was Done: Allahabad HC', *Quint*, 27 April 2018. Available: https://www.thequint.com/news/india/gorakhpur-infant-deaths-dr-kafeel-khan-granted-bail.

223 **'... there is no material on record, which may establish medical negligence':** Omar Rashid, 'Allahabad High Court rules out negligence charges against Gorakhpur doctor Kafeel Khan', *The Hindu*, 26 April 2018. Available: https://www.thehindu.com/news/national/other-states/allahabad-high-court-rules-out-negligence-charges-against-gorakhpur-doctor-kafeel-khan/article23682129.ece.

230 **I did no wrong, only did what a father, a doctor, a Hindustani would have done:** '"My Future Depends On Yogi Adityanath": Doctor Accused In UP Child Deaths', NDTV, 29 April 2018. Available: https://www.ndtv.com/india-news/gorakhpur-baby-deaths-out-of-jail-after-8-months-dr-kafeel-khan-says-his-future-depends-in-cm-yogi-a-1844393.

232 **The people who should have been prosecuted are the ones who filed the FIR:** Recordings where the author is heard making this statement are available on the internet.

238 **I will not leave Gorakhpur. I will not leave India. This is my home, my soul resides here, in this soil:** Mumtaz Alam, 'I will not leave Gorakhpur. I will not leave India. This is my home, my soul resides here, in this soil', Clarion India, 9 May 2018. Available: https://clarionindia.net/i-wont-leave-gorakhpur-nor-india-my-soul-resides-in-this-soil-dr-kafeel-khan/.

239 **did not want his son's death to be the cause of further hatred:** Sukriti Dwivedi, 'Father Of Delhi Man Killed By Muslim Girlfriend's Family Hosts *Iftaar*', NDTV, 5 June

2018. Available: https://www.ndtv.com/delhi-news/father-of-delhi-man-ankit-saxena-killed-by-muslim-girlfriends-family-hosts-iftaar-1862189.

240 **the picture of him in uniform touching the chief minister Yogi Adityanath's feet had gone viral:** 'UP Cop Kneels Down at Yogi Adityanath's Feet, Photo Goes Viral', *Quint*, 28 July 2018. Available: https://www.thequint.com/news/india/viral-photos-uttar-pradesh-police-officer-kneels-down-at-cm-yogi-adityanaths-feet.

242 **'The brother of Dr Kafeel, accused in the BRD oxygen tragedy, has been shot':** Anoo Bhuyan, 'Kafeel Khan's Brother Shot at Thrice in Gorakhpur', *Wire*, 11 June 2018. Available: https://thewire.in/health/kafeel-khan-brother-shot-at-thrice-in-gorakhpur; Yusra Husain and Arjumand Bano, 'Dr Kafeel's brother shot at in Gorakhpur', *Times of India*, 11 June 2018. Available: https://timesofindia.indiatimes.com/city/lucknow/dr-kafeels-brother-shot-at-in-gorakhpur/articleshow/64534831.cms; Sadiq Shaban, 'How Dr Kafeel Khan's brother was shot near high-security Gorakhnath temple', Wion News, 11 June 2018. Available: https://www.wionews.com/india-news/accused-in-gorakhpur-encephalitis-tragedy-kafeel-khans-brother-shot-at-in-gorakhpur-143617

244 **An FIR was filed against 'unknown assailants' who had shot at my brother:** Omar Rashid, 'Kafeel Khan's brother shot at in Gorakhpur', *The Hindu*, 11 June 2018. Available: https://www.thehindu.com/news/national/other-states/kafeel-khans-brother-shot-at/article24133149.ece.

244 **Adeel bhai met the CM in the janta darbar at Gorakhpur:** PTI, 'Kafeel Khan's brother meets UP CM during "janta darbar", seeks CBI probe into attack on family member', Business Standard, 29 June 2018. Available: https://www.business-standard.com/article/pti-stories/kafeel-khan-s-brother-meets-up-cm-during-janta-darbar-seeks-cbi-probe-into-attack-on-family-member-118062900981_1.html.

245 **'The response to an RTI filed by an activist':** Sayantani Nath Nath, 'RTI Response Proves There Was Oxygen Shortage In BRD Hospital, Dr Kafeel Khan Arranged For Cylinders', Logical Indian, 19 August 2018. Available: https://

thelogicalindian.com/news/rti-response-dr-kafeel-arranged-for-cylinders/; 'RTI response reveals BRD Medical College in Gorakhpur ran out of oxygen cylinders before 60 children died during treatment', *Firstpost*, 14 August 2018.

246 **The issue of deaths at BRD hospital had been blown out of proportion due to internal politics at the hospital:** 'BRD Hospital Tragedy Blown Out of Proportion Due to Internal Politics, Says Yogi Adityanath', News18, 25 August 2018. Available: https://www.news18.com/news/india/brd-hospital-tragedy-blown-out-of-proportion-due-to-internal-politics-says-yogi-adityanath-1856807.html; 'Gorakhpur infant deaths: There was no shortage of oxygen at hospital, says Adityanath', *Scroll.in*, 26 August 2018. Available: https://scroll.in/latest/891969/gorakhpur-infant-deaths-there-was-no-shortage-of-oxygen-at-hospital-says-adityanath; 'Yogi Adityanath on Gorakhpur infant deaths: Tragedy a result of internal politics, not shortage of oxygen', *Indian Express*, 26 August 2018. Available: https://indianexpress.com/article/cities/lucknow/yogi-adityanath-gorakhpur-hospital-infant-deaths-5325597/.

246 **I called his statement 'incorrect':** 'Gorakhpur tragedy: Yogi Adityanath misleading people, alleges Dr Kafeel Khan after CM says there was no shortage of oxygen', *Indian Express*, 27 August 2018. Available: https://indianexpress.com/article/india/gorakhpur-infant-deaths-yogi-adityanath-oxygen-supply-kafeel-khan-5327408/

246 **If the entire episode had been about 'internal politics' and 'there was no shortage of oxygen', why did we languish in prison for close to a year?:** Ibid.

248 **statement that internal politics at BRD had fuelled the controversy:** Qazi Faraz Ahmed, 'BRD Hospital Tragedy Blown Out of Proportion Due to Internal Politics, Says Yogi Adityanath', News18, 25 August 2018. Available: https://www.news18.com/news/india/brd-hospital-tragedy-blown-out-of-proportion-due-to-internal-politics-says-yogi-adityanath-1856807.html.

246 **there had been no oxygen shortage at all at BRD:** Yogi Adityanath on Gorakhpur infant deaths', *Indian Express*, 26 August 2018.

247 ***'Ab teri bari hai, bachega nahi ab tu* (It's your turn now. You**

cannot escape).': '"It's Your Turn Now": Death Threat for Dr Kafeel Khan After Attempt to Shoot Umar', NewsClick, 14 August 2018. Available: https://www.newsclick.in/its-your-turn-now-death-threat-dr-kafeel-khan-after-attempt-shoot-umar.

249 **The government was calling the cause of the deaths a 'mystery illness'**: 'Bahraich: Mysterious fever claims lives of 71 kids in 45 days', *Times of India*, 21 September 2018. Available: https://www.youtube.com/watch?v=KLnZQlfpIBM; 'Mysterious fever reportedly claims life of 71 children in 45 days in UP's Bahraich', *Business Standard*, 21 September 2018. Available: https://www.business-standard.com/multimedia/video-gallery/general/mysterious-fever-reportedly-claims-life-of-71-children-in-45-days-in-up-s-bahraich-71260.htm; '75 children dead in 45 days in UP; Doctors blame "mysterious fevers"', TimesNowNews.com, 24 September 2018. Available: https://www.timesnownews.com/videos/news/india/75-children-dead-in-45-days-in-up-doctors-blame-mysterious-fevers/10549; 'Bahraich witnesses 71 children's death because of Mysterious Fever', OneIndia, 21 September 2018. Available: https://www.oneindia.com/videos/bahraich-witnesses-71-childrens-death-because-of-mysterious-fever-343256.html; Bhim Manohar and Rahul Yadav, 'Malaria, mystery fever in Uttar Pradesh leaves 30 dead in two days; hospitals ill-equipped to tackle crisis', *Firstpost*, 21 September 2018. Available: https://www.firstpost.com/india/malaria-mystery-fever-in-uttar-pradesh-leaves-30-dead-in-two-days-hospitals-ill-equipped-to-tackle-crisis-5236141.html; 'Uttar Pradesh on high alert after 'mystery fever' claims several lives, Bareilly worst affect', TimesNowNews.com, 21 September 2018. Available: https://www.timesnownews.com/india/article/uttar-pradesh-on-high-alert-after-mystery-fever-claims-several-lives-bareilly-worst-affect/288165.

250 **were symptomatic of Acute Encephalitis Syndrome**: Jeevan Prakash Sharma, '"UP Police Undressed Me, Beat Me Badly On My Bum So That I Couldn't Sit": Kafeel Khan', *Outlook*, 7 September 2020. Available: https://www.outlookindia.com/website/story/india-news-i-am-against-nrc-not-caa-dr-kafeel-khan/359942.

251 **After two years of endless enquiries, the honourable Allahabad high court stayed that suspension on 9 September 2021:** Sparsh Upadhyay, 'Allahabad HC Stays Dr. Kafeel's 2nd Suspension Order Based on Allegations of Forcibly Treating Patient, Criticizing Govt. Policy', LiveLaw.in, 14 September 2021. Available: https://www.livelaw.in/news-updates/allahabad-hc-stays-dr-kafeel-2nd-suspension-order-allegations-forcibly-treating-patient-criticizing-govt-policy-181599; PTI, 'Allahabad HC stays second suspension order against Kafeel Khan', *The Hindu*, 15 September 2021. Available: https://www.thehindu.com/news/national/other-states/allahabad-hc-stays-second-suspension-order-against-kafeel-khan/article36467088.ece.

254 **starting receiving half of my salary:** For references to this, see Biswas, 'Kafeel Khan: National threat or symbol of repression?', BBC News, 3 September 2020.

256 **Two to three children were lying in each bed:** '75 children dead in 45 days in UP; Doctors blame "mysterious fevers", TimesNowNews.com.

256 **Upon reaching, I was horrified to see the conditions in the hospital:** KJ Saquib, 'Crisis deepens as encephalitis death toll in Bihar touches 128, *Hindustan Times*, 20 June 2019. Available: https://www.hindustantimes.com/india-news/crisis-deepens-as-encephalitis-death-toll-in-bihar-touches-128/story-SMckPnbgsU4TVHKLwuVtzM.html; 'Death Toll Due to Encephalitis Mounts to 128 in Bihar; Supreme Court to Hear PIL on Outbreak Soon', india.com, 19 June 2019. Available: https://www.india.com/news/india/death-toll-due-to-encephalitis-mounts-to-128-in-bihar-supreme-court-to-hear-pil-on-outbreak-soon-3694013/.

257 **The promise of a virology centre and a 100-bed encephalitis treatment:** G. S. Mudur, 'Five years later, Harsh Vardhan makes same promise', *The Telegraph*, 19 June 2019. Available: https://www.telegraphindia.com/india/five-years-later-harsh-vardhan-makes-same-promise/cid/1692718.

262 **I wrote to the chief minister of Uttar Pradesh:** Yusra Husain, 'Suspended BRD college doctor to Uttar Pradesh chief minister Yogi Adityanath: Reinstate or sack me', *Times of India*, 21 December 2018. Available: https://timesofindia.indiatimes.com/city/lucknow/suspended-brd-college-doc-to-cm-reinstate-or-sack-me/articleshow/67185601.cms.

262 **Dr Bhupendra Sharma, associate professor of the paediatrics department:** Tarique Anwar, 'Is Dr.Kafeel Being Unjustly Accused in Gorakhpur's Children's Death Case?', *NewsClick*, 20 April 2018. Available: https://www.newsclick.in/drkafeel-being-unjustly-accused-gorakhpurs-childrens-death-case

263 **in no way involved in the tender/supply/payment/order/maintenance of either liquid oxygen or jumbo oxygen cylinders:** Omar Rashid, 'Gorakhpur infant deaths: departmental inquiry clears Dr. Kafeel Khan', *The Hindu*, 27 September 2019. Available: https://www.thehindu.com/news/national/other-states/gorakhpur-infant-deaths-departmental-inquiry-clears-kafeel-khan/article29528392.ece.

264 **concluded his enquiry on 15 April 2019, which stated that the following:** Shoaib Daniyal, 'Gorakhpur child deaths: Probe absolves Dr Kafeel Khan of all charges, praises him for saving lives', *Scroll.in*, 27 September 2019. Available: https://scroll.in/latest/938688/gorakhpur-child-deaths-probe-absolves-dr-kafeel-khan-of-all-charges-praises-him-for-saving-lives; '"Huge Relief" – Kafeel Khan On UP Government's Decision To Withdraw Re-Inquiry', Citizen, 8 August 2021. Available: https://www.thecitizen.in/index.php/en/newsdetail/index/15/20731/huge-relief---kafeel-khan-on-up-governments-decision-to-withdraw-re-inquiry.

266 **Dr Kafeel Khan Jailed Over UP Child Deaths Cleared:** Video available on NDTV, YouTube, https://www.youtube.com/watch?v=AjS4hXfgjY4.

266 **'Yes, a hero but in the eyes of the termite clan':** Yusra Husain, 'Ex-BJP MP Paresh Rawal apologises to Dr Kafeel Khan', *Times of India*, 2 October 2019. Available: https://timesofindia.indiatimes.com/city/lucknow/ex-bjp-mp-paresh-rawal-apologises-to-dr-kafeel-khan/articleshow/71407576.cms; '"I Apologise": Paresh Rawal To Gorakhpur Doctor Kafeel Khan For His Tweet', *Outlook*, 3 October 2019. Available: https://www.outlookindia.com/website/story/i-apologise-paresh-rawal-to-gorakhpur-doctor-kafeel-khan-for-his-tweet/339878.

266 **'There is no shame in apologizing when one is wrong':** Twitter. Available: https://twitter.com/SirPareshRawal/status/1179259215527006209?ref_src=twsrc%20per%20

cent5Etfw%20per%20cent7Ctwcamp%20per%20cent5Etweetembed%20per%20cent7Ctwterm%20per%20cent5E1179259215527006209%20per%20cent7Ctw-gr%20per%20cent5E%20per%20cent7Ctwcon%20per%20cent5Es1_&ref_url=https%20per%20cent3A%20per%20cent2F%20per%20cent2; 'Paresh Rawal apologises to Gorakhpur doctor Kafeel Khan after two years', India TV, 3 October 2019. Available: https://www.indiatvnews.com/entertainment/celebrities/paresh-rawal-apologises-to-gorakhpur-doctor-kafeel-khan-after-two-years-554063.

267 **the government opened another enquiry:** PTI, 'Uttar Pradesh govt withdraws re-inquiry against Dr Kafeel Khan in Gorakhpur case', *The Print*, 8 August 2021. Available: https://theprint.in/india/uttar-pradesh-govt-withdraws-re-inquiry-against-dr-kafeel-khan-in-gorakhpur-case/711258/.

270 **'A complete reading of the speech prima facie':** 'Full text and video: This is the speech for which Kafeel Khan spent seven months in prison', *Scroll.in*, 1 September 2020. Available: https://scroll.in/video/971960/full-text-and-video-this-is-the-speech-for-which-kafeel-khan-spent-seven-months-in-prison.

270 **'justify the continuance of the order of suspension which has continued for more than four years':** 'Gorakhpur deaths: Justify Dr Kafeel Khan's suspension from hospital for over four years, HC tells UP', *Scroll.in*, 3 August 2021. Available: https://scroll.in/latest/1001915/gorakhpur-deaths-justify-dr-kafeel-khans-suspension-from-hospital-for-over-four-years-hc-tells-up.

271 **"guilty of laxity":** 'Four years after crib deaths, UP sacks Kafeel for "laxity"', *Times of India*, 12 November 2021. Available: http://timesofindia.indiatimes.com/articleshow/87655986.cms?utm_source=contentofinterest&utm_medium=text&utm_campaign=cppst

273 **'the Government of India declared that no deaths had occurred':** 'No State has reported deaths due to oxygen shortage: Health Ministry', *The Hindu*, 10 August 2021. Available: https://www.thehindu.com/news/national/no-state-has-reported-deaths-due-to-oxygen-shortage-health-ministry/article35840910.ece.